Proust among the Nations

THE 2008 UNIVERSITY OF CHICAGO
FREDERICK IVES CARPENTER LECTURES

Proust among the Nations

From Dreyfus to the Middle East

JACQUELINE ROSE

The University of Chicago Press ✳ *Chicago and London*

JACQUELINE ROSE is
professor of English at
Queen Mary, University of
London. She is the author
of many books, including
*The Last Resistance, The
Question of Zion,* and
Albertine: A Novel.

The University of Chicago Press, Chicago 60637
The University of Chicago Press, Ltd., London
© 2011 by The University of Chicago
All rights reserved. Published 2011.
Printed in the United States of America

20 19 18 17 16 15 14 13 12 11   1 2 3 4 5

ISBN-13: 978-0-226-72578-9 (cloth)
ISBN-10: 0-226-72578-2 (cloth)

Library of Congress Cataloging-in-Publication Data
Rose, Jacqueline.
    Proust among the nations : from Dreyfus to the
Middle East / Jacqueline Rose.
        p. cm.
    Includes bibliographical references and index.
    ISBN-13: 978-0-226-72578-9 (cloth: alk. paper)
    ISBN-10: 0-226-72578-2 (cloth: alk. paper)
    1. Proust, Marcel, 1871–1922—Criticism and interpreta-
tion. 2. Dreyfus, Alfred, 1859–1935. 3. Beckett, Samuel,
1906–1989. 4. Genet, Jean, 1910–1986. 5. Arab-Israeli
conflict—Literature and the conflict. I. Title.
    PQ2631.R63Z83645 2011
    843'.912—dc23
                                        2011019002

⊗ This paper meets the requirements of ANSI/NISO
Z39.48-1992 (Permanence of Paper).

for Irving Rose (1925–2009)
and for Frank Kermode (1919–2010)

Contents

Acknowledgments

This book grew out of the Frederick Ives Carpenter Lectures, which I delivered at the University of Chicago in November 2008. My thanks to Bill Brown for the original invitation, to Jay Schleusener for hosting the lectures, to W. J. T. Mitchell, Debbie Nelson, and Mark Miller, to Erin Glade and Samuel Brody of the Middle East History and Theory Workshop, to Daniel Benjamin of Yalla, and to Naomi Patschke, all of whom contributed to making my visit so intellectually valuable and enjoyable. Thanks to Alan Thomas at the University of Chicago Press for his encouragement and for seeing the project through to publication. A research leave award from the UK Arts and Humanities Research Council in Spring 2010 allowed me to complete the further research and writing of the book. Queen Mary, University of London, continues to offer invaluable support. I owe a great deal to its unflinching commitment to the humanities in hard times. I am much indebted to Ronit Tlalim and to Mohammed Shaheen for their expert guidance in Hebrew and Arabic, respectively. Responsibility for any remaining errors is, of course, my own.

A version of chapter 1 was delivered as a New York Thirtieth-Anniversary Lecture for the *London Review of Books* in April 2010 and subsequently published in the paper (32:11, 10 June

2010). Thanks to Mary-Kay Wilmers, Nicholas Spice, and Jeremy Harding. Chapter 2 was originally delivered as the P. K. Ghosh Memorial Lecture in Calcutta in January 2008. I am enormously grateful to Naveen Kishore for inviting me to give the lecture, to him, to Sunandini Banerjee, and to the staff at the extraordinary Seagull Press for their kindness and hospitality, and to Aveek Sen and Supriya Chaudhuri for much valued discussions during my visit. My thanks to Elizabeth Cowie for hosting my visit to the University of Kent in March 2008, where a version of chapter 2 was delivered as the Annual Lecture at the Kent Institute for Advanced Studies in the Humanities, and to the Centre for Theoretical Studies in the Humanities and Social Sciences at the University of Essex, where a version of chapter 3 was presented as the Annual Distinguished Lecture in May 2008. I have much appreciated my dialogue with Esther Shalev-Gerz and thank her for permission to reproduce images from her works *Daedel(us)* and *Oil on Stone, Tel Hai*.

Warm thanks to Sally Alexander, Leo Bersani, Neil Hertz, Jonathan Sklar, and to distinguished Proust scholar Ingrid Wassenaar, who have all, at various stages, read and commented on the book. And once more to Mia Rose, for her presence and forbearance.

The book is dedicated to Irving Rose, with whom I had fierce and loving arguments on these matters, and who gave me gifts untold, and to Frank Kermode, whose supervision of my work as a graduate student played such a key role in my intellectual journey.

London, December 2010

A Note on Translations and Editions of Proust

For translations of Proust's *À la recherche du temps perdu* I have mostly used the standard Scott-Moncrieff and Terence Kilmartin 1981 translation, revised by D. J. Enright (London: Chatto, 1992), simply because this is the translation with which I first familiarized myself. I have, however, also referred as appropriate to the excellent new Penguin translation under the general editorship of Christopher Prendergast that appeared in 2002. All translations have been subject to occasional modification. For the French original, I have referred throughout to the three-volume Pléiade edition (Paris: Gallimard, 1954).

Esther Shalev-Gerz, *Oil on Stone, Tel Hai* (1981/83).

Proust among the Nations

Introduction

Sitting in his cell on Devil's Island off the coast of French Guiana, Alfred Dreyfus penned the first entry of his diary on Sunday, 14 April 1895. To ensure they could be properly checked, each piece of paper had been numbered and signed by the authorities in advance. The diary, addressed to his wife, would never reach her. (He would himself retrieve it only on his return to France in 1899.) Without knowing it, Dreyfus was writing into a void. "Until now," he writes, "I have worshipped reason, I have believed there was logic in things and events, I have believed in human justice!"[1] Dreyfus had lost faith, not in the army or nation—his loyalty to both remained undimmed throughout his ordeal—but in the principles of human justice as he had hitherto believed them to be etched into the reasoned consciousness of mankind. In his former life, anything "irrational" or "extravagant" had found "difficult entrance" into his "brain."[2] He had been a man of reason—upright, steadfast; like reason itself, we might say. He had believed that to be such a man would be enough to guarantee his place as one of France's true sons. In fact, reason and nationhood were in some way commensurate: in the court of reason, he was—surely—a respected Frenchman and not a hated Jew. With the loss of this belief, things fall apart: "Oh, what a breaking down of all my beliefs and of all sound reason!"[3]

Behind the hyperbole, there is an ambiguity which is eloquent for the purposes of this study. Dreyfus's loss of belief and of his own sound reason ("toute ma saine raison") reaches out in two directions—to personal conviction as much as to political life. It sweeps up the public, manifest injustice of the world and the shattered inner landscape of the mind. But perhaps we should also ask whether to worship, or make a cult of, reason (the French is "J'avais jusqu'à présent le culte de la raison") might not be a type of folly in itself.

As Dreyfus begins to write the diary of his "dreadful" (épouvantable) and "tragic" life, he is swamped with "questions and enigmas" about what he is doing: "But what could I do with it? Of what use could it be to me? To whom would I give it? What secret have I to confide to paper?"[4] Dreyfus's Calvary—and many, including Jewish commentators, will describe his story in such terms—precipitates a collapse of faith, not only in justice, but in the cohesion and purposefulness of thought. In this strange state, and indeed as part of it, the only pull Dreyfus feels—he describes it as a "tyranny"—is toward the sea: "I have again a violent sensation, which I felt on the boat, of being drawn almost irresistibly toward the sea, whose murmurous waters seem to call me with the voice of a comforter."[5] (It is all the more ironic that a palisade will eventually be raised around his compound to prevent him from seeing the sea.) More than thirty years later, in a famous exchange with Romain Rolland, Sigmund Freud will write of the "oceanic feeling" where the ego merges with the cosmos and all sense of boundary between self and other is lost—a feeling of which he himself professes personal ignorance or which he avoids at any cost.[6] Dreyfus is way ahead. Most obviously, and understandably given the circumstances, his impulse is suicidal. But he is also describing, or rather experiencing in his flesh and blood, how easy it is to slip from the world of reason into a more watery, "murmurous," form of mental embrace. (The French "mugissant" is even stronger, less murmur than roar.) Throughout his five-year imprisonment, Dreyfus was kept in ignorance of the drama which his conviction had precipitated across the whole of France.

That drama is the topic of my first chapter. Nonetheless, one way of thinking about such moments of historical rupture—for Léon Blum, the Dreyfus Affair was as violent a crisis as the French Revolution and the Great War—might be the collapse which they precipitate in our most cherished distinctions: between the highest, reasoned principles of the world and the innermost call of the deep.

Dreyfus and Freud are contemporaries. It is central to the argument of this book that we have much to learn from this coincidence, that the pitfalls of justice—Dreyfus can fairly be claimed as one of the most famous miscarriages of justice in history—cannot be understood in isolation from the perils of the mind. In the year that Dreyfus started writing his diary, Freud completed his first major work, the *Project for a Scientific Psychology* of 1895. In terms of French history, the link is far more than theoretical. The hatreds unleashed by the Dreyfus Affair and an early hostility toward psychoanalysis in France ran in tandem, spawned from the same prejudices and fears. From the outset, psychoanalysis in France found itself up against anti-Semitism masquerading as anti-Germanic chauvinism. Famously, Freudian psychoanalysis unsettles a whole tradition of French philosophical thought—thought in the service of reason—by displacing the rational Cartesian cogito from its throne. In the words of Jacques Lacan, who became France's most renowned and controversial psychoanalyst, the discovery of the unconscious produces a subject whose "I think, therefore I am" must now be translated into "I am there where I do not think to be." (Although it can be argued that Lacan's status in France relied on the fact that he inscribed his challenge to the cogito so perfectly within its own terms.)

At the start, however, the psychoanalytic emphasis on human sexuality and the unconscious meant that Freudianism was considered an assault on reason and Frenchness in one and the same blow. In the eyes of his French detractors in the early years of the twentieth century, Freud and his science represented those debauched and degenerate, alien, forms of Jewishness from which the assimilated Jews of France had spent the past half a century and more trying to differentiate themselves. Before the Affair, it was possible to believe—as Dreyfus had believed—in the carefully nurtured distinction between the "Israelite," the refined, assimilated French citizen of Jewish faith, and the "Jew," the vulgar, corporeal prototype of an inferior, barbaric race. Like Dreyfus, Freud, together with all he represented, was despised in France because he was a Jew. In the first volume of her monumental history of psychoanalysis in France, *La bataille de cent ans*, Elisabeth Roudinesco places psychoanalysis firmly inside the grid of the ethnic hatred that had fueled the Dreyfus Affair:

> At the moment Freudianism was being introduced into France, the Israelite had become the polished, elegant, version of the Jew, an assimilated citizen above all "restrained in his desires." Someone capable of dominating his instincts and repressing his pernicious libido, that same libido which stirred the thoughts of his strange Germanic, Viennese, Hungarian fellow creatures. Thus crudely could the so-called "pansexualism" of Freud be denounced under the triple banner of germanophobia, unconscious judeophobia and cartesianism. In other words, anti-pansexualism, pitting itself against the Freudian doctrine of sexuality, is always the expression, whether overt or attenuated, of a race psychology which will not speak its name.[7]

Roudinesco is not, of course, arguing that hostility toward psychoanalysis is by definition anti-Semitic (which would be absurd). She is, however, suggesting that revulsion against Freud's universalizing, estranging, vision of sexuality is often fueled by national or ethnic exclusivity. If psychoanalysis spares none of the world's citizens from the wild, dissolute components of who we are, it becomes all the more urgent to preserve some one, some one group, from the taint—like the story of the American woman, recounted by Freud in *The Interpretation of Dreams*, who, at a lecture by Ernest Jones on the egoism of dreams, said that he could only speak for Austrians, she was certain all her dreams were strictly altruistic, and that none of it applied to her country.[8]

Dreyfus will never know, of course, that at the same time as he is struggling against a vicious racism that has destroyed the reason of the world, a new way of thought is struggling to emerge that will make its founding principle the need to understand, rather than to judge or expel, the forces of unreason that inhabit every human mind. Nor, given his adherence to reason as an ideal, however broken, would Dreyfus have probably been able to grasp the psychoanalytic insight that reason is never more endangered than when it refuses to countenance anything other than reason itself.

In the pages that follow, our other, and in many ways leading, companion will be the French writer Marcel Proust, who gives this book its title, *Proust among the Nations*, which is also my tribute to the work of the brilliant Proust scholar Malcolm Bowie, *Proust among the Stars*.[9] "Without Proust," wrote the avant-garde publisher and writer Jacques Rivière in 1924, "Freud cannot be understood."[10] If Proust completes the circle, it is also because he was, again like Freud, the contemporary of Dreyfus, whose saga struck its roots deep into the heart of Proust's writing. In this, Proust becomes exemplary of the traffic between politics and writing, the outer and inner life, between justice and reason, in Dreyfus's words, or in more Freudian terms, between the perversions of the world and of the mind. Hannah Arendt made Proust's depiction of the Affair in *À la recherche du temps perdu* central to her account of the case in *The Origins of Totalitarianism*, first published in 1951.[11] In her reading, Proust's portrayal provides the most prescient foretaste of the eventual fate of the European Jews. She is, of course, writing with hindsight, after Hitler's genocide, but she is also suggesting that art can be the hidden reservoir of a not yet discernible historical truth. Most simply, Proust was a Dreyfusard, sacrificing—some critics argue—his neutrality as a writer on this one issue like no other. He organized a petition in support of Dreyfus and attended the trial of Émile Zola, who had been charged with criminal libel for the publication of his famous letter, "*J'Accuse*." More, by choosing to support the Jewish artillery captain, Proust was going against some of his own most fervent identifications, siding with his mother against his father, contradicting his insistence elsewhere that it was the paternal, Catholic lineage that defined him, and not that of his Jewish mother which would make him—unanswerably in Jewish eyes—a Jew.

If Proust is central to what follows, it is, however, not despite these equivocations of the soul, but because of them. Proust is as drawn to, as he is repelled by, the latent violence of the anti-Semitic Parisian salon, the famous turn-of-the-century literary and artistic drawing room in which he passed so much of his time. That is why he is so alert to that violence and can plumb its depths with such insight. He has the peculiar gift of being at once precise in his historical and political judgments—in *À la recherche,* the anti-Dreyfusards are unambiguously more foolish, blind, and poisonous than the Dreyfusards—while also requiring all of us to question our certainties no less than his own, to worry to the very edge of our convictions. For Proust, this is an ethical task or priority, just as, I will be suggesting, it should be for us today. It is our effort at "perpetual sincerity," he writes at the end of his account of Zola's trial in his early autobiographical portrait, *Jean Santeuil,* that obliges us to distrust our own opinions: "Jewish, we understand anti-Semitism, partisans of Dreyfus, we understand the jury in condemning Zola."[12] This is one reason why reading him is at moments to experience that state of "intellectual bewilderment" that Freud, in one of his few pronouncements on aesthetics, defined as the necessary condition of all great art (although it is only with great reluctance, he comments, that he can bring himself to believe in such a necessity).[13]

Above all, Proust, like Freud, does not idealize, flatten out, or subordinate to reason the vagaries of who we are. It is not in the name of the perfectibility of reason that Proust was fighting for Dreyfus. When Émile Combes, French prime minister from 1902 to 1905, started pushing his anticlerical agenda, largely in response to the appalling hate-driven conduct of the Catholic press throughout the Affair, Proust was dismayed. It was the first stage in the separation of Church and State, without question a progressive move—the left called Combes "*le petit père*." (By 1904 ten thousand religious schools had been closed.) Proust himself was anticlerical to a fault. Nonetheless, he feared that a falsely secularized and unified France, blind to irreconcilable differences, would simply drive hatred in deeper: "A unified France would not mean a union of Frenchmen," he wrote in a letter to Georges de Lauris in July 1903.[14] It is a warning that those attempting to impose unity on France in the name of secularization would do well to heed today (Nicolas Sarkozy's banning of the burka being, by his own account, part of his attempt to foster a singular "French identity").[15]

Although Proust and Freud never met or read each other's work, at moments, as we will see, it is almost impossible to tell them apart. Like Freud, Proust immersed himself in the nighttime of the mind. He therefore never made the fatal mistake of believing that those who struggle for justice need to see themselves as innocent of the ills of the world. "In all of this, we are talking only about other people, about those who hate us," he wrote in the same letter to de Lauris, "But what about ourselves—have we the right to hate too?"[16] Proust is not, as I read him, promoting hate as a way of life, but he is suggesting that to suppress or deny our own capacity for hatred—to split it off to use the terms of the next-generation psychoanalyst Melanie Klein—can be deadly. When contemplating a title for his lecture "We and Death," delivered to the Vienna lodge of the Jewish community organization the B'Nai Brith in 1915, Freud first proposed "We Jews and Death," to show that Jews, like everyone else, were prey to the aggressive drives.[17] Today, we urgently need a new vocabulary, a way of thinking that allows us to remain attuned to the iniquities of the world, while never losing sight of the worse that we might have done and that we might still be capable of. And if this is the case for the individual, then it is no less so for the polity—for state and nation—as the Dreyfus Affair also starkly demonstrates. One of the key lessons of the

Affair, I suggest, is just how hard it is for the state, in relation to its own acts, to sanction, even less itself to deploy, a language of moral accountability.

In the pages that follow, I pursue these questions across the scarred landscape of our contemporary world, from the heart of Europe at the turn of the twentieth century to the Middle East, where the legacy of Dreyfus is still being played out to this day. Because of Dreyfus, therefore Israel—the argument is often made, and for many it is unanswerable: that the crimes perpetrated against the Jewish officer heralded, for those who could bear to listen, the end of the dream of emancipation for European Jews. Jewish nationalism would then be the most important lesson of the Affair and Israel its historic redemption. (In Israel it is Dreyfus as much as the Shoah that makes this unavoidably clear.) Like reason, however, redemption always runs the risk of being seduced by its own powers and wiping out the world's contradictions. No one nation or people has the *ratio* of history on its side, and to believe that it does so is to risk placing itself beyond the reach of justice. However urgent, the creation of Israel was a catastrophe for another people, the Palestinians, whose suffering as a people the ruling voices in Israel seem to find harder and harder to acknowledge by the day. What happens if instead we run the line: because of Dreyfus, therefore justice, or rather the struggle for justice, crucially for the Jews, a universal and endless affair? What happens if, like Bernard Lazare, a key player and for me a hero of this drama, we make justice a defining priority of what it means to be a Jew?[18] Then the journey from Europe to the Middle East will not be the story of redemption for any one people, but rather of continuous vigilance.

On this journey, I will be accompanied throughout by writers who all share the capacity to force the inadmissible part of thinking into the world of politics. When French philosopher Jacques Rancière defines such thought as "involuntary," he is aligning it with the world of Proust, for whom the involuntary part of the mind was the sole engine of mental freedom. This may not have been intentional. His explicit reference is to Freud and the unconscious as the site of a "confused knowledge," of "thought which does not think," which can only break bounds and rise to the surface of the mind as a form of savagery. (For all the attempts to transform it into an aesthetic object, the unconscious is not a thing of beauty.)[19] Although they don't make their appearance until the final chapter, Samuel Beckett and Jean Genet are presented here as the two writers who push the boundaries of the unthinkable in this sense to its furthest extreme. Crucially, however, they push this boundary not as transcendence of the world—which is how Beckett is so often read—but as part of their immersion in some of the blackest moments of its history. Although it is not often discussed—Marjorie Perloff is one exception—at the end of the Second World War, Beckett worked for the Irish Red Cross at Saint-Lô in Northern France, a town so destroyed by Allied bombing that the French called it the "capital of ruins," and to which he dedicated a poem in 1946:

> Vire will wind in other shadows
> unborn through the bright ways tremble
> and the old mind ghost-forsaken
> sink into its havoc.

As Perloff points out, it is almost impossible to make sense of this poem—even when we know that the Vire was the river running through the town. What trembles? What is unborn? Of what shadows are these the "other" shadows? (We also want to read "through" as "though," although it does not really help.)[20] It is as if Beckett were piling loss upon loss and then casting into the mind's depths to see what it can, and cannot, tolerate. This is not trauma as the ineffable, as one dominant strand of recent literary theory would have it. In this context the idea would appear as something of a luxury. Rather, these are the ravages of history, hyper-present on the page, playing havoc with everyday speech.

Against the advice of all who knew him, Beckett stayed in France throughout the war. He was, therefore, witness to the ultimate capitulation of the country to the anti-Jewish hatred that had first shown its colors at the time of the Dreyfus Affair. At almost the same time—*The Maids* was written in 1946—Genet will start ripping off the façade of French society, in this he is the heir of Proust, who was Genet's favorite writer (although he dramatically raises the heat). Specifically, in *The Screens,* which he first drafts in 1956, he shreds the official face of the army, whose conquest of Algeria between 1830 and 1847 predated, but also simmered beneath the surface of, Dreyfus. For some Dreyfusards, it was the conduct of the army in Algeria that formed the bedrock of, and in many ways licensed, its self-sacralizing and vicious omnipotence during the Affair. Exposing this link became a mission of the Parisian literary journal *La revue blanche* which plays a key role in what follows. But Genet also goes to Palestine—his first visit is in 1970—where he falls in love with the Palestinians, as he had with the Black Panthers earlier that year, making the justice of their cause his own. Together, Beckett and Genet face each other at either end of the taut wire that binds Europe to the Middle East. "There is no doubt," Genet writes in his last work, *Un captif amoureux*, the story of his sojourn with the fedayeen in the hills of Jordan, "that the Palestinians precipitated a breakdown of my vocabulary." (Published in 1986, it is his last work and barely complete when he dies.)[21] In Genet's hands, language is not subjected to the same form of decay as in Beckett, but he is no less witness to the devastation wrought by history on the norms of thought. Genet also knows that his mere presence as a European in the Middle East risks corrupting everything he sees. He is no innocent—Genet is, of course, never an innocent—in Palestine.

Both Beckett and Genet can be described as types of exile, whose relationship to homeland, state, and language was fundamentally awry. Their oblique, discomforted posture gives its unique quality to their vision. This is something they share with nearly all the writers who appear in this book, even those who, by dint of being as it were born into the conflict, might be seen as having a right to the authority that Genet refuses to claim on his own behalf in Palestine. In 1936, at the age of twelve, Yehuda

Amichai, considered by many as Israel's greatest modern poet, fled Würzburg, Germany, with his family for Palestine when it was still under the British Mandate, before the creation of the state. He then fought for the Haganah in the war of 1948, as he would fight in the Israeli army in the 1956 Sinai Campaign, the 1967 war, and the Yom Kippur war of 1973. Mahmoud Darwish, the most renowned Palestinian poet of his time, was six when his family fled the village of Birwe, in Upper Galilee, which was taken over and then destroyed by the Israeli army in 1948. When his family returned after the war, they were too late to be included in the Israeli census and found themselves classified as "present-absentees." Darwish then traveled between Palestine, Jordan, and Europe for much of the rest of his life.

There is no symmetry between these histories—there can be no equation between the industrial genocide of the Jews and the ethnic transfer of the Palestinians—but, as these stories make clear, they are irrevocably intertwined, first in the passage of suffering from Europe to the Middle East and then as the establishment of the state of Israel leaves a new, still unresolved, injustice in its wake. These are not two people apart. To know that is already to know much. "The problem is that we are not alone in this land," Amos Oz writes in a recent article, "and that the Palestinians are not alone in this land."[22] The problem, surely, is that this is seen as the problem. For this reason, I have focused in what follows on those moments in the poetry of Amichai and Darwish when they make their way across enemy lines at those points in Israel's history—its crushing victory in the 1967 war, for example—when to do so posed the greatest risk. Whether, in the case of Amichai, by simply acknowledging the presence of the Arab and his felt history in the newly conquered East Jerusalem of 1967 or, in the case of Darwish in the same year, by writing a poetic dialogue with an enemy soldier or, even more scandalously perhaps, lamenting a lost Israeli lover, their intimacy crushed by the contempt for the Palestinian which accompanied the rhetoric of conquest. (Although not all his readers apparently picked up that this lover was also a member of the Israel Defense Forces

(IDF), Darwish was fiercely criticized for both of these poems by some of his most passionate former admirers in the Arab world.)

What literature can do is, therefore, an abiding question of this book. It remains an open question, even if it is answered in part—there could not be a definitive answer—by the force with which each of the writers of the conflict offer their riposte to the frozen logic and vocabularies of a seemingly unending war. This is not utopian. None of them are crafting an idyll out of place and time. They are each far too deeply immersed in this history and would be the last to be seduced by such a vision. For the same reason, the idea of spontaneity where we might want to locate the possibility of the political seems inappropriate here. In a world where all spontaneity has been crushed, politics can only proceed as painstaking, laborious thought, of the kind Alain Badiou reads in Samuel Beckett.[23] Thus, Yizhar Smilansky, the godfather of Israeli letters, unpicks—as if in slow motion—the ethos of the founders of the nation, an ethos with which, as a native-born *sabra,* he should in fact perfectly identify. Yizhar's famous story *Khirbet Khizeh,* which narrates the story of the expulsion of Palestinians from their village in 1948, sent shivers across the nation when it appeared the year after the war. The story of its reception is in itself an object lesson in the struggle to tame and temper a recreant, albeit true, version of a nation's past. In one of its most shocking moments, the soldier narrator makes an analogy—it strikes him like lightning—between the fate of the Palestinians and the historic exile, *galut,* of the Jews. In fact, one of the most surprising things to appear in what follows is the number of Israelis who, in times of crisis—the Sabra and Chatila massacre of Palestinians in Lebanon in 1982 will be another—do not hesitate themselves to make the comparison between the sufferings imposed on the Palestinians and the history of the Jews, comparisons that uncritical defenders of Israel in the West view as anathema. Those who make the link, I would argue, however, are simply laying claim to an ethic of justice without borders. They are granting to—or requiring of—the Jew, precisely because of this history, that she or he should display that constant vigilance which, for Bernard Lazare, was the lesson of the Dreyfus Affair.

Always, it is the immense effort, the cost of the dominant narrative of state and nation, which these writers reveal, the work which it has to do to hold itself, unanswerably, in place—although only ever with partial success. At each point of crisis, one can also see that narrative stretched to breaking point (the law never so frail, nor so brutal, as when it knows only one version of events). The victory of 1967 precipitated Israel from despair in the previous year to an exultation one of whose tasks was to wipe out all memory of the somber mood that had gone before. (According to historian Tom Segev, neither the despair nor the exultation was justified.)[24] Amichai responds by laying the vanished melancholy across the euphoria of the present. In this, his poetry of 1967 is also an act of remembrance. And 1982, the year of Israel's invasion of Lebanon, was the moment that planted the first profound doubts among many of Israel's citizens toward the ethos of self-defense that had hitherto been the army's and nation's unquestioned rationale. The mass demonstration of 300,000 against the government after Sabra and Chatila—which came to be known as the "four-hundred-thousand protest"—was of a magnitude never seen before or since. (It says much about the current climate of dissent that the only demonstration to come anywhere close is the hundred-thousand–strong protest in June 2010 of Orthodox Jews against the High Court ruling that required the integration of orthodox Ashkenazi and Sephardic girls in the Beit Yaakov school in the West Bank settlement of Immanuel.)[25] These are, we might say, some of the highs and lows of a nation that, even when it has achieved exceptional military prowess and become an occupying power, has never ceased to justify its actions in terms of the historic vulnerability of its people—which is not to ignore the extent to which Israel as a nation feels itself to be constantly under threat. In their different ways, all the writers and artists presented in this book play havoc with the official version of history. Most simply, they choose to remember what Israel as a nation has wanted to forget. (The curriculum handbook issued by the education ministry to all Israeli teachers in June 2010 omits any mention of the 1982 war in Lebanon.)[26] Writing *Khirbet Khizeh* in the thick of the 1948 war, Yizhar composes his story as a reluctant memory on the part of the soldier, as if even at the moment it was happening, he could already feel it slipping all too keenly into the past, as if he were predicting Israel's reluctance to acknowledge the cruelest components of its own beginnings. For when in time this story makes its way onto the country's school curriculum, it only does so as a tale that transcends its own history.[27]

There is always more than one version of the story. Contrary to one Western cliché, this is no less true for the Palestinians, who are so often dismissed as mired in a single narrative of their past. At a key moment in *Gate of the Sun*, or *Bab el Shams*, the 1998 Palestinian saga by Lebanese novelist Elias Khoury, the narrator says, "I am scared of a history that has only one version. History has dozens of versions, and for it to ossify into one leads only to death."[28] Nor is memory a problem only for one side of this conflict. *Gate of the Sun* is the first novel to tell the story of 1948 from the point of view of the Palestinians. Previously, according to Khoury, writers had only hinted at what had happened "as if they are referring to something that everyone knows but nobody dares to say."[29] Palestine lacked its epic. *Gate of the Sun* "came to fill a gap and to open the debate on Palestinian memory. It was like a key that everyone had lost."[30] In the final chapter of this book, Khoury's novel appears alongside the signature film, *Divine Intervention*, of the Palestinian-Israeli filmmaker Elia Suleiman. Both Suleiman and Khoury are artists whose vision has been sharpened by exile. "I have two countries," said Khoury in discussion with Jeremy Harding at the World Literature Weekend in London in June 2010, "the country where I was born, Lebanon, and the country of my choice, Palestine, both of which do not exist." In his afterword to the earlier *Little Mountain*, Edward Said describes Khoury as "orphaned by history" and the novel in

Lebanon as existing "largely as a form recording its own impossibility."[31] "Palestine does not exist," Suleiman has stated, "it has no borders" (a country with a past and a future, but no present).[32] As a voluntary exile, Suleiman left Nazareth for the United States in 1982, his strange filmic slant on the conflict the child of this split vision. But it is only in his most recent film, *The Time That Remains*, newly released at the time of writing, that he too has been able to return to 1948.

Psychoanalysis began with a patient who could not bear to retrieve a forbidden, guilty thought from the unconscious recess of her mind. It begins with the anguish of remembrance. This is just one reason why to invoke psychoanalysis, whether for the individual subject or in the wider sphere of states and nations, is to soften, rather than thicken, the contours of judgment—without losing sight of the dangers when memory is too brutally repressed, without diminishing the struggle for justice. The suggestion in *The Question of Zion*, first published in 2005, that psychoanalysis can help in the understanding of Zionism was felt by some critics to offend both the suffering of the Jewish people and the reason of (their) history. In the preface to the 2007 Hebrew edition, I wrote: "To try and understand the specific psychic components or fantasies that play their part in one group or identity is neither to accuse, insult nor degrade it. The founding principle of psychoanalysis is that no one is—*ever*—demeaned by the unconscious. Restoring the 'dignity'—*die Würde*—of the psyche was Freud's stated aim in interpreting dreams."

Throughout his work, and increasingly toward the end of his life, Freud explored the traffic between the public and private domain. It was in fact his first intellectual passion. Looking back in 1935, in the postface to his *Autobiographical Study*, he describes how his interest has returned to the cultural problems "which fascinated me long before, when I was a youth scarcely old enough for thinking."[33] When he goes on to conclude that the events of human history are "no more than a reflection" of the inner dynamics of the mind, "the very same processes repeated on a wider stage," we should, however, be suspicious. The model is too neat, the relation between the two domains will not easily submit to such reduction (as has also been pointed out—how can something which expands its scope and dimensions possibly stay exactly the same?)[34] The problem is not, therefore, the *whether* of the link between psyche and polis, but the *how?* In the vexed relationship between them, there is in fact no one theoretical model that will do the trick: we are not cruel simply because of the injustices of the world, any more than the worst of the world is simply the offshoot of who we are (neither one exempt, neither the other's sole cause). Nonetheless, we should listen to Freud as he traces this link, which he never abandoned, to a moment in his own life before conscious, deliberative thought (like an involuntary memory, as we might say). At the very least, we are far from the tradition—traced by Arendt to early Greek thought—that insists on the "gulf between the sheltered life in the household and the merciless exposure of the *polis*," although even then the line could be blurred, with Socrates often drawing his examples of the polis from everyday, private life.[35] For psychoanalysis, we are caught in the world of the other, potentially violently, from the outset—it was how to negotiate this that became Freud's increasing concern. It is, then, a founding premise of psychoanalysis that the personal and political are intertwined more or less from the moment we are born.

In this book, the key questions are: How do psyche and politics control the equivocations of their world and then, given that they are bound to fail, how ruthlessly do they respond to that failure? How, as individuals and as citizens of nation-states—since there is no sign, not even under the pressure of globalization, that national identification is on the wane—do we countenance, and then take responsibility for, the most disturbing versions of our own histories?

Figure 1 is a photograph of a sculpture by the Lithuanian-born artist Esther Shalev-Gerz. Out of a piece of Jerusalem stone, she has carved the relief of a soldier in such a way that he then casts his shadow in fragments or ruins on the ground. The sculpture is situated at Tel Hai, the site of one of the most famous moments

FIGURE 1. Esther Shalev-Gerz, *Oil on Stone, Tel Hai* (1981/83).

in Israeli national memory, when the hero Trumpeldor fell in 1920 in a clash with Arabs while defending an isolated Jewish farm. Now a permanent exhibit, it was built at the time of the Israeli invasion of Lebanon in 1982 while bombs were falling on the surrounding villages. Shalev-Gerz lived for twenty-three years in Jerusalem, from 1957 to 1980, before moving to New York and then Paris, where she now lives and works. In Europe, one of her most famous works is the "Monument against Fascism," a lead-covered column that she constructed with her then husband, the sculptor Jochen Gerz, in the German town of Harburg in 1986. The inscription on the column reads:

We invite the citizens of Harburg and visitors to the town, to add their names here to ours. In doing so, we commit ourselves to remain vigilant. As more and more names cover this 12 meter high lead column, it will gradually be lowered into the ground. One day it will have disappeared completely and the site of the Harburg monument against fascism will be empty.

In the long run, it is only we ourselves who can stand up against injustice.[36]

By traveling from Lithuania to Israel to Paris, Shalev-Gerz moves across all the spaces covered in the journey of this book, from the East, home to so many of the Jews who first migrated to Palestine, into Israel's present political landscape, and from there back into the heart of Europe's fascist past. Finally, or for now at least, she ends up in Paris—where this story will now begin—carrying the quest for justice, like so many on this journey, wherever she goes.

Proust among the Nations

So, Monsieur Drumont, what are you going to do with the Jews?
«BERNARD LAZARE, letter to Edouard Drumont[1]»

In the same way as science is the religion of the positivists, justice is the religion of the Jews.
«LÉON BLUM, *Nouvelles conversations de Goethe avec Eckerman*[2]»

And since bad people are armed in every fashion, it is incumbent on the just to do likewise, when justice would otherwise perish.
«MARCEL PROUST, *Jean Santeuil*[3]»

Proust in the Courtroom

About halfway through *Jean Santeuil*—Proust's autobiographical novel, precursor to *À la recherche*—the eponymous hero is sitting in the Chamber listening to a debate about the Armenian massacre of 1894. The discussion has just ended. France will do nothing. Whereupon, the deputy Couzon rises to his feet to excoriate his fellow ministers. (He is modeled on Jean Jaurès, future leader of the French Socialist Party.) In uproar, the Chamber bays at him to be silent. When the president reminds him that he must limit his remarks to a response to the previous speaker, he replies: "Let me assure you, if I have to wait an hour for this clamour to subside, I intend to exert my right to the full." "You have just assassinated two hundred thousand Christians," he then declares. "We are going to tell the people, and the people, whom you have taught to use a rifle, will avenge them."[4] The ensuing frenzy is "indescribable": "Such words have never before been pronounced in a French Chamber," the minister of agriculture proclaims. "Jean understood," writes Proust, "that Couzon had been driven to speak by that feeling for Justice which at times overtook him completely like a form of inspiration."[5]

Watching Couzon, Jean is overcome with excitement. His heart pounds. As Couzon, on his short ungainly legs, hastens to the dispatch box with no grace (the French word is *disgracieusement*), Jean feels that "no human body has ever expressed such dignity and grandeur."[6] When the deputies rattle their desks, he wants to kill them, to stone them, as he once wanted to "massacre"—his word—the police for abusing their power by roughing up a young, vulnerable thief. There is no limit to what he imagines himself doing to those who would stifle justice— justice whose voice he describes as "palpitating" and "ready to sing."[7] In Proust's vocabulary, justice is an inspiration, a song, and a beating heart. But this lyrical vision of justice does not blind Proust to its ruthless dimension. When justice is threatened, it must take up arms by whatever means. To those who argue that it is precisely by disregarding the question of means that justice is most likely to perish, the narrator observes that justice would never have won any of its victories had the great revolutionaries of history been so cautious.

It is not customary to associate Proust with such forms of passion. We tend not to imagine him most obviously sitting in the corridors of power, cheering on—at least inside his head—a deputy pleading on behalf of a massacred people; nor indulging in fantasies of political violence, and justifying such violence in the name of such a people who have been abandoned by France, indeed by the whole of Europe and the rest of the world. A twenty-first century reader might also be surprised to discover, in this sequence which was omitted from the first published edition of *Jean Santeuil*, a reference to the Armenian massacre at all. Today we tend to associate such an event with what has come to be known, no less controversially, as the Armenian Genocide of 1915, an event to which today's political powers have also gone to great lengths to turn a blind eye.[8] But it will be my argument throughout this book that Proust not only inhabits this world, vibrantly and urgently, at numerous points throughout his writing, but that in doing so, he can help us understand some of the deepest, most persistently difficult components of our contemporary political world. Just how many of our current preoccupations can we watch unfolding in this episode? From the right to speak out, to the legitimate means for redressing injustice (Couzon might today be accused of incitement: "the people, whom you have taught to use a rifle, will avenge them"), to national and ethnic violence, to our responsibility for the sufferings of others in seemingly remote parts of the globe. The young Jean feels these concerns in his body—he breaks out in a sweat and then falls back in his seat, happy and smiling, when Couzon has finished speaking, unclenching the fists with which he had imagined himself pummeling these raucous, cruelly indifferent ministers. Only the rules of the Chamber prevent him from bursting into applause.

At its most simple, for Proust, politics is always a question of passion. There is no dividing line between the trials of the world and of the mind. In the earliest pages of *À la recherche*, the narrator runs a line from his horror at the cruel teasing dealt his beloved grandmother by his great aunt (whom he wants to beat as a consequence) to what he knows will become in adulthood an even crueler indifference to human suffering: "all these things were of the sort to which, in later years, one can grow so accustomed as to smile at them and to take the persecutor's side resolutely and cheerfully enough to persuade oneself that it is not wholly persecution."[9] Later he will describe our indifference to the suffering we inflict on others as "the terrible and most lasting form of cruelty."[10] Proust may believe in justice, he may, as it were, be on the side of the angels, but he is no innocent. He knows his own potential for violence. Indeed, in the Armenian episode, he describes it with something akin to relish. Being on the side of justice and knowing one's own cruelty—the two are unlikely companions which do not often sit together in the political vocabularies of our time. Those who proclaim the justice of their cause do not normally wish to taint that cause with the complex, often ugly, vagaries of the heart. I would suggest, however, that in politics the rhetoric of innocence is deadly. One of the things I will be arguing in what follows is that there is much to be gained from a way of seeing that does not require those struggling for a better world to persuade themselves that they have done no wrong or to believe in their own inner perfection.[11]

In 1898 Proust attended the trial of Zola, charged with libel after the appearance of his famous open letter to President Félix Faure, known today under the title *"J'Accuse"*—it was a stroke of genius of the editor of *L'Aurore*, the paper in which it appeared, to splay these words in a bold headline across the front page. Zola had written the letter in response to the acquittal of Major Ferdinand Esterhazy, a low-life womanizing swindler, who had been uncovered by Colonel Georges Picquart as the true author of the *bordereau*, or missive, that had precipitated the Affair. The missive, discovered in a wastepaper basket at the German Embassy in Paris by a cleaner working for French intelligence, revealed that classified military information was being passed from France to Germany. Wrongly—willfully as it turned out—it had been attributed to the young Jewish artillery captain, the rising star at the General Staff headquarters of the French army, Alfred Dreyfus. To put it most simply, Dreyfus had been framed. In 1894, he was convicted of treason, court-martialed, and deported to Devil's Island, the tiniest of three tiny *Iles de Salut*, or Salvation Islands, off the coast of French Guiana, where the climate was so intense that deportation there was considered a death sentence. By the time of Zola's trial, he had already been languishing on the island for three years, in conditions that can fairly be described as inhuman. It almost killed him. He would remain there for another two years until he was brought home for his 1899 retrial, where he would be reconvicted "with extenuating circumstances" by a court set up by the army to vindicate itself. Given that by then everyone knew he was innocent, this was a conviction in many ways more shocking than that of 1894. Today the case is known as one of the most famous miscarriages of justice in history. Dreyfus was pardoned in September 1899 and then fully exonerated and reinstated in the army in 1906, earning a Légion d'Honneur for combat in the First World War (although his experience came close to destroying him and he was a broken man).

Zola was sparked into his famous protest when Esterhazy walked clear. As the world watched the events in France with growing dismay, Zola, along with the rapidly expanding number of Dreyfusards, had believed that the inevitable conviction of Esterhazy would be the beginning of redemption. Dreyfus would be granted the retrial that would exonerate his name and set him free. Instead, it was a whitewash for Esterhazy and for the army. In fact, Esterhazy had himself requested the court-martial, so confident was he of acquittal.

By the time of Zola's letter, Hubert-Joseph Henry, the main forger of the documents against Dreyfus, had been exposed and cut his throat in prison. As well as perjuring himself at the original trial by falsely claiming inside knowledge of Dreyfus's treason and forging the main incriminating document ("le faux Henry"), he had led the General Staff witch hunt against Picquart, who was now imprisoned in a fortress pending a formal investigation into his conduct. The suicide of Henry was a turning point in the Affair. Zola, who had originally shown little interest in Dreyfus,[12] was tapping into a new surge of opinion that Dreyfus must surely be innocent, although even after Dreyfus was pardoned in 1899, this was not the majority opinion across France. Zola knew, however, that by charging a military tribunal with having knowingly acquitted a criminal (Esterhazy), he was himself courting a charge of criminal libel, a prospect he welcomed with enthusiasm: "Let there be an inquest in the full light of day!" he ended his letter, "I am waiting." He also knew that, as the question of what the tribunal knew or did not know would be virtually impossible to settle in law, he was almost certain to be found guilty.[13]

"It is impossible," writes Louis Begley in his recent study of the Affair, "to overstate Zola's courage."[14]

Zola's trial was the high spot of fin-de-siècle Parisian political and cultural life. Indeed, it is not going too far to describe it as a type of literary salon, a caricatured microcosm of the upper-class drawing room that plays so crucial a part in *À la recherche*. Proust would have been at home there. Joseph Reinach was the author of a nine-volume study, *Histoire de l'Affaire Dreyfus*, in many ways still unsurpassed to this day—Proust was an admirer, in one of his letters to Reinach praising "your beautiful history of the Affair."[15] This is how Reinach described the scene: "Never had such a numerous, more passionately agitated, crowd invaded the Assizes chamber. Lawyers were piled on top of each other, some clinging to the high ramparts surrounding the reserved enclosure or to the window sills; and mingling with them, crushed to suffocation point, in the emotion of the spectacle absorbing the whole world's attention, elegant ladies, journalists, officers, men of leisure, actors, 'Everybody who was anybody—all, the cream, of Paris.'"[16] The world of the salons, we could say, minus the luxury and comfort, as if we were staring, somewhat sadistically, at the members of Parisian high society trampling all over each other, or with their faces—a little like a Francis Bacon painting—crushed and distorted against a window pane. Jean attends the trial with his friend Durrieux. They arrive first thing each morning with a few sandwiches, a small flask of coffee, and remain, "fasting, excited, emotionally on edge [passionné]" until five o'clock in the evening. In Jean's eyes, they are two fifteenth-century Florentines or Athenians, "or any of those whose burning preoccupation it is to play a part in the thrilling events [affaires passionnées] of the city."[17] Jean sees himself as a dedicated man of the polis. Proust's own word—twice—is "passionné." This makes *Jean Santeuil* unexpectedly something of a throwback to true, Athenian citizenship as envisioned by Hannah Arendt. There can be no greater passion than public life.

It may be hard today to imagine such intensity of engagement—as Tony Judt has eloquently argued, the idea of the political collective has become a type of debased currency in our time.[18] But in late nineteenth-century France, the Dreyfus Affair raised public life to the pitch of frenzy. Proust was not alone. "The *coups de théâtre*," Reinach wrote of the Zola trial, "one after the other without interruption, sparked intense emotion, passions, so fermented, were roused to madness. . . . Brains pounded with the fever."[19] For the Dreyfusards, the Affair unleashed a type of joy, made life, in the words of Léon Blum looking back in 1935, not just "tolerable, but happy." The intense value that living acquired at the time could be measured by the fact that "life, for me, for my friends, no longer counted," so willing were they to be sacrificed in the cause of truth and justice.[20] Émile Durkheim, the famous sociologist, and Charles Péguy, influential poet and essayist, saw it as a moment of "conscience humaine" (the French *conscience* is both consciousness and conscience) that introduced into political life a new level of moral seriousness.[21] It was a view shared by Tolstoy. According to Reinach, he sent his greetings to France, congratulating it on its "great fortune" that such a crisis was presenting itself to the nation, a unique opportunity, unrivaled since the Reformation, to give politics a moral hue.[22] All these writers were bearing witness to a momentous, even monstrous, collision of public affect: a belief in human justice and the rule of law, set against the corruption of army and government and a hatred of untold viciousness against the Jew.

Proust was directly involved. Within a week of his letter appearing in *L'Aurore*, Zola received hundreds of signatures to his petition for a reopening of the case: "We the undersigned, protesting against the violation of legal process at the 1894 trial, against the iniquities surrounding the Esterhazy affair, persist in demanding Revision." The signatures were collected by a group of young writers that included Fernand Gregh, Elie and Daniel Halévy, André Rivoire, Jacques Bizet, and Marcel Proust.[23] "When I think," he writes to the Comtesse de Noailles in 1906, slightly embellishing his memory, "that I organised the first list for *L'Aurore* to ask for a revision of the trial."[24] Proust, alongside his mother but against his brother and his father, was a committed Dreyfusard. "Tell them I have not deceived them about the Affair," he writes to his mother at the time of the second trial, following Dreyfus's reconviction. If Dreyfus were a traitor, the judges would not have imposed such a mild sentence: "Extenuating circumstances" he insists, were "the obvious and vile admission of their own doubts."[25] Like a political pundit calculating odds on election results, he observed with satisfaction in September 1899 that *le Matin* "is coming round to *our side.*"[26]

At moments—although this is of course not the whole story—writing for Proust appears to take on the character of a political task. Dismayed that some had read *Le côté de Guermantes* as anti-Dreyfus, he promises, in a letter of 1920, that *Sodome et Gomorrhe* will be "entirely Dreyfusard and corrective."[27] Proust will later describe the Affair as his only incursion into politics, but comments like this show that it shadowed his whole life as a writer. In the wonderful phrase of Malcolm Bowie, Dreyfus was Proust's "great experimental laboratory."[28] The portrayal of the Affair in *À la recherche*, as it infiltrates the life of the salons, will be a central part of the next chapter. Here, as I examine the complex exchange between politics and writing, as well as a form of political ethics we might do well to revive today, it is *Jean Santeuil* that gives us the key—Dreyfus in the raw, before the Affair is finessed by Proust into the "kaleidoscope" of Parisian social life. (In *À la recherche*, it is Bloch rather than the narrator who attends the trial.) *Jean Santeuil* offers a vision of justice, and the endless fight to secure it, that will be the constant theme of this early book.

If Zola's courage is remarkable and duly famous, it is Colonel Picquart, less known to posterity, who can fairly be described as the true hero of the Affair. His role in pressing Dreyfus's innocence at the General Staff was all the more noteworthy insofar as he was considered, before the Affair, to have been an anti-Semite. "He's an anti-Semite!" Zola is reported to have exclaimed when told by Georges Clemenceau, founder of *L'Aurore* (also its most eminent columnist and a future prime minister), that Picquart had been the first to cast doubts on Dreyfus's guilt. "From birth," writes Reinach, "he shared the atavistic prejudice, one that had long existed in Alsace, against the Jews." In a footnote, however, he quotes Anatole France insisting, against Zola, that Picquart had always been a stranger to all fanaticism and hatred.[29] Either way, faced with the evidence, Picquart put any prejudice to one side. When General Charles-Arthur Gonse said to him, "What do you care if that Jew rots on Devil's Island?" Picquart replied, "What you are saying, General, is abominable. I will not in any case take this secret with me to the grave."[30]

It was Picquart who discovered that the writing on the *bordereau*, the sole evidence against Dreyfus, corresponded to that of Esterhazy. (Esterhazy famously wrote in a letter, later uncovered, that he would happily die if he could run through the odd Frenchman with his saber and would personally have a hundred thousand Frenchmen killed with pleasure: "What festive delight!"[31]) From the moment of his discovery, Picquart stopped at nothing, including the destruction for ten years of his own career, in his attempts to redeem an injustice which he saw as threatening the integrity, if not the existence, of France as a nation. As he put it in his statement at Zola's trial, he did not think his country, or indeed the army, was best served by "wrapping oneself in blind faith": "Tomorrow perhaps I will be driven out of this army which I love and to which I have devoted twenty-five years of my life! This has not stopped me from thinking it my duty to search for truth and justice. I have done so in the belief that I was thereby doing greater service to the army and to my country."[32] For Picquart, in a distinction that will become more and more important as we proceed, blind faith in army or nation was the enemy of justice and truth. On 14 September 1896, Picquart wrote to Gonse, "If we wait any longer, we will be overtaken, trapped in an inextricable situation, and we will no longer have the means to defend ourselves nor of establishing the true truth (*sic*) [la vérité vraie]."[33] "It was we who defended the real and permanent interests of the army," Reinach would later insist, "by refusing to separate them from the cause of justice."[34] "We honour the army," wrote Georges Clemenceau, "by requiring it to respect the law."[35]

Picquart's nobility of soul seems to have been limitless. "You should not pity me," he is reported to have said to a woman who accosted him in the street a few hours before his arrest, "after all, I really did something: I wrote a letter to the Council President denouncing the forgeries. . . . It is the other one [Dreyfus] you should pity, the one crushed by a penalty he does not owe, who has done nothing, nothing, nothing." Whereupon the woman's eyes filled with tears, while Picquart maintained an unruffled calm.[36] "He feels himself to be worthy of all," Reinach comments, "but is capable of being nothing"[37] (worthy of all, he can also efface himself). According to Maurice Paléologue, representative of the foreign ministry at Zola's trial, Picquart also excited untold hatred from his enemies: "A strange thing and one that I have noticed frequently, is that Dreyfus is not an object of hatred for the officers. . . . As for Picquart, the name alone of that renegade is enough to arouse them; they detest, loathe, and execrate him to the point of fury."[38] As Begley puts it, Picquart was nearly destroyed by the army because he was the whistle-blower. At the time of Zola's trial, Picquart was being detained in a fortress pending an army investigation into his conduct. He had already been sent on a mission to Tunisia where—although this was of course denied by his superiors—the hope was that he would be killed by the natives. (Picquart resigned from the army after Dreyfus's second court-martial, was reinstated after Dreyfus was exonerated, and then served as minister of war in Clemenceau's 1906 cabinet.)

Picquart did not quite raise his distinction between blind faith in army and nation, and truth and justice, to the level of an abstraction, but nothing makes the import of this distinction clearer and more powerfully than the Dreyfus Affair. Nor, given the army's final and total climb down, does anything show quite so clearly the price to be paid by an army for its own machinations, cover-up, and self-deception. Bernard Lazare described the judiciary as having been subjected by the army to a "moral terror."[39] The army lied. More important, once its prestige and standing had been compromised by the first lie—the wrongful accusation of Dreyfus—to cover its tracks, it became even more important for it to lie over and over again. For a nation crushed by its defeat against Prussia in 1870 and the loss, as a consequence, of Alsace Lorraine (home to both Dreyfus and Picquart), the army had to be infallible—"an inexplicable fetishism," in the words of Lazare. "The army," he wrote "must be infallible when it judges" (the unintended implication being that the army acts as judge and jury in its own cause).[40] That is why many anti-Dreyfusards believed that, *even if Dreyfus were innocent*, there must be no second trial. Reading the accounts of the Affair is to watch an army dig itself deeper and deeper into a morass of its own making, like the hero of a Russian novel, in Reinach's graphic image, who enters a house with the intent to burgle and leaves it a murderer, "having killed the two women who surprised him in the act."[41] Under interrogation at Zola's trial, Major Alexandre-Alfred Ravary of the Paris military tribunal declared, in an extraordinary outburst, "Military justice does not proceed like your justice." At which Albert Clemenceau (brother of the future prime minister) expostulated, "There is only one justice, not two." "Our code," replied Ravary, "is not the same."[42] In his account of the trial, Reinach congratulates Ravary on his "beautiful frankness": "Clemenceau's protestation was groundless. It was Ravary who was right. There were indeed two justices, two conceptions of duty and honour, two mentalities, two nations of France."[43] (Georges Clemenceau would famously say later: "Military justice is to justice what military music is to music.") Today such a distinction between military justice and the law also finds its advocates. In the words of Scott Brown, the Republican elected to Ted Kennedy's presumed-safe Senate seat in the upset U.S. election result of January 2010: "It's time we stopped acting like lawyers and started acting like patriots." (He was arguing against court trials of alleged terrorists.)[44]

For Jean Santeuil, Couzon became a fallen hero, as his idea of justice lost its outreach (to Armenia we might say) and slowly but surely constricted itself around his own person: "He fought only for himself, 'himself' now including on his own behalf his ideas of justice and social equality."[45] Narrow, or shrunken, justice would then be a contradiction in terms. In Proust's typology, this makes justice—for the good of the other or for nothing—the flip side of cruelty, which turns a blind eye to the suffering of others which we ourselves have caused. You cannot have it both ways, although it is one of Proust's insights, as we have already seen, that we often and easily do. Fighting for justice does not, for the most part, exonerate the soul or purge us of our darker passions. Victory in the world's courts of justice has never stopped anyone from putting themselves on trial in their dreams. But Proust is not immune, any more than the rest of us, to the pull of idealization, of other people, if not of himself. Picquart gave him his opportunity. He was, by all accounts, a true hero—Francis de Pressensé's book on Picquart is entitled *Un Héros, le Colonel Picquart*; Reinach's 1899 pamphlet, *Une conscience, le Colonel Picquart*. "No man," wrote Blum of the moment Picquart persuaded him of Dreyfus's innocence, "so naturally ever 'possessed' another."[46] In the words of Jean Recanati, he was "beautiful, like an aristocrat, and just, like a Jew."[47] Compared with the description of Couzon, Proust's portrayal of Picquart—to whom he devotes a chapter in *Jean Santeuil*—is a love-affair raised to the pitch of identification. In his biography of Proust, Jean-Yves Tadié calls it a "cult": "With the appearance of Colonel Picquart, everything changes."[48] Picquart will also haunt Proust's future writing, as he lavishes on his person trait after trait which will eventually bedeck the characters of Robert de Saint Loup and Albert Bloch, as well as the narrator of *À la recherche*.

In *Jean Santeuil*, the "mysterious" Picquart enters the courtroom—which had been awash with rumors that he would or would not appear—with "something of the charm of a bird released for a moment from his cage."[49] With a "resplendent" hat, worn at an angle, and catching the rays of the sun, he gives the impression of a man far away, a head "not so much rigid as motionless, even when it turned to right or left," and a bodily carriage that produced in the spectator "a feeling of lightness and speed held for the moment in check."[50] In fact Picquart makes his entrance twice over, as if Proust could not settle on his figure, which first sways "from side to side."[51] In another passage, omitted from the first edition, the mobility of his eyes and head make his entrance a rehearsal for that of Robert de Saint Loup.[52] Picquart's arrival in the courtroom is flight rather than landing, even while Jean experiences it as a shock, a brute jolt of reality, an unalterable physical fact that does violence (his word) to the version of the colonel he has long coaxed and cherished inside his head. For Jean, Picquart is an internal object. He knows him. In the pages before Picquart appears, Proust has been pouring scorn on those who take up a political cause, vote for a certain party, put their name to a manifesto "no matter what fine sentiments of justice and pity it may contain," as a substitute for an inner life.[53] If such acts are devoid of anything "genuinely personal," then humanity will "relapse into barbarism," the dead will be neglected, "the innocent would be allowed to suffer for the guilty, and the governments of this world would turn harsh and dishonest."[54] Dishonest government and the innocent suffering for the guilty will do nicely as a description of the Dreyfus Affair. Proust will use the hero Picquart to drive home his distinction between paying lip service to justice and serving a cause with one's own internal flesh and blood. If we truly want to save the world from miscarriages of justice and corrupt government, we must hand over to politics not just a name and a face but the deepest parts of ourselves.

If Picquart is a hero for Proust, it is because, in Picquart's head, as it inclines from side to side, Proust reads the passage of thought. Not deliberate thought, of the kind that had tried to mould and control Picquart before he appeared, but the kind of thinking over which our conscious minds can do little. "All those things which do not form part of what is generally called a correct attitude, but are personal to those who are preoccupied not with the outside but with the inner world," he continues, "are freely agitated by the unconscious and involuntary movements which instinctively follow those of thought and will, expressing them far more faithfully than if they were under their deliberate direction."[55] It is our involuntary gestures that give us away, open the path to who we really are. Although these gestures are physical, Proust is describing a form of movement not staged for the benefit of the courtroom, indeed not staged at all, since it is directed by our inner world. Such movements are "unconscious, involuntary." In this passage, Proust comes close to endowing Picquart with the power of involuntary thought, which he will place at the heart of memory and the creative process in *À la recherche*. It is worth pausing at this. In *Jean Santeuil*, Proust offers us the somewhat unlikely, indeed surreal, opportunity of considering what the world would be like—how justice would not have miscarried—if the involuntary life had been allowed to seed in the corridors of power and to take up its place in the minds of judges and army generals.

Picquart is a poet and a philosopher. Reinach describes him as "a meditating type and an artist": "Complex thoughts inhabited that extended brow; he had the refined, agile hands of, not a swordsman, but a musician."[56] Pressensé writes of his "clear, clairvoyant, precise mind," doubled, "in a fortunate and rare combination, with the imagination of an artist and the sensibility of a poet."[57] (What strikes a modern reader in all of this is, despite his self-effacement, or perhaps because of it, just how seductive Picquart must have been.) Even his enemies concurred, Gonse describing him as that "insubordinate, that evil mind driven by who knows what 'philosophical opinions.'"[58] Picquart inhabits the world of memory, a dreamer, prone to reverie, who calls on his memories of his Alsace childhood—this is, of course, Pressensé's own imagining—as antidote to the vicious betrayals of an army which, like Dreyfus, he never ceases to love.

Sixteen years old when the war broke out with Prussia, Picquart then made his way through the military ranks, again like Dreyfus in a meteoric rise, with the Germans in occupation of his homeland and France "lying prone on the ground like a wounded noblewoman."[59] And yet, in Pressensé's portrait, this history did not rob him of the sense, peculiar to the inhabitants of Alsace, that France was a window onto Germany, that the world was a bigger, more deeply connected place than the struggle over Alsace, a cause to which Picquart was of course devoted, allowed the two peoples to recognize. Likewise, the invisible traces of Judaism were, according to historian Jean-Marie Mayeur, more deeply implanted in Alsace than other regions of France[60] (according to Reinach, it was also home to anti-Semitism). Proust's mother was an Alsatian Jewess. The borders of Alsace were atypically porous. In 1871, the young Picquart had boldly and somewhat foolishly led a group of friends on a two-day hike into the mountains, swarming at the time with German troops. Pressensé offers the anecdote as an example of his open spirit, his inner resources, and his poetry.

Proust seems to draw on all this, but then goes further, as if this colonel—worthy of all, capable of being nothing—is the canvas on which he first elects to paint the inner life of the mind which will become the raison d'être of his entire life's work. Projection is not quite the right word here, although there is undoubtedly an element of that. It is something more radical, as Picquart becomes a template for the breadth, and sensuous embodiment, of human thought (in that sense in which Julia Kristeva describes Proust's writing as giving flesh to human time).[61] At moments in this chapter of *Jean Santeuil*, it is easy to forget that we are meant to be inside a courtroom, with the future of the nation— or indeed, as he puts it at one point, "the fate of Europe"—at stake.[62] In the following lines, the narrator is describing the vague, thankful smile that he imagines Picquart, during his military assignments, bestowing like an act of grace on the landladies, who steal away happily nurturing the memory of leaving him locked in his thoughts: "the vague smile, the look of affection which accompany all great upsurgings of thought, which in the stretched movement of our lips, in the dilation of our pupils, we feel still hovering above us as we work, as we write, while the only sign of our body's life is a gentle rhythm, like the quiet breathing of a sleeping child. Look, smile, breath—like the child's breathing, each give witness by their calm to the innocence of the hidden life of such moments."[63] We are already in Combray, in the famous opening sequence of the whole of *À la recherche*, with the solitary figure sleeping in his bed, as the "sequence of the hours, the order of the years and worlds"—and in this case of nations— all revolve around him.[64] Body and soul, Picquart has submitted to a lost inner landscape. He has become a writer—a devotee of what Proust describes earlier in the novel as the "sympathetic ink that is thought."[65] As the passage progresses, the sleeping child grows into a young poet. His father indulges him as long as his poetry is simply a pastime that excites the praise of adults but is roused to fury when the young man refuses all conventional professions and claims writing as his true and only life's vocation. (At this point the biographical references to Proust's own life have become unmistakable.)

Like Jean, like the young narrator of *À la recherche*, and like Proust himself, Picquart is an eccentric who, faced with social absurdity—in this case his interrogators—lets his mind go, as his thoughts follow a method, which is not quite a method, since it is the one "our mind unconsciously forms so as to be able to think, as a bird makes use of his wings for the purpose of flying."[66] Picquart belongs to a different species from his accusers, lives on another planet. Which does not prevent his thoughts from taking wing, so that, faced with men who would destroy him, he can enter into their minds: "putting himself inside every being he has to deal with, ceasing to be himself, making the other's soul his own, moving instinctively, inevitably, towards the actions of the other."[67] "Ceasing to be himself," Picquart *becomes* the other, makes the other's soul his own, even when he holds that other in utter contempt. (Like Proust in the salons, he makes his way into all the available social space.) This is empathy in the ser- vice of justice (the outreach of the heart). Proust has given a political twist to the craft of fiction. He has turned the art of the writer, who is nothing if he cannot make such leaps of imagina- tion, into a life and death matter. He has run a direct line from the power of thought to make illicit crossings—say, across the French-German border—to the struggle against a corrupt and deadly form of political power, one which at this point had nearly the whole of France under its sway. By the end of the chapter,

Jean and Picquart are brothers in arms, two philosophers lost amidst "some two hundred persons with nothing of the philosopher about them."[68] Jean would have killed for Couzon. When Picquart is in the dock, he is ready to let himself be killed, should anyone dare to touch a hair on the head of a man whom he now describes as his brother.[69]

What is most striking in this moment is the deceptive ease with which Proust slides between courtroom and fantasy, between politics and spirit, between the law of the world and of the inner life. In many ways, it is the transparency of the identification that makes the portrayal so compelling. "The person of Picquart has to submit," writes Recanati in his study of Proust's Jewishness, "to a set of particular and persistent fantasies"; it has to, he continues, "if the lieutenant-colonel is to be more his brother, more his double."[70] Recanati also believes that, far more than a partisan of Dreyfus among others, Proust "*is* Dreyfus," because he feels his sufferings inside his own body.[71] The Affair would then give us the first taste in Proust's writing of what it means to lose oneself, body and soul, in the cause or place of another. *À la recherche* will also display the counterimpulse, or even fear, as the narrator ceaselessly pulls back from such vertiginous proximity in order to delimit his subjectivity or risk losing himself.[72]

A final detail, key for what is to come. When Picquart enters the courtroom, one of the first features to strike Jean is "his slightly too hooked nose." Extraordinarily, the French phrase— "un peu trop busqué"—is translated as "aquiline" in the English edition of 1955. It seems that the translator could not tolerate this Jewish trait, clichéd as it is—which Proust will pass on to Albert Bloch in *À la recherche* and the dying Swann—and thought it better, in a gesture which can only be described as one of forced assimilation, to rectify it. This man, we are then told in the next paragraph, has something in his appearance of an "Israelite engineer"—a description so unexpected that it explodes, in the words of Recanati, "like a shot going off in the middle of a concert" (a paraphrase of Stendhal's famous comment that politics in the midst of matters of the imagination is like a pistol going off in the middle of a concert).[73] In a passage omitted from the first edition of *Jean Santeuil*, the phrase is repeated almost verbatim—"that fair, slightly reddish head of an Israelite engineer."[74] Why "engineer" is not clear, but the Jewish reference, albeit refined by the use of Israelite, is unambiguous. ("Israelite" was the term used to distinguish the assimilated, mostly French-born Israelite from the alien Jewish migrant.) As if Proust, who may or may not have known that Picquart was thought to have once been an anti-Semite, felt driven to welcome Dreyfus's strongest advocate into the Jewish fold.

In a famous letter to Robert de Montesquiou, model for Baron de Charlus in *À la recherche*, Proust wrote, "If I am Catholic like my brother and my father, my mother, on the other hand, is Jewish."[75] Supporting Dreyfus, alongside his mother, against his father and brother, therefore placed him askance this declared affiliation. (He sides, one might say, with his impulses). You are Jewish, of course, if your mother is Jewish, even if you have been baptized, as Proust had been. Famously, he made the narrator of *À la recherche* a non-Jew. But might not this cast a new light on the child's desperate yearning for the mother, out of which the whole work is spawned—the embrace of the mother, the most longed-for return, as being received back into the arms of the faith? Another moment in *Jean Santeuil* suggests this might not be too far-fetched. The chapters before those dedicated to Dreyfus narrate the corruption scandal of a deputy and former government minister, Charles Marie, whose wife—"an exquisite creature, a ravishing and witty woman, a sublime wife and mother"—before her premature death from consumption at the age of thirty, was befriended by Jean's mother. Dying, she places her husband and son in Jean's mother's safekeeping: "She was a Jewess. Only the prominence of her charms and the experience of her virtues had made it possible for Mme Santeuil, who came from a milieu where the deepest distrust weighed down upon the Jews, to become attached to a Jewish woman as a sister."[76] The Israelite Picquart is Jean's brother; a Jewess is his mother's sister. Despite the strength of that claimed detachment in the letter to

Montesquiou—or perhaps because of it—in *Jean Santeuil*, Jewishness is a family affair. Proust would have known that sentiments such as those expressed in the following lines—remember this is just before the chapters on Dreyfus—were scandalous to the point of sacrilege: "Even the most bigoted peasant woman would have surely felt that the soul of such a Jewess was a more pleasant perfume to Our Lord than all the souls of Christians, curates and saints."[77] He knew that the established Catholic Church had been foremost in condemning the "Jew traitor" and that the worst anti-Semitism came out of the Catholic press."As if the defenders of the Altar," he wrote in a letter of 1898, "shouldn't have been, before all others, the defenders of truth, pity and justice."[78]

Perhaps Proust could go so far because of the efforts he was willing to make in order to understand what he was up against. "In our attempts at perpetual sincerity," he writes at the end of the sequence on Zola's trial, "we do not dare trust to our own opinion, so we side with the opinion least favourable to ourselves. And Jewish, we understand anti-Semitism; partisans of Dreyfus, we understand the jury in condemning Zola."[79] This might also offer one way of reading those moments in *À la recherche*, so cogently analyzed by Malcolm Bowie, where Proust's portrayal of his Jewish characters seems to cross over into unmistakable, at moments cruel, Jewish stereotype (even as, Bowie also insists, he knows that the darkest and deadliest must be repudiated).[80] It takes a particular kind of mental promiscuity—the same artistic gift he ascribes to Picquart—to entertain all the psychic options, to be willing to enter so fully the enemy's mental space. At such moments, Tadié comments, it is as if Proust held in his possession the "craziest part of truth."[81]

"Neither Justice nor Pity"

The publication of "*J'Accuse*" and Zola's trial were the occasion for the most vicious outpouring of anti-Semitism across France. According to Jean-Denis Bredin, the day after publication, anti-Jewish riots, attracting up to four thousand people, broke out in Nantes, Nancy, Rennes, Bordeaux, Moulins, Montpellier, Angoulême, Tours, Poitiers, Toulouse, Angers, Rouen, Châlons, and Saint-Mâlo, as well as in Paris. Jewish shops were attacked and synagogues besieged, Jews were assaulted in the street, effigies of Dreyfus and Zola were burned. In Paris, during the trial, the anti-Semitic agitator Jules Guérin, founder of the Ligue antisémitique, orchestrated his troops on the Left Bank and all round the Palais de Justice. "I can still see," writes Reinach, "the furious young woman who came after me, trying to tear off my *Légion d'honneur* ribbon, while the demonstrators screamed out: 'Death to the Jews! Death to traitors!'" Similar cries from the crowd had greeted Dreyfus's court-martial. (Following his indictment, many called for the reinstatement of the death penalty for treason.)[82] According to Reinach, the police, mainly consisting of former soldiers, smiled at the rioters, who took care to accompany their declarations of Jew-hatred with cries of "Long live the army!" Anyone daring to counter with "Long live the Republic!" was immediately threatened. (One such was apparently set upon by one of the judges who had acquitted Esterhazy.) Reinach has no doubt that the outbursts were orchestrated, a combination of ugly but deeply felt sentiment and calculated, paid-for violence. "For two weeks," he writes, "the court, the pavement, the streets, belonged to Ratapoil [*rats à poil*, skinned rats]," a reference to the unscrupulous political agents who connived to help Louis Napoleon rise to power.[83]

Algeria saw the worst outbursts. One Algerian newspaper published the statement: "A Jewish sow has just given birth to two swine." The same week, a band of anti-Semitic youths, encountering a pregnant Jewish woman in the street, stripped her and urinated all over her. For Edouard Drumont, author of the bestselling 1885 anti-Semitic diatribe *La France juive*, all this was the expression of the noble rage of a people who would like to throw all Jews into the river or roast them: "Except that grilled Yid must stink," wrote his newspaper, *La Libre Parole*.[84] The Catholic newspapers, the *Croix*, the *Pèlerin*, and the *Gazette de France*, all made themselves the vehicle for anti-Jewish hatred. "With very few exceptions," wrote Lazare in the 1897 edition of his pamphlet *Une erreur judiciaire*, "the press was anti-Semitic."[85] For a country that, according to Reinach had lost the habit, the riots were remarkable for unleashing "the brutality of wild beasts."[86]

But that was perhaps too easy. It ignored the extent to which these outbursts were drawing on the underside of other, more civilized, passions. For socialist Alfred Naquet, anti-Semitism was simply an affiliate of normal feeling pushed to breaking point and owed its strength to its ability to suck out of every sentiment its "bad, subversive" element: "From religion, it borrows fanaticism; from the conservative idea of capitalism, it borrows envy and fear; for any appeal to socialism, it relies entirely on dread of disorder; it takes from patriotism only suspicion and hatred."[87] "They are stirring up France," Zola wrote of the army's appeal to national sentiment, "hiding behind her legitimate emotions, clamming mouths shut because the heart has been vexed, perverting minds. I know of no greater civic crime."[88] For Reinach, anti-Semitism was "descending into the lower depths, into the old bedrock where it has flowed for centuries."[89] The image is important. If we look carefully, we can see that this is not the vague image of an eternal, unchanging anti-Semitism that Hannah Arendt warned against for placing Jewish life outside history and politics—which always involves a claim for its inevitable recurrence and stokes a regime of perpetual, ineffective fear. Anti-Semitism always belongs in time. There is a bedrock, but it takes a historical crisis, flush with the needs of the moment, to go looking for it and bring it to life.

Worse was to come. In 1898 the *Libre Parole* launched a fundraising petition for "the widow and orphan" of Henry, after his prison suicide, to "defend the honour of the 'French officer killed, murdered by the Jews.'"[90] The donations allowed Henry's widow to file charges against Reinach for having accused him of being Esterhazy's accomplice in treason. In the relative privacy provided by the petition, which came to be known as the Henry "monument," there were no bounds. "Long live the sabre that will rid us of all the vermin," one contributor wrote; another:

"For God, for his country and the extermination of the Jews."[91] According to Stephen Wilson, in his monumental breakdown of anti-Semitism at the time of Dreyfus, calls for expulsion and extermination were endless. But they were ritual, rather than in search of enactment: "The translation of such a 'final solution' into practice was not necessarily implied or intended." There was, however, a clear logic of extermination.[92] In an 1897 article on "The Syndicate" (the mythical brotherhood of the Jews purported to be in control of the whole country), Zola had also talked of a "war of extermination."[93] Running through the Henry monument, Jean-Denis Bredin concludes, was "the latent justification of genocide."[94]

Zola's own diagnosis was that this anti-Semitism, apparently unleashed by his intervention, was in fact the cause of the Affair: "Anti-Semitism. Now that is the culprit."[95] Certainly it does not seem, as some commentators have suggested, that anti-Semitism was dormant in the early 1890s until it was sparked by the Dreyfus Affair. As early as 1891, that is, three years before the charges against Dreyfus, Jules Simon, who had briefly been prime minister of France in 1876–77, complained in an article in *Le Petit Marseillais* that his people, neither bloody nor violent, often well-disposed even toward their enemies, were rushing to embrace the calumnies being heaped upon the Jews: "For them, there is neither justice nor pity."[96] (He was writing about the reception of *La france juive*.) The Jew Dreyfus could be handed over defenseless, wrote Lazare, "because he had already had all human sympathy withdrawn from him."[97]

In this, France's humiliation by Germany in 1870 was crucial, since it had sowed the idea of treachery inside a nation which, like any other nation, could not bear to see itself as responsible for its own defeat. Idolization of the army was the barely concealed cover for catastrophe. This is worth noting. There is no army more dangerous or ruthless, more prone to internal corruption, than one haunted by the specter of failure. Only under conditions of disaster, past or threatened, does an army turn into a god. After 1870, the newly modernized army—modeled in many ways on the victorious Prussian army—was the fulcrum of the nation. An Ecole Supérieure de Guerre was created that admitted officers via open competition. The General Staff, where the Affair had originated, was also a post-1870 creation. Oddly, or perhaps symptomatically, given the rampant anti-Semitism, it was known as "La Sainte Arche," or "Holy Ark," an unmistakable Jewish reference. It was because it offered traineeships to the top twelve graduates from the Ecole Supérieure that Dreyfus had arrived there in 1893. Under the Republic, the army was open to all. These facts provided the opportunity for orchestrated resentment against Jewish officers, whose numbers were hugely exaggerated by the anti-Semitic press. Although there were nothing like the three to four hundred thousand Jews in France reported by the right-wing *Gazette de France* in 1894 (the number was closer to seventy-five thousand) or the fifty to sixty it insisted were admitted annually to the most prestigious military schools, the Ecole Polytechnique and Saint Cyr (Dreyfus had trained at the first, Picquart at the second), it was true that Jews were disproportionately successful in gaining admission.[98] "Since we cannot describe them as cretins, the least we can do is cast them as spies," wrote one commentator. "Therein lies the source of the entire Dreyfus Affair."[99]

At the heart of this anti-Semitism, one belief stands out from all the rest—the conviction that the Jew was not a Frenchman. He was therefore inherently a traitor. Seen in this light, the Dreyfus Affair was the fulfillment of an anti-Semitic dream—"an immense grace," in the words of the Catholic paper *La Croix* after Dreyfus's 1894 court-martial, "proffered to France."[100] "'Why would God have created the Jews,'" Drumont cites Bismarck, "'were it not to serve as spies?'"[101] But then he asks, "Does this in fact constitute either spying or treachery for the Jew? In no way. They cannot betray a country which is not theirs."[102] (When Dreyfus was arrested, Drumont declared he had been "prophetic.") "As a Jew, Dreyfus had not betrayed his country," commented another anti-Dreyfusard, "which is the temple of Jerusalem."[103] Reinach called it the "moral expulsion" of the Jew.[104]

No French Jew escaped the charge, not even the French-born, successfully assimilated Jew, as Dreyfus—rich, educated, rising up the military hierarchy—had thought himself to be. Why on earth, his defenders repeatedly asked, would he have wanted to jeopardize so much? The patriotic feeling of the true Frenchman, wrote Drumont, was inscribed on his heart "like a name carved into the bark of a tree"[105] (a graphic variant of the idea of patriotism rooted to the soil of the nation). "It is clear," wrote the *Petit Journal* after the judgment of 1894, "that the entire nation would have despaired of the future if it were conceivable that a Frenchman, of indisputable lineage, could descend to the ignoble depths whose full horror the atavism of Captain Dreyfus perhaps prevented him from fully grasping."[106] Such sentiments were as comforting as they were brutal. "For a people betrayed," Lazare comments, "having someone who can be accused of treason, in their capacity as a Jew, is the only consolation."[107]

Assimilation, on which the French Jew prided himself, was therefore a myth, since overnight one Jew had become—in the terms of Arendt—a pariah from having been a parvenu. "The theoreticians of anti-Semitism," wrote Blum, "had in fact presented the Jewish contribution to society as the introduction of a foreign body, a body impossible to assimilate, to which the organism's natural response was a defensive reflex." (The "theoretical postulate," he added, was identical to that of "hitlerite racism.")[108] In this context, the worst offense of the Jew was no longer that of embodying the world of money, to which his talents and history had consigned him (not that such views ever included any recognition of Jewish history). If the Jew's crime was that of being a foreigner, a far worse sin was to think he might cease to be one. "We used to attack them for being nothing but usurers," wrote one commentator. "Today people want to strike at the Jews because they now claim to be foreigners at nothing."[109]

It is a conviction that survives well into the twentieth century. A 1966 French poll of public opinion, conducted by the French Institute, uncovered that 19 percent of the French believed that the Jews were not fully French like other Frenchmen. In a famous episode in 1980, when an attempted bombing was carried out against a Paris synagogue in the rue Copernic, Prime Minister

Raymond Barre pronounced the assault: "A hateful attack which wanted to strike at the Jews who were in that synagogue, and which struck *innocent French people* who were crossing the street" (which managed to imply in one breath both that Jews were not French and that they were guilty).[110]

Excluding Jews from the army became a priority of the anti-Dreyfusards. As early as 1892, when Drumont's *La Libre Parole* had published a series of anonymous articles denouncing the increasing numbers and privileges of Jewish officers, a crowd of two thousand supporters escorted him to his office.[111] "They will be undisputed masters of France," thundered one anti-Semite, "from the day they take control of the army."[112] It is one of the tragic ironies of the Affair that there was in fact no more loyal officer than a Jewish officer—rising up the ranks of the army being a way of proving that the Jew was one of France's true sons. For the same reason, Dreyfus's undimmed wish throughout his ordeal was rehabilitation into the army.

How then—the question must arise—did the Jewish community of France respond to the Affair? Above all by avoiding it. French Jews feared that any intervention on their part would further inflame anti-Semitic opinion, that they would jeopardize any painfully won status they enjoyed in French society, and above all that Jews would be seen as rallying to the defense of a traitor purely because he was a Jew. (For the first few years after the 1894 conviction, there was little reason in the public mind to question the court's judgment.) None of these fears were groundless. "What Jewish officer and what Jewish official," asked Isaiah Levaillant, "has not wondered at any given moment whether the condemnation of the ex-captain would hinder his own career?"[113] According to Blum, the French Jew dreaded having imputed to him any distinction or solidarity based on race. Note, observed one Dreyfusard in response to an article linking Dreyfus and Rothschild, "the solidarity assumed between Dreyfus and 'all Israel.'"[114] The hardest thing for the French Jew was to relinquish his faith in the Republic that had emancipated him in 1791. "We are convinced," wrote Louis Lévy in 1898 in *Univers Israelite*, "that

France will soon pull herself together, will be ashamed of the deviation which she has let herself take, will shake herself free of her error."[115] The result, for the most part, was silence. "Generally speaking," Blum commented, "Jews did not talk about the affair among themselves; far from raising the topic, they studiously avoided it. A great misfortune had befallen Israel. You submitted to it silently, while waiting for time and silence to wash away its effects."[116] Correctly perceiving the link between Dreyfus and anti-Semitism, the Jews saw the first as fueling the second, rather than the other way round.[117] Very few took Zola's position—that anti-Semitism was the *cause* of the Affair.

Even when anti-Semitism was at its height, not one Jewish organization spoke out or organized in favor of Dreyfus. But for any Jew reading this today, before she rushes to judgment, the question must be, as always in relation to such predicaments: What could have been done? What would *I* have done?

Looking back, Blum's criticism was unflinching. To his mind, it was this attitude that constituted the real danger for the Jewish people, at the time of Dreyfus but even more when he was writing in 1935: "Rich Jews, middle-class Jews, Jews in the civil service, they were all frightened of actively engaging in the struggle for Dreyfus in exactly the same way that today they are frightened of fighting against fascism. They understood no more then than now that no precaution, no role-playing, would fool the adversary and that they remained the proffered victims, as much of a victorious anti-Dreyfusism, as of triumphant fascism."[118] Blum was both right and wrong. Ultimately, the Dreyfus Affair was a defeat for anti-Semitism. Dreyfus ended up freed and reinstated. Prejudice was finally trumped by the law. Blum himself would become the first Jewish prime minister of France in 1936 and was again prime minister in 1938 and 1946–47. But Blum's fears for French Jews, under the threat of an incipient fascism, would turn out to be hideously justified. (Justice, as Derrida has argued, is an infinite affair.)[119] The factors feeding anti-Semitism in Occupied France were at once very similar (military defeat) and very different (a financial crash in 1931 on the heels of the world crash of 1929, a massive influx of impoverished migrant Jews). In rushing to adopt anti-Semitic measures, France would this time be identifying with the enemy—in this they could not have been further from 1870—while at the same time reenacting many of the ugliest tropes of its own past. "A giant step will have been taken toward justice and national security," wrote arch anti-Semite Robert Brassillach in 1938, "when the Jewish people are considered a foreign people." In November of that year a law was passed allowing French nationality to be stripped from those already naturalized should they be deemed unworthy of the title of French citizen. (The minister of the interior explained the law as permitting a "filtering of the frontiers.")[120] One of the first legal measures of the Vichy regime was the *Statut des Juifs*, passed on 3 October 1940, excluding Jews from top positions in public service, from the officer corps, and from the ranks of non-commissioned officers. In a cruel irony, the right to hold menial public service positions would be reserved to Jews who had once served in the army.[121]

The day after the *Statut des Juifs* was passed, Jewish former deputy Pierre Massé, interned at Drancy before being deported to Auschwitz, wrote to Marshall Pétain:

> I would be obliged if you would tell me if I must remove the stripes from my brother, sub-lieutenant of the 36th Infantry Regiment, killed at Douaument in April 1916; from my son-in-law, sub-lieutenant in the 14th Dragoons, killed in Belgium in May 1940; from my nephew Jean-Pierre, killed at Rethel in May 1940. May I allow my brother to keep the medal he won at Neuville-Saint-Vaast, with which I buried him? Finally, can I be sure that no one will take away my great-grandfather's Sainte-Hélène medal? I want very much to abide by the laws of my country, even when they are dictated by the invader.[122]

"We Protest"—the Politics of Writing

"I thought there was a better way to serve a cause than to wrap oneself in blind faith"—if we now return to Picquart's words at

Zola's trial, we find that they received the strongest support from what might appear at first glance to be an unexpected quarter. *La revue blanche*, France's leading intellectual and literary fortnightly, founded in 1889, was home to some of Proust's earliest writing and boasted Blum as one of its foremost contributors. Over time its writers included Stéphane Mallarmé, Claude Debussy as music critic, and Alfred Jarry. Up until 1898, it seemed to share no aesthetic or ethical principles, no communal identity, except, perhaps—for some of its writers—the sense, in the words of A. B. Jackson in his book on the magazine, "of belonging to the race of Israelites."[123] Thadée Natanson, its proprietor, a wealthy Polish-Jewish art dealer who had settled in Paris in 1880, was a friend of Reinach's. Gustave Kahn, Julien Benda, and Bernard Lazare all wrote for the journal. On 1 February 1898, two weeks after the publication of "*J'Accuse*," the *Revue* published a "Protestation," proclaiming its belief that Dreyfus was the victim of a judicial error and its "nausea" at the Affair: "For the first time in judicial history, neither an infinitely probable error, recognised by many, nor the persistence of men with the authority or glory to point it out, is enough to ensure that a trial be judged according to the elementary forms and guarantees of equity."[124] If *La revue blanche* is exemplary, it is also because it was one of the few public forums in which Jews were willing to speak out in defense of Dreyfus.

In January 1895, Félix Fénéon, the anarchist and aesthete, had taken over the main editorial work. Acquitted of terrorism and sedition at the famous 1894 "Trial of the Thirty" against French anarchists, he considerably raised the journal's political profile, launching a small monthly column, *Passim (Here and There)*, exclusively focused on politics. The column's first entry referred to "lynching fury" at the degradation of Dreyfus. (Fénéon's biographer refers to him as a "Dreyfusard before the term was invented.")[125] In October 1896, the *Revue* published an article by Cuban anarchist revolutionary Tárrida del Mármol on his time spent in a Spanish jail (the first of fourteen articles by Tárrida to be published in the journal over the next fifteen months).[126]

Nonetheless, the "Protestation" on behalf of Dreyfus marked a turning-point. Overnight the *Revue* became a publication in the service of a political cause.[127] Zola accused. The *Revue* protested (its statement punctuated, like Zola's "*J'Accuse*," with the repeated formula "Nous protestons"). There was no rivalry, of course. The *Revue* saw itself as paying tribute to Zola. They published an article in his honor by Gustave Kahn on 15 February and an "Homage" on 1 March 1898, following the guilty verdict at his trial: "The verdict obtained on the 23rd February 1898, by the government signifies that, in France, one can no longer protest against moribund theories if a few officers choose to revive them; nor against monstrous procedures, as soon as they become the deed of a few superior military officers."[128] In an outburst that nothing in the five previous years of publication could have anticipated, *La revue blanche* picked up Zola's baton and ran with it. Even if Zola turned out to be wrong—a rhetorical concession since they were convinced he would not be—the youth of France could not fail to be moved by the "generous beauty of his act."[129]

In this they were appealing to what had always been an aesthetic dimension to the Affair. Reinach described it as a great poem (which had also inspired mediocre writers to poetry).[130] According to Lazare, Zola's early indifference turned to passion only when the Affair moved into the realm of melodrama: "Grace fell on Zola only when Esterhazy the traitor, Picquart the good genius, Dreyfus the martyr seized his imagination." "Our factual accounts became poetry for Zola," wrote Scheurer-Kastner, looking back on the Affair.[131] In fact, Zola's critique of anti-Semitism started earlier: his "Lettre à la jeunesse," excoriating French youth for its anti-Semitism, appeared in 1897, and his article "Pour les juifs" the year before.[132] Nonetheless, Lazare's was a judgment with which Zola himself concurred. "What a poignant drama, and what superb characters!" he opened a letter to *Le Figaro* of November 1897, a year before "*J'Accuse*," "Faced with documents of such tragic beauty, my novelist's heart leaps with passionate admiration. I know of no higher form of psychology."[133] Later he is somewhat embarrassed: "One will note in these first pages that the professional, the novelist, was above all seduced and exalted by such a drama," he writes in a note appended to a later publication of the letter. "And," he continues, "that pity, faith, the passion for truth and justice all came later."[134]

For anyone considering the Affair in relationship to the politics of writing, the *Revue* must surely constitute one of the most extraordinary resource books of its time. Certainly it tightens the link between justice and the world of literature with which we began. Proust wrote for it; although he had stopped doing so by 1898, he was unquestionably part of its milieu and was writing *Jean Santeuil* throughout the period of the journal's political agitation. *La revue blanche* was home to intellectuals, a term we in fact owe in its modern meaning to the Dreyfus Affair. "Manifesto of the Intellectuals" was the name of the petition in favor of Dreyfus which Proust had played his part in organizing. A quarter of a century later in 1927, Julien Benda, one of the *Revue*'s writers, was the author of the famous *Trahison des clercs*, or, as it is translated, *Betrayal of the Intellectuals*.[135] For the anti-Dreyfusards, the intellectuals were the chief culprits: "To the extent that a people becomes intellectual [*s'intellectualise*], it perishes," ultra-nationalist Maurice Barrès had written, "military virtues alone constitute the force of a nation."[136] Used by Barrès as a term of opprobrium, it was Georges Clemenceau who turned it into a badge of honor.[137] Barrès had been an important contributor to the *Revue*, but when he refused to support the *Revue* over Dreyfus, it published an open letter to him from Lucien Herr condemning his stance on the Affair. "I am one of those 'intellectuals,'" the letter opens, "whose protest has so distracted you."[138] "Do not count, in your least tolerable fantasies, on the support of hearts who once indulged you."[139]

In the eyes of the *Revue*, it was the writer's role to redeem the political disaster engulfing France: "It is the writer who is restoring to a diminished country a share of its former glory."[140] Or more prosaically, because patriotism will in fact be the target of the *Revue*'s most impassioned critique: "Justice, like charity, like solidarity, must always be able to count on writers."[141] It knew it was sticking its neck out. A basic mindset had taken hold of France: unconditional faith in nation and army; the belief that any challenge to the army threatened the stability of all national institutions and would fatally weaken the country; and finally, the deepest suspicion of intellectual life, a rejection, in the words of Robert Gauthier, key chronicler of the Affair, "of free enquiry masquerading as a call to action."[142] (This is perhaps the best definition of anti-intellectualism one could hope to get.) "To tolerate that an external force," writes Gauthier, "that of intellectuals, professors, writers and unaccountable journalists, that is, the force of mere opinion—be allowed to exert pressure on decisions taken by our authorities, is to open the door to subversion."[143]

Looking back, Blum described how they would meet every evening to plan their next move, commenting on the latest news as if it was a dispatch from the front.[144] To this extent, even if metaphorically, Proust was one of the crowd. Like Proust, the *Revue* drew its politics at least partly from the realm of the night: "Should action be the sister of the dream?"[145] (Siding with Dreyfus, it answered its own rhetorical question.) "What writer has not caressed the dream of bringing to life for a moment Paris in thought . . . , has not felt the desire to write down the evening of her thought" (le désir d'en écrire le soir de pensée).[146] Because it was the "simple right to thought" that had been assaulted by the Affair, the *Revue* could be said to have raised the power of thought, in its nighttime mode, to something of a political principle.[147] "Well may [those proclaiming his guilt] try to forget," Reinach had written in his 1896 pamphlet on Dreyfus on Devil's Island, "thought returns."[148] Picquart, as depicted by Proust, was not therefore the only character for whom the inner life was one of the strongest weapons against injustice.

In a run of articles—"The Peril," "The Dreyfus Affair and the Principle of Authority," "The Nationalist Idea," "The Traitor," "The 'Disciplot'" (*sic*), "The Tourniquet," and others—the *Revue* dismantled one by one the shibboleths of French nationhood—army, race, and nation—on which the case against Dreyfus had been built. (In this they were picking up the strand that had begun with Tárrida's prison account of 1896 and continued with reports of Fénéon's own experience—after being acquitted of sedition, he had posed for a series of drawings by Maximilien Luce illustrating the life of a prisoner in solitary confinement.)[149] "La 'Disciplote'" and "Le Tourniquet," two articles on the brutality of the French army toward its disciplined soldiers, were pieces of investigative journalism that laid out in graphic detail the forms of often fatal physical and psychological torture to which these prisoners were subjected. If, in the words of Jean Jaurès, it was known that soldiers were shot "without pardon or pity for a momentary lapse or act of violence" (he was arguing for restoration of the death penalty for treason at the time of Dreyfus's first trial), this was something else.[150] "By recording undeniable facts," "La 'Disciplote'" stated on the first page, "we will give an idea of the penitentiary institutions of the French army." *Exposés*—since that is what they were—they appeared in July and August 1900, the year after, therefore, of Dreyfus's pardon of 19 September 1899. For many of his family and many of his supporters, the pardon was a disaster. A pardon is only granted to the guilty. It spelled the end of the struggle for justice, while allowing the army—once more and wickedly—to save face. (Not until 1906 would Dreyfus be fully exonerated and reinstated in the army.) Aware, surely, of the echoes of the Affair that was now meant to fall from memory, the articles turn on the army in the remotest parts of the globe, exposing an unaccountable military authority without checks or balances, the "omnipotent" disciplinary counsel to which there is no appeal, and an inhuman regime that reduced men to wild animals: "Man is annihilated, only the beast exists." In the outreaches of empire—most of the stories come from Africa—the French army was reducing its own soldiers to Giorgio Agamben's "bare life." "The word torture is not exaggerated."[151]

Such practices, these articles insist, were routine—for instance, the use of grain silos to house the prisoner, which meant effectively burying him in the ground, a practice dating from the conquest of Algeria of 1830–1848. (Silos, *mesmour'ha* in Arabic, were the grain stores of the indigenous Arabs.) Some of these tortures—being cut off from the light, food and sleep deprivation, iron shackles—were treatments meted out to Dreyfus during the five years he spent incommunicado on Devil's Island. Reinach was not alone in describing Dreyfus's life on the island as a living tomb: "The Chamber thought to seal the tombstone over the Jew on Devil's Island for ever." (He was "shut inside a tomb," wrote Lazare, "from which he was never meant to reappear.")[152] Dreyfus also described himself as buried alive in a sepulchre.[153] "I have not had to do with judges," he is purported to have said after his trial, "but with executioners."[154] He opens his diary by describing his five-year incarceration as the time "when he was cut off from the world of the living."[155] Likewise, one of the prisoners in "La 'Disciplote'" is reported as building his own tomb: "The expression is no longer a metaphor."[156]

Again, the allusions must surely have been intentional. As Begley points out, the treatment of Dreyfus was an infraction of the law as regards the treatment of deportees whose freedom could be curtailed only to a level that would prevent escape and which did not allow for the incarceration of detainees. In 1899, at the heart of the Affair, Reinach had himself published a pamphlet claiming a miscarriage of justice in the cases of five prisoners subjected to forced labor who had clearly been condemned for their anarchist political opinions. (*Torture* was also his word.)[157] If treating a Jew inhumanely might—just—pass muster, the systematic brutalization of the nation's soldiers, even for disciplinary infractions, was surely something else. Reinach's pamphlet already indicated that miscarriages of justice were systematic. The articles in *La revue blanche* were ripping the cover off an institution that had blithely trusted in the belief that no one, in the words of General Gonse, would care a toss if a Jew was rotting on Devil's Island. This was a military machine out of control. A brutal colonialist army was treating its own disciplined soldiers like conquered natives. (Remember, the victims are Frenchmen, not even, say, Iraqis in Abu Ghraib.)

To write like this in 1900 was to attack a sacred object. As I have already discussed, for the anti-Dreyfusard, the fate of France as a nation depended on the glory of the army. (Barrès: "Military virtues alone constitute the force of the nation."[158]) "The famous *special honour of the army*," observed "Le Peril" on 1 June 1898, "is a cover for the privilege of lying, of treachery, of thieving with glory, and assassinating with impunity."[159] The political analysis offered by the *Revue* was focused and precise. France had become a military state: "All at once, we can see the State, in its terrifying power as military State. . . . The rule of law is over. . . . The despotism of the sword has begun."[160] The government was no more than a "vain shadow, fading away in the face of the Generals."[161] With uncanny prescience, the *Revue* was diagnosing the seeds of a totalitarianism that would come to fruition in 1940. Ze'ev Sternhell has described the anti-Dreyfusard League of Patriots as the first protofascist organization: "French fascism," he writes in *La droite révolutionnaire*, "is the direct heir of Barrès and Drumont."[162] France had submitted to the yoke of its generals. The rule of law was in thrall to an army. Raised to a "theocratic," "sacerdotal" principle,[163] it was idealizing itself in direct proportion to the violence it was meting out, not just to its own soldiers but also to other peoples: "To prove our indomitable courage, we go off and kill defenceless negroes . . . prey to the murderous insanity that fatally seizes a man with weapons."[164] "Scrape beneath your national patriotism," Herr wrote in the letter to Barrès, "you will find haughty, brutal, conquering France, pig-headed chauvinism . . . , the native hatred of everything that is other."[165]

Like Couzon in the Chamber in *Jean Santeuil*, the *Revue Blanche* rails against France's dereliction of duty toward the Armenians. (As with Proust, the *Revue Blanche* treated the collapse of justice in the case of Dreyfus as also an international affair.) In play is a world economy—again the echoes of today are striking: "Ministers in the pay of international High Finance, and a press which treats massacres in the East as if they were suicides in Monaco, lovingly nurture the bestiality of the crowd."[166] This is war as big business: "Everywhere the International of the Sword rouses and excites itself: the Church promotes it; Finance sustains it."[167] Likewise Georges Clemenceau had warned, "If absorbed by the idea of national defence, civil society abandoned itself to military servitude, then we might still have some soil to defend, but we would have abandoned everything which had given France her glory and renown in the world, ideas of liberty and social justice."[168] There was, the *Revue* insisted, no way to stand back "without degrading parts of the soul."[169]

If the Jew is not truly French, the question then arises, who is? Or where, in the words of Gustave Kahn in "The Nationalist Idea," "does France end, where does it begin?"[170] Without anti-Semitism, the absolutist state and its brutal army would lose a founding rationale. (The glory of the nation depends on its abjected other.) The critique of despotic army and state therefore entailed a no less spirited assault on ethnic hatred of the Jew. "It is not true," the "Protestation" asserted, "that the Jews belong to one race and the rest of France to another."[171] Nor should this be read simply as a demand for the right of the Jew to be a French citizen like any other (the assimilationist plea). At stake was a deconstruction of the very concept of nationhood as a metaphysical error—the idea of ethnic purity as an "ethnic metaphysic" that had laid hold of the whole nation.[172] Wedded to this "metaphysical idea of reality," the nationalists mistakenly believed in the idea of "*la France,* feminine, with a heart, arms, children and a past," in exactly the same way "as the salons believe in High Society."[173] The analogy is telling. Proust's exposure of high society, as relentless as it was devoted, can be read as a form of iconoclasm directed at the nation's most lofty vision of itself. Nationalism corresponded to "no need, no theoretical truth."[174] Against such constricted national passion, the vision of *La revue blanche* was inclusive. "You should know," Herr wrote to Barrès, "that if the word 'race' has any meaning, you, like the rest of us, are not the man of one race, but the product of three, six or twelve, melted together and indissolubly mixed in your person."[175] This is to take the blood of the nation—the racist, nationalist, metaphor par excellence—and pollute it in the name of humanity. Only at those times when it had been generous and reached out to the world had the soul of France ever been truly great and strong.[176] A people will only survive, I read them as saying, if it embraces the stranger it already is. There is, of course, a vital part of Jewish tradition in this: "Thou shalt neither vex a stranger nor oppress him. For you were strangers in the land of Egypt" (Exodus 22:21; also Deuteronomy, 10:19).

Mixed blood, no frontiers—you do not know where one nation, one race, ends and another begins. We can make the link from here straight back into the heart of Proust's writing. The first of his pieces, published in *La revue blanche* in 1893 and reprinted in *Les Plaisirs et les Jours*, subjects the frontier to the fluidity of natural life. "Études" tells the tale of the narrator's walk with a young love across the Swiss-Italian border, whose frontier, they are surprised to discover, is marked by no visible alteration in the landscape: "If the nature of the soil were to change, it would do so imperceptibly and we would have become acclimatised to it before arriving at the summit." "We fell in love," the story begins, "in a lost village in Engandine with a name of two-fold sweetness: the dream of German tones expiring in the voluptuousness of Italian syllables." Eros as a medley of tongues (the idea that love knows no boundaries in its linguistic mode). The lovers sit watching butterflies—"a tiny pink butterfly, then two, then five"—moving from one side of the riverbank to the other, vaulting over the lake, repeating time and time again their "adventurous crossing."[177] Remember that it was the quality of Alsace in Picquart that allowed him to see across the border and past the national and racial boundaries underpinning the Dreyfus Affair. (Mayeur describes Alsace as possessing a "mémoire frontière.")[178]

As always with Proust, such transgression is always also sexual. In the next tale—"Avant la nuit"—a dying friend of the narrator confesses her lesbianism to him, fearful of his response, but reassuring herself by recalling his own words to her on an earlier occasion: "How can we be indignant at habits which Socrates—who swallowed poison rather than commit an injustice—gaily recommended to his favourite friends? . . . Love, even of the sterile kind, knows no hierarchy and it is no less moral—or rather no more immoral—for a woman to find pleasure with another woman rather than with someone of another sex."[179] These are the first stirrings of the Proustian discourse on homosexuality, which will reach its apogee in *Sodome et Gomorrhe*. But even at this early stage (in fact, he is more emphatic on this matter here than he will be later), Proust is insisting that you will find no hierarchy, no clear-cut—let's say metaphysically sanctioned—distinctions in either nature or sex. Nor can there be any place for persecution of minorities in such a vision: "Who is to say that, just because most people see as red, objects that are classified as red, that those who see them as violet are mistaken?"[180]

On Being a Jew

Although many of the writers at *La revue blanche*, as well as its proprietor, were Jewish, they did not name themselves as Jews. "It was despite his Jewish origins," writes Tadié, "that a Jewish intellectual sided with Dreyfus."[181] The fight for justice, the critique of ethnic hatred, and the case for Dreyfus were all mounted in the name of universal humanitarian values in which we can already see the outlines of human rights discourse today. (For Drumont, an "inexorable universalism" was one of the most important failings of the Jew.)[182] We have to recognize, however, that for the Jewish defender of Dreyfus, such appeals to universality could also be a form of camouflage, a way of not standing out in the crowd, of covering up an identity which—it was sincerely felt—would do neither the case for Dreyfus nor the Jews of France any favors. To that extent, many Jews at the time, where they did not simply lie low, were drawn into a posture that could be mistaken for a betrayal of their people. On this topic, the most scathing of critics was Bernard Lazare, the first public defender of Dreyfus—his pamphlet, *Une erreur judiciare*, which had been commissioned by Dreyfus's brother Mathieu, was written in 1896, two years before "*J'Accuse*." (Three thousand copies were secretly printed abroad and then sent in sealed envelopes to members of parliament, notables, lawyers, and the press.) Throughout the whole saga, he never ceased to identify himself as a Jew: "Let it be said," he wrote in an open letter to the former minister of justice Ludovic Trarieux, "that the first who spoke, the first who stood up for the Jew martyr was a Jew, a Jew who suffered in his own flesh and blood the sufferings of that innocent man, a Jew who knew to which disinherited, wretched people of pariahs he belonged and who drew from this awareness the will to fight for justice and for truth."[183] "I am a Jew," he wrote in his account of his polemic with Drumont (they fought a duel), "having been born a Jew."[184] "Lazare spoke in the name of the Jew," the *Mercure de France* observed in their retrospective tribute of 1933, "at a time when it had all but been forgotten."[185]

Lazare had not been raised with a strong sense of Jewish identity, but to his mind this only made his task as Jew all the more pressing: "I am a Jew and I know nothing about the Jews," he wrote in one of his aphorisms. "Henceforth I am a Pariah and I know not out of what elements to rebuild myself a dignity and a personality. I must learn who I am and why I am hated and that which I can be."[186] For Lazare, therefore, being a Jew did not mean an exclusive ethnic identity. It was more like a project, an identity to be discovered and forged against hatred, as well as a form of continuous self-education (an *éducation sentimentale*, as one might say). Lazare belonged to those Jews, described by Léon Blum, deeply, eminently, capable of faith even when lacking in religious conviction: "But in what could such a non-religious faith consist? In a word, Justice. Just as science is the religion of the positivists, justice is the religion of the Jew."[187] "I belong to the race of those," Lazare said "who were first to introduce the idea of justice into the world.... All of them, each and every one, my ancestors, my brothers, wanted, fanatically, that right should be done to one and all, and that injustice should never tip unfairly the scales of the law. For that, over centuries, they cried out, sang, wept, suffered, despite the outrages, despite the insults spat at them. I am one of them and wish to be so. And that being the case, don't you think I am right to speak of those whom you haven't even dreamt of?"[188]

In a scathing attack, Lazare accused the Jews of France—"well do I know them"—of abandoning all solidarity with their own people and rejecting foreign-born Jews, on whom they dumped their own failings. Thus, they had become "more jingoist than the French people of France" (amongst whom he clearly has no desire to include himself or any Jew). Even if a few dozen may have come to the defense of "one of their martyred brothers," thousands more would have been willing to mount watch on Devil's Island along with the "most devoted champions of the fatherland": "The Jews have drawn away from each other, and shame of the Jewish name has come upon them."[189]

And yet, what is crucial about Lazare—and the reason why he brings the journey of this first chapter to its end—is that he demonstrates so clearly that to fight for justice as a Jew, against a pseudo-universalism in which any sense of being a Jew is lost, requires no restriction—indeed quite the opposite—of either your ethical or political vision. "I do not address those who are indifferent to either the iniquity or misfortunes of others," he wrote at the end of his introduction to the second edition of *L'erreur judiciare*. The worst of all, who inspired him with horror, were not only those who, declaring their concern for all humanity, turn aside from individual misery, but equally those who "only confer on their own unhappiness, or on the unhappiness that befalls one of their family, tribe, party or sect, the status of a universal calamity."[190] On this basis, he issued a warning still resonant today: "Do you think that I am acting only for those among Israel who suffer? Do you think the ancient prophets spoke for Judea alone? You are a Jewish patriot. Are you dreaming for your people only a miserable and selfish life? If one day you bring the debris of Israel back to Palestine to make a people of merchants and farmers whose minds are restricted to their fields and trading counters, then Israel will perish. A people can live only if it works on behalf of humanity."[191] For Lazare, there could be no exclusivity—not of family, party, sect, or tribe. "I have spoken out for one man's salvation, but in the name of all; so that freedom will be restored to an imprisoned man, but so as to safeguard the freedom of each and every citizen."[192] It was therefore possible—indeed, this is the wager of Bernard Lazare—to fight *as a Jew* for *all* humankind. According to Charles Péguy, there were two Dreyfus Affairs: "The one to emerge from Colonel Picquart was very fine. The one to come out of Bernard Lazare was infinite."[193] Proustian scholarship has also uncovered that Proust knew about and appreciated Lazare. A passage in the first draft of *Time Regained* laments the fact that Swann, "like so many others, died before the revelation that would have most moved them (Bernard Lazare, the Dreyfus Affair)."[194]

There is a line, we are often told, that runs from the Dreyfus Affair to the creation of Israel as a nation. It is true that, for many, Dreyfus signified the end of the dream of Jewish emancipation. Theodor Herzl, founder of political Zionism, was a journalist in Paris at the time of Dreyfus's first trial and would later describe this moment as inspiring his vision (although his reporting and diaries suggest that he made little connection at the time between the events in Paris and the fate of the Jews and was far more concerned with the electoral rise of Austrian anti-Semitism).[195] For a while, Lazare also became a Zionist, although he would finally fall out with Herzl and reject a political program in which he could no longer envisage a viable future for his people. What Lazare wanted above all was for Jews to acquire the status of free citizens, to gain the right, wherever they found themselves, to stand up and enjoy the sun. This was no metaphor. Following a wholly unfounded rumor of his escape planted in a newspaper by his brother in hopes of keeping the case alive in the public mind, Dreyfus's jailors raised an eight-foot high palisade all around his compound, cutting off all light and preventing him from seeing the sea. If we read the following passage in this context, then there can be no doubt that Lazare took his vision—all-inclusive, nonterritorial—from the Jew languishing on Devil's Island who has been my focus in the opening pages of this book:

For a Jew, the word *nationalism* should mean freedom. A Jew who today may declare, "I am a nationalist," will not be saying in any special, precise or clear-cut way, I am a man who seeks to rebuild a Jewish state in Palestine and who dreams of conquering Jerusalem. He will be saying, "I want to be a man fully free, I want to enjoy the sunshine, I want to have a right to my dignity as a man. I want to escape the oppression, to escape the outrage, to escape the scorn with which men seek to overwhelm me." At certain moments in history, nationalism is for human groups the manifestation of the spirit of freedom.[196]

The story: because of Dreyfus, so Israel, is not without some truth; what happened in France at the turn of the century was in many ways the forerunner of Vichy. But it is not the only story, and those who tell it risk blinding themselves to what Israel, as the nation for the Jewish people, has become. If the only lesson we learn from anti-Semitism is more and more anti-Semitism— of necessity, eternally, and as the core and limit of Jewish life— then we have learned nothing. A different version of the story would instead take from Dreyfus a warning—against an over-fervent nationalism, against infallible armies raised to the level of theocratic principle, against an ethnic exclusivity that blinds a people to the other peoples of the world, and against govern-ments that try to cover up their own crimes. In the chapters that follow, it is this story that I will tell, one that takes us from the heart of Dreyfus to Palestine, where the legacy of that dreadful saga is still being played out to this day. As we proceed, I will also be suggesting what vision of mental life—Proust's, to which we will now be adding Freud—can best help us make the journey. I will start with Freud, because of what psychoanalysis has to tell us about the cruelest divisions of the world and of the mind.

2

Partition, Proust, and Palestine

Though all human beings have many affiliations, with many distinct patterns of sharing (including the important commonalty of a shared human identity), these multiple identities are systematically downplayed in the cultivation of group violence, which proceeds through privileging exactly one affiliation as a person's "real identity," thereby seeing people in an imagined confrontation against each other across a single line of prioritized divisiveness.

«AMARTYA SEN, "We Can Best Stop Terror by Civil, Not Military, Means"[1]»

Impulses appear which seem like those of a stranger. . . . The ego says to itself: "This is an illness, a foreign invasion."

«SIGMUND FREUD, "A Difficulty in the Path of Psycho-Analysis"[2]»

Generally speaking, what we call the world, whenever we might observe it, is divided, like a cake one might have cut into two pieces, not necessarily equal but seeming to be separated forever.

«MARCEL PROUST, "Notes for *Time Regained*"[3]»

In the sky of the Old City
a kite.
At the other end of the string,
a child
I can't see
because of the wall.

We have put up many flags,
they have put up many flags.
To make us think that they're happy.
To make them think that we're happy.
«YEHUDA AMICHAI,"Jerusalem"[4]»

A Rift in the Mind

Minds, like nations, divide. If in the last chapter, I was able to appeal to the inner life against a corrupt law and state, now we must turn to its darker, more recalcitrant, side. Otherwise we make our task too easy. As if the mind itself cannot be implicated, at the deepest level, in the social order from which it suffers most. Psychoanalysis begins with the recognition that the mind is a divided terrain—miming, if not at times engendering, the antagonisms of the outside world. Tracing the evolution of Freud's thinking on this question will allow me, before returning to Proust and Dreyfus, to probe further what the mind is capable of doing, not only to others, but also to itself. It will allow us to understand more deeply the violent lengths we will go to in order to rid ourselves of what—both in the world and in the heart—we cannot bear.

Anna O was the first psychoanalytic patient—her analysis with Josef Breuer opens Breuer's and Freud's *Studies on Hysteria*, which effectively inaugurated psychoanalysis when it was published in 1895. (Psychoanalysis is a contemporary of the Dreyfus Affair.)[5] Faced with the anguish of her own thoughts, Anna O's body froze and she started babbling in tongues. Then she started living in two times, exactly a year ago and the present, switching from one to the other, as if, instead of being two related moments of a continuous history, they were different worlds. She cut in and back, like a character from Phillip Pullman's *His Dark Materials*, rending the sleek, deceptive, surface of the everyday. It is a paradox inherent in psychoanalysis that it will struggle to link the different parts of the patient's torn inner landscape while teaching us, through the theory of the unconscious, that the mind is not its own home. In our mental lives, we are fundamentally inhospitable to ourselves.

In the earliest stages, Freud treated the symptom as an unwelcome intruder. His task was not wholly unlike that of the exorcist. "*Hysterics*," he famously wrote, "*suffer mainly from reminiscences*."[6] Call up the dreaded memory, and the symptom, in a flash, would be gone. "*We found, to our great surprise at first*," he wrote with Breuer in the 1893 "Preliminary Communication" to *Studies in Hysteria*, "*that each individual symptom immediately and permanently disappeared when we had succeeded in bringing clearly to light the memory of the event by which it was provoked and in arousing its accompanying affect, and when the patient had described that event in the greatest possible detail and had put the effect into words*."[7] It was, Breuer comments, "a therapeutic and technical procedure which left nothing to be desired in its logical consistency and systematic application."[8] We should, however, be suspicious. The idea of "leaving nothing to be desired" is, to say the least, a radically unpsychoanalytic thought (not to speak of "logical consistency" and "systematic explanation"). For psychoanalysis, it is a delusion to think that anything, ever, is completely dropped or lost from the mind.

As so often, we do not have to wait long for Freud to become suspicious himself, to question this early confidence which, in the beginning, he had shared with Breuer. By the end of the *Studies on Hysteria*, he knew that things are not as easy or clear as this. (He and Breuer had also parted ways.) As the "beauty" and "completeness" of the earlier therapeutic procedure started to crumble, it was nothing less than the theory of unconscious process that began, hesitantly and tantalizingly, to emerge. Freud suspected that the processes he started to outline in his concluding essay to *Studies on Hysteria* might one day acquire the value of raw material for the whole dynamics of thought. Between the earliest trauma and the symptom, the mind had taken flight, weaving a web of thoughts, memories, and desires that could no longer be held to some mythic, originary place. Something has started to radiate and grow that could lead anywhere. You cannot simply, with surgical precision, lift the foreign body out of the mind. You cannot remove, extirpate, expel what you don't like— or who you don't like, we might add. "We have said," he writes, "that [the pathogenic material] behaves like a foreign body, and that the treatment, too, works like the removal of a foreign body from the living tissue. We are now in a position to see where this comparison fails."[9]

As always with Freud, failure is eloquent. Imagine something so embedded in the tissue surrounding it that to remove it would be to endanger what is healthy as much as what is ill. Looking back on the Dreyfus Affair, Proust uses almost exactly this image when critiquing the post-Dreyfus abolition of religious education, which was central to the new separation of church and state initiated by Prime Minister Émile Combes, who came to power in 1902. Anticlerical politics, Proust wrote in a letter to Georges de Lauris in 1903, was dividing France in two and the gulf was widening by the day: "You can answer me by saying that if you have a tumor and live with it, in order to remove it I have to make you very ill. . . . Such indeed was my reasoning during the Affair." But now he knows better. The struggle for Dreyfus had not redeemed France, whose divisions remained deep inside the nation. The new law, he believed, would exacerbate the hatreds it was designed to placate. ("If I thought that once the religious teaching orders were destroyed, the ferment of hatred among the French people would be destroyed as well, I should consider it a very good thing to do; but I think exactly the opposite.")[10] In a bizarre footnote to this moment, the banning of headscarves in French schools and more recently the burqa or niqab on the street is likewise intended to guarantee the secular unity of the nation, and in so doing eliminate religious-cum-political tensions which it is most likely to intensify.[11]

Like Proust, Freud comes to realize that his early idea of cleaning out the stables of the mind had been a dream (a white-wash, as one might say). "The pathogenic idea," he writes, cannot "be cleanly extirpated from the ego," because its "external strata" pass in every direction into the ego: "In analysis the boundary between the two is fixed purely conventionally, now at one point, now at another, and in some places it cannot be laid down at all."[12] There is no fixed boundary between the pathogenic idea and the rest of the mind. Now he describes the pathogenic idea as an "infiltrate" and analysis as making resistance to that idea's presence "melt," so that "the circulation" can "make its way into a region that has hitherto been cut off."[13] We are talking—again— about border crossings (like the Alsace frontier or the lost border village of Engandine). Defying territorial propriety, the contents of the mind shift from place to place. Imagine a house, a land, with moving walls.

Here as elsewhere, Freud's vocabulary carries an unmistakable political weight. What he is really discussing, and this will become a crux for future psychoanalysis, is how far we should recognize what is foreign and unwelcome, as an inherent part of ourselves (impulses "like those of a stranger"; the ego says "this is a foreign invasion").[14] Hence, the central concept of this second chapter—Partition—which has such global resonance today. It is an act of partition that brings the state of Israel into being, at the same time as—indeed, almost simultaneously with—the act of partition that creates India and Pakistan. Although there are key differences, both these events, coming close on the heels of the Second World War, had as their antecedent and prior model the partition of Ireland after the First.[15] In the case of Israel-Palestine and India, what was involved was an actual or putative eviction of peoples as a political solution whose violent consequences are with us to this day. Significantly, Freud touches on this domain and deflects it from such an outcome, or rather deflects it precisely insofar as this outcome is one that psychoanalysis also had first to reckon with and even to some extent entertain. In the brief space of two years (Freud writes his final essay of *Studies on Hysteria* in 1895), we have moved from fixed borders and foreign bodies to bodies merging and liquids that circulate and flow. You get rid of nothing. Instead, it becomes the task of analysis to create movement into once inaccessible territories where you thought you had no right to go ("a region that has hitherto been cut off"). Freud's geographic terrain has undergone a seismic shift. In fact, we can see this as a shift between two languages of militarization—one close to classical defensive strategies, the other sounding more like the lightning incursions of guerilla war. Something infiltrates, crossing over enemy lines.

I think it is no coincidence that psychoanalysis finds itself struggling over this ground. Certainly, as I will argue in this chapter, the fact and way that it does so has the utmost relevance for anyone trying to think about the divided, contested worlds we live in today. We are the offspring of partition—worlds not so much crumbling as cracking into parts that petrify and freeze. (The wish to expel the Jews at the time of Dreyfus thus stands at the historic beginning of the journey this book will now trace.) And once so formed, it seems to be almost impossible for the shape, let alone the people, to give, or let go. Group violence, writes Amartya Sen in my opening epigraph, cultivates "a single line of prioritized divisiveness."[16] Or in Proust's striking image, the world is like a cake cut into unequal pieces that appear—but only appear—to be separated for ever ("qui semblent à jamais séparées").[17] Psychoanalysis proper begins, one could argue, with two insights whose relationship will then color the whole of psychoanalysis to come: the mind is divided, but the boundaries between one part of the mind and another are strangely porous. We could then perhaps say that in that first overconfident moment of 1893, when Breuer and Freud were boasting of the efficiency and beauty of their procedure, they were acting not on the hysteric, so much as *with* her: trying and failing, like her—like all of us—to extirpate the unwanted part of the mind. By 1895, Freud knows better. The foreign body will not be expelled. We are all the failed ethnic cleansers of our own souls.

Psychoanalysis will not recover from this insight. Or to put it another way, the question of how to think about division will divide the psychoanalytic community in turn. Freud's famous posthumously published essay "The Splitting of the Ego in the Process of Defence" is a crucial case in point. This deceptively slight, unfinished paper was written near the end of 1937.[18] Freud was writing it on the eve of the year of the Anschluss, which would force him to leave Austria, at the same time, therefore, as he was trying to complete *Moses and Monotheism*.[19] That most tormented of his final works argued not just that Moses was an Egyptian (thereby, as he acknowledged in the opening lines, depriving the Jewish people of the man they regard as the greatest of their sons) but also that there had been two Moses and that two historic moments and figures were at the origin of the faith (another iconoclasm, to deprive the Jewish people of one divinely sanctioned genesis).[20] It is as if the question of what unites and divides a people—the Jewish people—and what coheres and splits the mind were inseparable in his own thought. From hysteria to *Moses* and the splitting of the ego, Freud's work begins and ends here. Something in both mind and world is radically torn. Unity of self and history is a myth. From the outset, this was an insight that put Freud on the defensive, as if he knew where it might lead. The idea of a divided mind is an affront to the ego that does not take kindly to thus being dethroned. (Later he would attribute hostility to psychoanalysis to this idea at least as much as to its account of sexuality.) "No one should object," he had written in his 1893 obituary for his great mentor Jean-Martin Charcot, "that the splitting of consciousness [die Theorie einer Spaltung der Bewustseins] as a solution to the riddle of hysteria is much too remote to impress an unbiased and untrained observer."[21]

"The Splitting of the Ego" is a caution, perhaps Freud's strongest statement against our belief in the consistency—one could say the safety—of our own minds. What Freud had uncovered was a challenge to his own thought, to his belief, or perhaps hope—one that will be consolidated in a whole psychoanalytic tradition to come—that the ego is the great synthesizer, the bearer of an ultimate consolation, something that transcends and resolves the clashes of the mind. This, he stated, is a mistake. We are in danger of taking for granted the "synthetic processes of the ego."[22] To put it more simply, we want to believe that the mind is a single place. "But we are clearly at fault in this."[23] Thus, a traumatized child will partially acknowledge an unwelcome, threatening reality even as he pushes it away with another part of his mind. But while he may thereby achieve a partial success in dealing internally with the problem, he will have done so "at the price of a rift in the ego which never heals but which increases as time goes on."[24] "The two contrary reactions persist as the centre-point of a splitting of the ego" (als Kern einer Ichspaltung bestehen).[25] It is a procedure, as Freud notes, "which we would prefer to reserve for psychoses."[26] "And," he concludes, "it is not in fact very different."[27] We are far from Proust's lyrical image of a child lost in slumber (Picquart creatively lost in his own thoughts). Freud's child is mentally tearing herself asunder.

Whether Freud could bear his own conclusion, and whether its difficulty played a part in the paper being left unfinished, can only be conjecture. Nonetheless, as the paper trails off, Freud has left us with a painful insight, a vision of the ego brushing against psychosis as it splits across the dilemma of whether reality can be borne. "We take for granted the synthetic nature of the processes of the ego. But we are clearly at fault in this." The ego splits. Psychosis, or something close, is the price the subject willingly pays to reject what it cannot abide. Or to put it another way, madness is the form whereby human subjects routinely police themselves. Armies who lie and generals who commit perjury are therefore the tip of the iceberg (the inflated or caricatured version of our proclivity to self-deceit). How much of our unconscious lives are any of us willing, or able, to own? In this last paper, the question with which we started—the question of the hysteric but also, remember, Freud's own—returns to haunt the final moments of his thought, to become the core—*das Kern*—of the ego: Can you expel the foreign body or is it, irrevocably, part of yourself? This was, of course, the question at the heart of the Dreyfus Affair. Remember Lucien Herr had written to Maurice Barrès in 1898, "You should know that if the word *race* has any meaning, you, like the rest of us, are not the man of one race, but the product of three, six or twelve, melted together and indissolubly mixed in your person."[28] To what lengths will the mind go to rid itself of a stranger, or to shut down the thought it does not want to hear?

And if the mind is torn apart by this question, then we should not perhaps be surprised, as we gaze on the scarred landscape of contemporary political life, that so too is our world.

Psychoanalysis will at once grow and flounder over this question. Thus, what might seem to be the most logical response to Freud's paper will be to fortify the ego, to give it the strength and coherence that, Freud is quite unequivocal here, it fundamentally if not constitutively lacks. Against this form of ego-psychology, in which his own analyst, Ralph Lowenstein, played an important role, the response of Jacques Lacan will be to go in the opposite direction, to insist that the problem is not the weakness of the ego but its delusion in thinking it is equal to the task. Crucially, in Lowenstein's case, the defensiveness—the belief that the ego must be stronger—has to be understood as the response of his flight, as a Jew, from Hitler's Germany: the mind fortifying itself in the face of horror. (What does the mind need to withstand the worst?)[29] But for Lacan, with no less an ear for the historical origins and resonance of his concepts, this is a false consolation. Only a duped ego—one struggling, and inevitably failing, to believe in its own indomitable powers—will try to master the complex life of the mind. To strengthen the ego is therefore to fall into the trap that the ego sets for itself. Instead, it should be the aim of analysis to help the patient acknowledge the ego's partial frailty and, with it, the destitution of a subject who will readily destroy the world in the attempt to hold him- or herself together. "Everything that disturbs order," proclaimed Charles Maurras in his preface to a line-by-line critique of Reinach's history of the Dreyfus Affair, "is an injustice."[30] (In his view, nobody since Barrès and Drumont had done more for France than the author of this volume-length critique.) Justice and injustice can be turned on their heads, twisted to any end, provided the world stays in shape. There is nothing more dangerous than the conviction that our overriding duty to the world is, at whatever cost, to get everything under control and to hold it all together.

Thus, while James Strachey translated Freud's famous formula: "Wo es war, soll ich werden" as "Where Id was, there Ego shall be," Lacan countered: "There where it was, so must I come to be." No false sovereignty. The subject must move back across the border, cede itself to the world it most fears. Think of the ego not as a wall—or "security barrier," to use the euphemism for the Wall that today carves through the lives and lands of the Palestinians—nor as the LOC, or Line of Control, snaking its way between the India- and Pakistan-controlled parts of disputed Kashmir. Rather, think of it as something more like a suspension bridge—perhaps the derelict wooden bridge across the Jhelum river, whose repair became something of a devotional project in April 2005 so that the restored bus service could, for the first time since 1949, ferry people from both sides of the border across the line. Or, think of the young French lover at the lost border village of Engadine in Proust's "Études," of my first chapter, relishing the mixed sonorities of the German and Italian tongues. It is sheer fantasy, Proust wrote to Mme Straus in January 1898, to believe that the French language is in need of protection. In fact, it is an assault on language that freezes it in an "apparent immobility which hides perpetual, vertiginous activity."[31] In response to such an assault, Proust offers us instead an unsettled world and an in-built resistance to all principles of social order and control. (Bowie describes this as a "hallmark" of his political vision.) However rigid the border, in the eyes of both Proust and Freud, the world is always stirring beneath: "matter constantly shifting about, unfit to be the landscape of political control," in the recent words of painter Thérèse Oulton to give an up-to-date rendering.[32] For Léon Blum, the best thing about the Dreyfus Affair was the forms of connivance, the secret ties of sympathy and understanding, which made their way beyond— "au delà"—the frontiers.[33]

Proust and Partition

In *Enlightenment in the Colony*, Aamir Mufti traces the historic link between the "Jewish question" in Europe, which has so far been my topic, and the crisis of partition and Muslim identity in India.[34] He is interested in how the most famous modern acts of political partition—India-Pakistan and Israel-Palestine—are grounded in the belief in a radical separation of peoples and the need to preserve their distinct racial and ethnic purity, a belief at the core of the Dreyfus Affair: the Jew is not a Frenchman whose patriotism grows from his heart, in Drumont's image, like a name carved into the bark of a tree. At the end of a discussion of George Eliot's *Daniel Deronda*, Mufti writes: "This manner of settling the Jewish Question is thus *the first instance historically* of those modes of thinking that seek resolution of the minority crisis of the (majoritarian) nation-states through a *partition of society*, modes of thinking that have become the norm globally in the course of the twentieth century."[35] Partition, he is arguing, is the offspring of the Jewish Question in Europe—for India, as much as for Palestine. This is to say far more than that India and Palestine are the legatees of British colonialism (Britain's policies having been at the origin of partition in both parts of the globe); it is to go much further than simply to stress that the crisis of Palestine today is the consequence of the Balfour declaration of 1917 or that the partition of India was heir to the ethnically based prescriptions and fostered divisions of imperial rule. Rather, it is to suggest that the very idea of partition, offered as the solution to a crisis of peoples, is in fact a repetition of the very mode of thought, the historical process which, in the case of the Jews of Europe, it was intended to resolve. In Mufti's important argument, it is because Europe could not, would not, assimilate the Jew that the lines of fissure that are India-Pakistan and Israel-Palestine today are etched over the land. There is an especially poignant irony in this in relation to the Middle East. More or less from the time of Dreyfus, the Jews actively sought a national homeland—they wanted, as Lazare put it, to stand up in the sun and be free: "At certain moments in history, nationalism is for human groups the manifestation of the spirit of freedom."[36] They did not stop to consider that by carving up the land, tearing it into two (more than unequal) parts, they were ushering into the Middle East the very principle—the partition of peoples— that, cruelly staged in Europe, had made their need so urgent.

Partition, therefore, begins at home. In fact, Theodor Herzl comes close to making the same point. He is famous for describing the envisaged Jewish state as an "outpost of civilisation as opposed to barbarism," but in "A Solution of the Jewish Question," published in the *Jewish Chronicle* in 1896, the same year as his historic pamphlet *Der Judenstaat*, barbarism makes another appearance, this time in the heart of Europe: "Two phenomena arrest our attention by reason of the consequences with which they are fraught," he writes. "One, the high culture, the other, the profound barbarism of our day."[37] And then he explains: "By profound barbarism, I mean anti-Semitism."[38] In commentary on Herzl, this second appearance of the term, unlike the first, is rarely mentioned. The two uses are, however, inseparable. Herzl has, as it were, diagnosed his own orientalist vocabulary. Barbarism is a European problem—as was made plain by the Dreyfus Affair (doubtless one reason why Herzl retrospectively insisted that it was the trial of Dreyfus that had made him a Zionist). The barbarism that the Jewish state is meant to redeem for the backward Arab people is in fact his own European legacy. Long before the horrors of the Second World War will offer its deadly confirmation to his insight, Herzl has more or less stated that barbarism—like partition, we can say—originates in the West. Writing much later, Hannah Arendt will make the same point: "The danger is that a global universally interrelated civilisation may produce barbarians from its own midst." She is writing of totalitarianism as a phenomenon "within, not outside, our civilisation": "Deadly danger to any civilisation is no longer likely to come from without."[39]

If we return to Proust, we can now watch the Dreyfus Affair laying its brutal dividing lines over the world of the salons. In *À la recherche*, politics becomes a form of refinement, of subtle barbs and innuendo, of barely concealed forms of cruelty, in many ways more repellent, and at times even more frenzied, than the head-on political portraits which took us directly into the courts and halls of government in *Jean Santeuil*. On Dreyfus, Proust— it is agreed by more than one critic—will sacrifice his neutrality as a narrator.[40] However foolish or even ridiculous they may appear at times, the Dreyfusards are never as repellent as the repeatedly ridiculed anti-Dreyfusards ("stupid" and "unprepossessing," as he described the conservatives in one of his letters to Reinach).[41] For Malcolm Bowie, Proust offers, through his narrator's take on the Affair, his own version of Zola's "*J'Accuse*."[42] "During the Dreyfus Affair," Proust writes in his notes for *Le temps retrouvé*, "the life of the salon took on the character of political meetings."[43] It is his particular gift to take the hushed voices of the drawing room and then to raise the volume, as if, instead of watching the most elegant members of Parisian high society as they glide around a ballroom or dinner party, we were witnessing them all screaming at a horse race.

As we have already discussed, Proust's relationship to his own Jewishness was ambivalent, an ambivalence expressed in the first instance by the simple fact that his narrator is not a Jew. Like his homosexuality, Proust's Jewishness is put under erasure only for both to surface as the abiding and, at moments, twinned preoccupations of *À la recherche*. Remember these words in his letter to Montesquiou of 1896: "If I have not replied to what you asked me about the Jews, it is for this very simple reason. If I am Catholic, like my father and brother, on the other hand my mother is Jewish."[44] Somewhere Proust knows that to have a Jewish mother is to be Jewish. Rejecting his Jewish identity, Proust renounces his maternal legacy, aligns himself with the world of brothers and fathers, whom he had opposed when supporting Dreyfus, and enters high society in disguise.

While this transformation can be read as evasion or even denial, I see it as central to Proust's genius, because it is a move that allows him, in the very form of the writing, to make a political point. However deep one's inward Jewishness, to be Jewish in Dreyfusard France is to be someone who strictly must only be observed from the outside, as if through a lorgnette. After all, Swann, the assimilated Jew par excellence, who betrays the salons with his support of Dreyfus, was "almost the only Jew anyone knew."[45] "And this is how he repays us," expostulates Monsieur de Guermantes, "a society that had adopted him, has treated him as one of its own. . . . We've obviously been too easy going, and the mistake Swann is making will create all the more stir, since he was respected, not to say received."[46] The tone, the narrator stresses, is inoffensive, not vulgar, rather that of a father let down by the misdemeanors of a carefully educated and much loved son. But although he may not be aware of it, M de Guermantes's distress arises from a sinister shift in the political climate. Anti-Dreyfusard opposition, the narrator tells us, has become more "violent," no longer just political, in the sense of alignments, but something that is insinuating itself into the very fabric of social life: "It was now a question of militarism, of patriotism, and the waves of anger that had been stirred up in society had had time to gather the force which they never have at the beginning of a storm."[47]

We then watch as a sense of personal betrayal slips into a more public, and potentially killing, judgment: "We were all of us prepared to vouch for Swann," Guermantes then continues: "I would have answered for his patriotism as for my own. He has proved that they're all secretly united and are somehow forced to give their support to anyone of their own race. It's a public menace."[48] Behind the figure of the one Jew, all Jews. The "traitor" Dreyfus, and each of his supporters, becomes the emblem for the treachery of the whole race. Dreyfus, as we saw, was taken to represent "all Israel" (tout Israël).[49] Remember too the calls for expulsion, and even extermination, that accompanied the Affair. Loosely, in the shadows, we can already see taking shape in these moments of Proust's novel one logic, or rather sublogic, of genocide: not as many Jews as possible, not even all Jews, although that, of course, was the intent, as if the issue were quantitative, cumulative; but the whole race struck down with the death of each and every one. Swann will be the scapegoat. By the time we have reached this point in the story, it is clear to everyone that he will soon die.

As Hannah Arendt describes in her analysis of anti-Semitism in *The Origins of Totalitarianism*, Proust lays out with stunning clarity that strange amalgam of treachery and viciousness that combined in the image of the Jew in late nineteenth-century

France, in such a way as at once to strip from him all true political belonging, open the doors of the salons to his presence, while making him utterly vulnerable to its most violent, degrading whims. "'Punishment is the right of the criminal',"writes Arendt, citing Hegel, "of which he is deprived if (in the words of Proust) 'judges assume and are more inclined to pardon murder in inverts and treason in Jews for reasons derived from original sin and racial predestination.'"[50] As we saw in the last chapter, the Jew is inherently a traitor. But if Jews are racially predestined to be traitors, then they are—perversely—absolved of all crimes. It is, of course, a poisoned chalice, for Jewishness then becomes the insignia of an inherent propensity to the very crime of which, formally at least, they have been absolved. Treachery slides into viciousness, something far more slippery, like an ink blot spreading across a clean white page. "As far as the Jews were concerned," Arendt writes, "the transformation of the 'crime' of Judaism into the fashionable 'vice' of Jewishness was dangerous in the extreme. Jews had been able to escape from Judaism into conversion; from Jewishness there was no escape. A crime, moreover, is met with punishment; a vice can only be exterminated."[51] Writing in 1950, Arendt traces the line from the divisions of early twentieth-century French society into the death camps of Europe.

It is obvious to Arendt that a society that tolerates the Jew on such terms is itself in love with murder and vice. Those most passionately attached to their mascot Jews, the so-called Philo-Semites, will be the ones who rush to expurgate France of its Jewish citizens when the time comes: "as though they had to . . . cleanse themselves of a stigma which they had mysteriously and wickedly loved."[52] Almost contemporaneously with Freud, but in my view always one step ahead, Proust is describing the logic of projection, while giving it its fullest social import. The Jew will be included, on condition of representing pure difference, and then got rid of (for the same reason) as a way of allowing French society to avoid confronting the truth about itself. The real lines of division, as they are rehearsed in the niceties of the Parisian salons, cut through the Frenchman's own soul. Freud does not quite say it in *Studies on Hysteria*, although it is a truism and he will get to it later, that we love and are profoundly attached to what we most hate. You cannot extirpate the foreign body, not just because it is embedded in the surrounding tissue, but because it is also a cherished part of who we are. Even when he tries to divide the world of the drives into Eros and Thanatos—the impulse to partition was not alien to Freud—he has to acknowledge that, while Eros is our best hope in binding our destructive impulses, an admixture of Eros can, instead of defeating them, greatly enhance their strength. "Aberrations are like our loves," Proust writes in *Time Regained*, "in which the germ of disease has spread victoriously to every part."[53] Aberration—Scott Moncrieff glosses this as "perversion"—is like a disease, is like love. It spreads, gets to you, everywhere. Counterintuitively (no one likes to think of love as a disease), but with immense political foresight, Proust is analyzing the erotic subtext of the worst anti-Semitic fantasies.

With startling precision, Proust charts the logic of projection across the Parisian social scene, including, as Julia Kristeva stresses in her study of Proust, its sadomasochistic underside. Like George Eliot in Aamir Mufti's reading—except that a quarter of a century later things are much worse—he also shows us how the Jewish question travels, if only in fantasy, to the East. (At the end of her novel, Deronda will travel to Zion to create a homeland for the Jews.) Thus, Baron Charlus, loyal to Drumont's *La france juive*, pays Bloch the dubious compliment of not being a traitor in supporting Dreyfus, since no Jew can be a Frenchman—a belief which, in the eyes of the anti-Semite, made Dreyfus's arrest an act of grace. This idea was repeated to me, more or less verbatim, when I found myself sitting next to a man who introduced himself as Charles de Gaulle's grandson in a restaurant in Paris a few years ago.[54] Then, in almost the same breath, Charlus expresses his desire—in words the narrator will characterize as "affreux et presque fous"—to witness a spectacle or performance of Bloch's Jewish nature: "some great festival in the Temple, a circumcision or some Hebrew chants."[55] As the pitch of his desire intensifies, he asks for more:

You might even arrange some comic turns. For instance, a contest between your friend and his father, in which he would smite him as David smote Goliath.

That would make quite an amusing farce. He might even, while he was about give his mother a good thrashing. . . . It would make an excellent show, the sort of thing we like, eh, my young friend with our taste for exotic spectacle, and to thrash that non-European bitch would be giving a well-earned punishment to that old cow.[56]

Thus, the Jew is lifted out of Europe. But, as with Herzl's barbarism, the hideous spectacle comes home to roost, shows its proper national affiliation. Charlus's dream will come true, but inflicted, willingly, on his own body. Sketched out in this imagined humiliation of Bloch are all the contours of the famous flagellation scene to come, set in Jupien's brothel during the war in *Finding Time Again*, in which Charlus, witnessed by the hidden narrator through a small oval window that opens the room onto the corridor, abases himself at the hands of a man who, it turns out, is simply pretending to be depraved. As with the Bloch fantasy, the pleasure resides crucially in the staging. Charlus becomes the master of ceremonies, as well as casting himself in the starring role, of his own hideous anti-Semitic dream.

If this moment risks—and by no means for the first time in Proust's book—twinning invert and Jew in their joint allegiance to vice, there is nonetheless a crucial asymmetry at play. The humiliation of Bloch is sheer fantasy, called up from the ugliest depths of Charlus's own mind. Vice is, therefore, the property of the Frenchman. It is not the "non-European bitch" but the European baron who truly deserves, longs for, a thrashing. Note too the key elements in the first part of Charlus's desired spectacle for Bloch, so easy to overlook once the going gets rough, as it were—"some great festival in the Temple, a circumcision or some Hebrew chants"—epithets which hand over the Jew to a degraded, parodic form of ancestral belonging: Temple, circumcision, and the Hebrew tongue. Barely concealed beneath these fantasies, there is, of course, a logic of expulsion. According to his wife, the Duc de Guermantes "has always maintained that all the Jews ought to be sent back to Jerusalem."[57] Remember the anti-Dreyfusard who insisted that Dreyfus had not betrayed his country, "which is the temple of Jerusalem."[58] Reinach had called it the "moral expulsion" of the Jew.[59] "For the repatriation of the dirty Jews in Israel"; "Treat the Jews as if they all had the plague and send them off to Palestine"—just two expressions of this sentiment from the Henry petition at the time.[60]

For Proust, on the other hand, such a vision is anathema. These are the two occasions in the novel in which the narrator is impelled to speak out, going so far as to characterize what he sees as insane. Charlus's words are "affreux et presque fous"—"hideous, almost insane" ("dreadful, almost deranged").[61] The narrator leaves us in no doubt that this form of anti-Semitism is repellent and disturbed, the symptom of the mind that produces it. Later on, as he is leaving the brothel, the narrator says to Jupien: "[This house] is worse than a madhouse, since the mad fancies (la folie) of the lunatics who inhabit it are staged as actual, visible, drama."[62] The madness of the inmates—"la folie des aliénés"—"is staged, it is played out, it is all on display."[63] Madness brought to life. Perversion as psychosis made flesh. (One definition of the psychotic is that it is someone whose dreams come true.) From the depths of the Frenchman's unconscious arises a bloody spectacle that you have to rub your eyes to believe: "there in the room . . . receiving the blows that Maurice rained upon him with a whip which was in fact studded with nails, I saw, with blood already flowing from him . . . I saw before me M de Charlus."[64] In Proust's hands, the dividing line between Jew and non-Jew, a division he charts with such meticulous precision, submits to a radical, sexual disorientation. In the unconscious at least, the partition of the nation fails.

And not only in the unconscious. Proust has the ability, like no other writer, I would say, to portray the most rigid social divisions at the same time as he puts us as readers at an oblique angle to them, so that they also seem, in the very moment we think we have grasped them, refracted by the light, to start shimmering and then dissolve. Raoul Ruiz's brilliant 1999 film of *Time*

Regained opens with Marcel lying on his deathbed dictating his novel to Céleste Albaret, his housekeeper and confidante. As the camera pans slowly on its axis round the room, it takes a few moments for the spectator to register that the movement of the furniture is not quite justified by that of the camera. Rather, the room is undulating and the furniture has a life of its own. Ruiz crafts these bold formal properties of his opening scene out of this one line from *Combray*: "Perhaps the immobility of the things that surround us is forced upon them by the conviction that they are themselves and not anything else, by the immobility of our conception of them."[65] The French is "notre pensée d'elles," translated in the new version as "the immobility of our mind confronting them."[66] Whether thought or mind, Proust is suggesting, as a type of opening gambit in *À la recherche*, that the fixity of the world is an illusion, summoned by the mental rigidity of the one who is facing it. And if it is only the immobility of our minds that secures the objects of the world, then he is also stating, against the most fundamental law of logic, but true to the logic of the unconscious, that things are both what they are and what they are not at the same time.

George Eliot, writing a quarter of a century earlier, did not, of course, have this formal option as a way of illustrating the disenchantment, not to say decadence, of her world. But while the end of *Daniel Deronda* may seem to fulfill the dream of Zion, I would suggest that she is more wary about her own solution, more alert than tends to be allowed to the strange and potentially unrealizable component of Deronda's vision—an aspect of their longing of which the founding fathers of Zionism were themselves all too aware.[67] Famously, *Daniel Deronda* is a novel that cannot hold itself together. It fails to contain its Jewish element and more or less splits apart under the strain.[68] But whatever the signs of struggle in the very form and texture of her last novel, and however wary, critical, and distanced she may be, Eliot cannot exert pressure on our perception of the knowable world to the point of its radical disintegration, to the point where society's distinctions become precarious, not just because they are false, or overstated, or fussy, but because nothing holds its shape once it passes through the multiple pathways, conscious and unconscious, of the human mind. Most boundaries are false, in the world and in the mind. The implications of this are as fully social as they are psychic. Group violence, as Sen put it, relies on cultivating "a single line of prioritized divisiveness." You draw up the lines and then you police them. You are only safe behind a wall. It is, of course, an illusion that only works—not that it works—on condition that you turn a blind eye to the damage you are inflicting on the landscape, on others, and on yourself. This is, as I have been suggesting, Freud's territory and makes, for me, the profound allegiance between the writing of Proust and Freud. "Without Proust," wrote Jacques Rivière in 1924, "Freud cannot be understood."[69]

If George Eliot couldn't go this far, Joseph Conrad—almost—does. In this, he is the transitional writer between Eliot and Proust. Most famously in *Heart of Darkness*, he renders the world of empire fragile by dint of the uncertainty of his language. "If Conrad can show that all human activity depends on controlling a radically unstable reality," Edward Said writes in *Culture and Imperialism*, "to which words belong only by will or convention, the same is true of empire, of venerating the idea and so forth."[70] In this reading, the end of European imperialism, a prospect Conrad would not live to see, is prefigured by what he does to words, by the pressure he exerts on language at the points where it seems to be surest of itself. "Come to an end it would," Said comments, "if only because—like all human effort, like speech itself, it would have its moment and then have to pass."[71] The arrangements we make for ordering reality are as precarious as the language through which we try to pin it down. (It is, in Proust's already cited words, an assault on language to try and arrest its "perpetual vertiginous activity.") The Jew is only what he is—stands distinct from the rest of the culture and from everybody else within it—because of the illusions we entertain about the permanence of words.

Seen in this light, the dread of social disintegration at the

time of the Dreyfus Affair can be better understood. If the Jew
was innocent, the conceptual schema of the knowable world, as
well as its founding institutions, would fall to pieces. If a Frenchman were capable of treason, an inconsolable nation would have
despaired. "The army would disintegrate," wrote Julien Benda in
"The Dreyfus Affair and the Principle of Authority" in *La revue
blanche* in 1899, "if the error was brought to light."[72] ("Everything
that disturbs order," wrote the critic of Reinach, "is an injustice.")[73]
At moments during the Affair, it was as if reality were decompos-
ing itself, subject to a scientific experiment gone awry—hence,
the beauty of Malcolm Bowie's image of the Affair as Proust's
"grand experimental laboratory."[74] "All political parties," Blum
observed, "decomposed and remade themselves with the trans-
posed elements. . . . All combinations, all alloys, fell apart."[75]

Go back to Proust, to his depiction of the Dreyfus Affair, and
what we then see on more careful examination is not so much, or
only, the divisions provoked by the Affair, the hardening of caste
and class, but those same divisions losing their clarity, becoming scandalously fuzzy as the wrong people start crossing over
the appropriate social dividing lines. While seemingly sharpen-
ing the distinction between Jew and non-Jew (although, we have
seen even that is sexually dubious), the Affair, we are told, is leading to a general collapse of social distinctions. "All this Dreyfus
business," Charlus expostulates shortly after his rant about Bloch,
clasping the narrator by the arm, "has only one drawback. *It de-
stroys society* by the influx of Mr and Mrs Cow and Cowshed and
Cow-pat, unknowns whom I find even in the houses of my own
cousins, because they belong to the Patriotic League, the anti-
Jewish League, or some other league, as if a political opinion
entitled one to a social qualification."[76] Siding against Dreyfus
provides a pass into high society for those who otherwise would
have had no chance whatsoever of crossing such a threshold. This
is, for the Duchess of Guermantes, an obscenity: "I do think it
is perfectly intolerable that just because they are supposed to be
right thinking and don't deal with Jewish tradesmen, or have

'Death to the Jews' written on their sunshades," she objects in the same scene, "we should have a swarm of . . . women we should never have known but for this business. . . . Now one finds all the people one has spent one's life trying to avoid, on the pretext that they are against Dreyfus, and others of whom you have no idea who they can be."[77]

In Scott Moncrieff's original translation, "Mort aux Juifs" was translated as "Down with the Jews," as if the ugliness, which is, of course, an affront to decency, should not pass into the English tongue. Proust was, however, being precise. As we have seen, this was the cry in the streets at Dreyfus's court-martial, outside Zola's trial, and then across the whole of France—even if having the words inscribed on society ladies' parasols is his unique, and somewhat surreal, embellishment. The implication is unmistakable, however, and the allusion to murder surely crucial. Death to the Jews will provide entry into the best houses in Paris, but it is a virus, spreading—like love and aberration—across society's most carefully monitored dividing lines. Dreyfus has forced the duchess not just to deal with people whom she would otherwise never have had to countenance, not only to meet those she has gone out of her way to avoid hitherto; it has led to a more fundamental crisis of social legibility, as she now has to deal with people "of whom you have no idea who they can be." It is the fixity of our perceptions which gives us the illusion that objects are what they are and nothing else; it is the fixity of our social divisions that allows us, no less misguidedly, to believe that we know who people really are.

In a key turning point in the novel, the first sign of the ascent and final triumph of the Dreyfusards, Swann is dragged off "with the force of a suction pump" to the end of the garden by the Prince de Guermantes—to "show the Jew the door" as certain observers wrongly inform the narrator.[78] In fact, the prince wishes to confide in Swann that he now believes in the innocence of Dreyfus. In confidence, he had asked the Abbé Poiré to say a mass on Dreyfus's behalf, only to discover that the Abbé had already been approached, also in confidence, by none other than his wife, the Princess de Guermantes. (They had both feared to give offense to the other's nationalist opinions.) Never quite believing his good fortune at having secured an invitation to this aristocratic soiree, the narrator tracks Swann throughout the scene, like a jealous lover, as if his life, as much as the fate of Dreyfus, depended on it. Only the narrator and we as readers are party to the revelation (what was really said in the garden). Dreyfus's innocence is not yet something that can be fully spoken or known. But it is the first sign of a truth that slowly but surely is making its way from the Parisian salon into the heart of government.

Against the murderous forms of certainty to which anti-Dreyfusards such as the baron and the duchess cling for dear life, Proust then offers us a wonderful counterimage. M de Guermantes has just uttered a vulgar expression, "with a name like": "with a name like the Marquis de Saint Loup, one isn't a Dreyfusard."[79] Such common usage sits ill with Guermantes, who prides himself, of course, on his linguistic, no less than his social, distinctiveness. Reflecting on this linguistic aberration on the part of Guermantes, the narrator begins to speculate on the laws of speech. One such law would dictate that a person's language can indeed be drawn from those of the same mental category rather than the same class: a duke can write novels in the language of a grocer, and a plebeian in the language of the aristocrat. This is extraordinary enough in itself—since the salon, as Arendt describes it, was the place where the equation between an individual and his social rank was most strictly enforced.[80] Behind this apparently liberal musing, there is also a sharp irony at Guermantes's expense: his use of the vulgar phrase—"with a name like"—betrays in his language the very in-mixing of social groups that he is protesting against (a French aristocrat should not be supporting a Jew). But there is a second law of language that merges its users along more suggestive, genuinely protean lines. As the image so beautifully encapsulates the issue of borders that is at the heart of this chapter, it is worth quoting the passage in full:

But another law of speech is that from time to time, just as certain diseases appear, vanish and are never heard of again, there somehow arise (either spontaneously or by some accident like the one that brought into France that American weed the seeds of which, caught in the wool of a traveling rug, fell on a railway embankment) modes of expression which one hears in the same decade on the lips of people who have in no way concerted their efforts to use them.[81]

Language travels by chance, speeding over national barriers, like a disease, like trains: freedom is a cross-border journey that can be curse or opportunity, epidemic or the intermingling of old and new worlds and words. It is impossible, surely, not to recognize here an allusion to Proust's own father—the famous epidemiologist responsible for creating the policy of the "cordon sanitaire." Proust, we might say, is having none of it. He is rewriting his father's law. This is no random image, even though randomness is what it, at least partially, evokes. At the very least, it seems to be no coincidence that Proust casts the seeds of new life and new death from a rug, via a passing train, onto an embankment from where, miles from its point of genesis, from any primary allegiance or belonging, they take root and start to grow on foreign shores. (For a more up-to-date version, we could compare Anne Michaels, whose heroine in *The Winter Vault* loves botany and yearns to know "how seeds had travelled—crossing oceans in the cuffs of trousers.")[82] Above all, it seems no coincidence that he deploys this image of mobility on the wind against the rigidly and violently held divisions of the Parisian anti-Semitic drawing room.

If we return for a moment to where this chapter started, it is exactly because disease is no respecter of borders that Freud knows a hysterical symptom when he sees one. "Hysterical paralysis," he writes in his 1893 "Some Points for a Comparative Study of Organic and Hysterical Motor Paralyses," "is characterized by *precise limitation* and *excessive intensity*."[83] A paralysis of the arm will be hysterical, rather than organic, he explains, if it is both isolated and total, that is, if it stops arbitrarily at the shoulder, freezing the arm like an effigy, cutting off the limb, whose tissues and muscles are not, of course, in reality detached from the rest of the body, as the symptom makes them seem. In fact, if the paralysis is organic, there will be a minor affection of the face and the leg. Hysteria, however, writes Freud, "is ignorant of the distribution of the nerves."[84] Once again hysteria mimes theory. Like Freud trying to excise the foreign body from the mind in his earliest case studies, the hysterical limb tries, and fails, to detach itself from the living, spreading tissue to which it belongs. The hysterical thought is "inaccessible to the free play of other associations."[85] Across mind and body, hysteria draws its false lines. Miles from the free-floating seedlings of Proust's imagination, the hysteric, her mobility lost, draws up the covers and hunkers down.

There are, of course, journeys, and journeys. At the end of *Daniel Deronda*, Deronda travels to Zion. As I have already indicated, I would make more than Said and Mufti of the fact that he doesn't actually get there and that his longing, precisely as it increases in heat and intensity throughout the last part of the novel, is somewhat frantic, if not deranged. Nonetheless, for George Eliot, nationhood for the Jews, indeed, for everyone, is a worthy ideal, rooted in her belief that the individual must be grounded in, must know, her own place. Eliot is on the side of what she terms, in her 1879 essay "The Modern Hep! Hep! Hep!" the "distinctive consciousness" of the Jews. She is opposed to the modern "tendency of things ... towards the quicker or slower fusion of races." To be deprived of nationality is "a privation of the greatest good."[86] But on the transition of this good into its concrete form as statehood for the Jewish people, Eliot is far more ambivalent than is often thought. Mordecai's call for the revival of an organic center, for example, in the passage picked out by Said in "Zionism from the Standpoint of Its Victims," bears all the tones, and many of the exact words, of Ahad Ha'am, whose spiritual and cultural Zionism took priority over the creation of a Jewish state in Palestine.[87] It is the "divine gift of memory," "the living force of sentiment in common," the foundation of all "national consciousness" that Eliot exhorts for all people, and hence for the Jews: "An individual man, to be harmoniously great, must belong to a nation of this order, *if not in actual existence* yet existing in the past, in memory, as a departed, invisible, beloved ideal, once a reality, and *perhaps* to be restored." "*If not in actual existence.*" "*Perhaps.*" Eliot—and this makes all the difference—is not sure. The nation is a haunting memory, like a "departed, invisible, beloved ideal." The question of its realization is suspended. Nor is Eliot blind to the colonizing impulses of a nation once empowered: "We do not call ourselves a dispersed and punished people: we are a colonizing people, and it is we who have punished others."[88]

Proust does not go there. If, for the rest of this chapter, we now travel to Palestine from the heart of Europe, we could say that Proust will, and will not, help us make the journey. It is the logical consequence of everything I have described in his writing so far that the solution to the Jewish Question will not in his imagination take on the contours of the Zionist movement, to which his only two references throughout the whole of *À la recherche* are unsympathetic to the point of disparagement. It is also significant that, as Proust scholar Annick Bouillaguet points out, in Proust's typology of Dreyfusards and anti-Dreyfusards, not one Jewish nationalist appears. (Remember that in his notes he refers to Bernard Lazare.)[89] Juliette Hassine even goes so far as to suggest that those moments when Swann's Jewish identity burns with almost excessive fervor at the end of his life should be read as a warning, an attempt by Proust to exorcise any idea of basing "the right to the city on the voice of the blood."[90] For Proust, no viable solution can come from transposing the boundaries of the Paris salons across to the East. He is the counterexample to Mufti's thesis. Partition is not a solution, not anywhere. For Proust, group identity is always defensive—like homosexuals huddling together against the hatreds of the world. It would, writes Proust at the end of the exordium to *Sodome et Gomorrhe*, be a "deadly mistake" (une erreur funeste) to propose "just as people have encouraged a Zionist movement, the creation of Sodomist movement" (elsewhere he refers to Zionism as a form of "apostolic zeal").[91] No one, or not everyone, would stay there, since homosexuality is a multifaceted, complex mode of being which, only in response to hatred, and against its most fundamental nature, can or should be held to one place. On this, although only on this, Proust is with Herzl, for whom the identity of the Jews as a people arose out of persecution: "We are one people—our enemies have made us one in our despite, as repeatedly happens in history."[92]

In this famous section of his book where the reference to Zion appears—the opening of *Sodome et Gomorrhe*, it is the culminating center of *À la recherche*, coming as it does slap in the middle of the whole work—Proust hands to the invert and the Jew a shared propensity to deception (both hiding from the light). But such deceit is uncanny ruse, the desperate strategy of the persecuted in a hostile world. It is also the case, as I have occasion to note every time I read this section of the book with my students, that Proust's depiction of the multiple identities and varieties of the homosexual makes Freud's account of the complexity of human sexuality seem truly tame in comparison. Sexuality and politics then each become the canvas on which Proust can best illustrate the fundamental vertigo of being human. What matters is that you somewhere know the mobility of your own soul—which is why the endlessly shifting kaleidoscope of the Affair in *À la recherche* does not contradict, but radically underpins, his political stance on Dreyfus, whose detractors saw themselves as defending a social order that was sacrosanct. For Proust, order is a (false) consolation, and our sense of belonging, the more tenaciously we hold to it, often a buttress against a truth that we cannot bear to face. Our most cherished affiliations can be a cover. The corrupt minister, Marie, in *Jean Santeuil*, prefers to think of himself as a "wretched sinner," which ushers him into the general communion of humankind, rather than acknowledge that he stole thousands: "The facts that set us apart from the rest of mankind," Proust comments, "remove none of our profound need to be united with them, to be worth no less than them, to be one of them."[93] In the end, it is his wariness about the most rigid forms of belonging—what Kristeva terms the perverse underside of all collective identities—that leads Proust away from Zionism at the same time as it enables him to give us one of the finest ever literary dissections of the vicious and deadly opprobrium heaped onto the figure of the Jew.

At the end of *À la recherche*, Proust seems to turn his back on his intense involvement with the Dreyfus Affair, as he insists that no political reality is worth the sacrifice of the subtlest components of art, nor of the single-minded dedication it takes to be a writer. The inner book of our thoughts, which requires the writer to plunge "into his unconscious like a diver," where he will flail and stumble, is the only book that matters: "Every public event, be it the Dreyfus case, be it the war, furnishes the writer with a fresh excuse for not attempting to decipher this book."[94] But in this moment—seized on by critics keen to sever the world of art from politics[95]—Proust does not seem to be aware that he himself has provided the most eloquent answer to his own charge: most simply because in *À la recherche*, Dreyfus is no distraction from writing but is a privileged *terre d'élection* for writing, the very ground on which it moves. In social terms, too, there is something disingenuous about the claim. As he so meticulously charts, the Affair was witness to the last gasp of the aristocracy and the rise of a newly cultured bourgeoisie most vividly personified at the end of the work by the dramatic social ascendancy of Mme Verdurin. We could say, then, that in relation to Dreyfus, it was the literary classes that won. If, to recall Proust's own formula, the salon took on the nature of a political meeting, political activity could also—as we saw in the case of the *Revue Blanche*—take on the guise of the literary salon. Proust was also a product of that world whose rise corresponds exactly to his birth as a writer. He is its witness, its ambassador, and its child.

Finally, we should not forget Picquart in the courtroom—whose interiority was the handmaiden to justice. In this chapter, I have gone further in exploring the anguish of that interiority, how it can also be prey to the most deadly of sentiments, can break apart, or seize itself and the world in a false vice, under the pressure of its own fears. In the end, I would argue, no one shows perhaps more clearly than Proust the impossibility of severing politics from the unconscious ("exploring my unconscious, my mind flounders like a plunging diver").[96] After all, we simply have to return to the beginning of *À la recherche*, to Combray, where a sleeping man holds in his orbit the chain of the hours, the years, and the heavenly bodies, to remind ourselves that the whole of *À la recherche*, including its meticulous and disturbing portrayal of Dreyfus, is drawn, like a long silken thread, out of the deepest recesses of the mind.[97]

Border Crossings

Proust will, and will not, take us to Palestine. The image we take from his writing shows him longing for a world of permeable boundaries, seedlings crossing over borders, the souls of the dead caught in an animal or plant, calling out to us for release, but only if we happen to pass by. Above all, in his account of involuntary memory out of which his whole work is spun, and to which I will turn in the next chapter, he longs for a world not subject to false forms of mental control. Like Freud, we could say, and unlike the frozen hysteric with which we began, he wants a world "accessible to the free play of other associations." For many of the earliest Jewish critics of political Zionism (Martin Buber, Ahad Ha'am, and Hans Kohn, for instance), it was the failure to countenance such associations—of Jew and Arab—that spelled tragedy over Palestine.[98] It was not nationhood as spiritual identity (a vision closer to George Eliot's than often thought), but the rigid parameters of a specific form of statehood—that is to say, the exclusiveness of the claim—that led to the partition of the land and to the expulsion of the Palestinians that was its drastic accompaniment. To say this is in no way to deny the urgency of the need for the Jewish people, nor the legitimacy of their national aspirations—all the more so after the genocide of the Second World War, a genocide already hideously sketched out in fantasy during the worst moments of the Dreyfus Affair. Vichy France would become the willing participant, although the extent of that participation was for a long time denied. No other European country, apart from Bulgaria, handed over Jews to the Nazis for deportation from areas not under German military occupation. According to Marrus and Paxton in their study of Vichy France and the Jews, the anti-Semitism of Vichy would require no German prompting or intervention. It was "a home-grown program that rivaled what the Germans were doing in the occupied north and even, in some respects, went beyond it."[99] In fact, the extent of this, specifically the role of Marshall Pétain, France's collaborationist leader, has only recently been fully revealed. An uncovered private memo indicates that he personally intervened in the drafting of the *Statut des Juifs*—enacted, in the words of lawyer Serge Klarsfeld, "without pressure from the Germans, without the request of the Germans: an indigenous statute"—to increase its harshness.[100]

UN resolution 181 of 29 November 1947 proposed the partition of Palestine into two entities, Jewish and Palestinian, the former constituting almost 56 percent of the land, of which, up to that point, the Jews had owned less than 10 percent. It included four hundred Palestinian villages and a population of 499,000 Jews and 407,000 Arabs. It is because the plan took no account of how far these realities, these numbers, vitiated the Zionist concept of Jewish statehood that historian Ilan Pappé holds the partition plan uniquely accountable for the ethnic transfer that followed.[101] Inside this crisis, another problem of boundaries was taking shape—that of the Palestinians who would become the alien to the new state, whether they were in fact inside or outside its borders. "Everything that did stay to challenge Israel," writes Said in "Zionism from the Standpoint of Its Victims," "was viewed not as something *there*, but as a sign of something *outside* Israel and Zionism bent on its destruction from the outside."[102] In the aftermath of 1948, it is the Palestinian who inherits that at once dangerous and most crushingly banal of stereotypes: the trope of the enemy, or foreign body, in our midst.

Today, this position is given its fullest expression by Avigdor Lieberman, minister for foreign affairs in Benjamin Netanyahu's coalition government, who has openly advocated the transfer of Israel's Arab population, or by historian Benny Morris, who first exposed the violence of the ethnic transfer of 1948 and then lamented it, not as an injustice, but because it did not go far enough.

My argument has been that both Freud and Proust allow us to glimpse other possibilities, where worlds and minds can escape their self-inflicted boundaries, where peoples do not have to entrench their borders and shut down, and where no national group has to subordinate its identity as citizen completely to the reason of state. In any case, such borders are disabling illusion. They simply fail:

> We have put up many flags,
> They have put up many flags.
> To make us think they're happy,
> To make them think that we're happy.[103]

These lines are from Amichai's "Jerusalem." which form one of the epigraphs to this chapter.

For those who live "at those terrifying frontiers where the existence and disappearance of peoples fade into each other," writes Said in *After the Last Sky*, what is required is "an unusual, and to some degree, unprecedented, knowledge" (a possibility glimpsed in the photographs by Jean Mohr that accompany Said's words on life in Palestine).[104] I will, therefore, end this chapter with two poets from the heart of the conflict in the Middle East who could be seen as offering some such knowledge. Both use language to work over this divided terrain in the opposite direction, undoing the rhetoric of statehood, writing from the other side of power. Yehuda Amichai, Israel's best-loved and most famous poet, and Mahmoud Darwish, the equally loved poet of Palestinian national aspiration, are in themselves the living emblems of the history I have been tracking. Amichai escaped Nazism by leaving Germany for Palestine in 1936; Darwish fled the Palestinian village of al-Barweh for Lebanon in 1948. When he returned a year later, having been unaccounted for in the first Israeli census, he was classified as a "present absent alien." Both are therefore exiles who have moved—under pressure—across borders. There is no symmetry, of course. There can be no equation between ethnic transfer and genocide. It is also the abiding dilemma of this conflict that national self-determination for the Jews would spell catastrophe (*nakba*) for the Palestinian people. Amichai's entry into the land will be the precondition of Darwish's eventual flight. Yet each of them knows what it is to be an alien in your own home, and each of them, in key moments in their poetry, blurs boundaries in favor of a scandalous intimacy between the two peoples on either side of the partition line.[105]

The two poems I will focus on are both taken from immediately after the 1967 war between Israel and its Arab neighbors, a key moment in the conflict, in the plight of the Palestinians, and in Israel's conception of itself. The exodus of thousands of Palestinians from the newly conquered land of the West Bank and Gaza was one of the war's consequences (250,000 from the West Bank, 70,000 from Gaza, 655,000 in total between June 1967 and 1986).[106] More immediately, in the heady euphoria of victory, two days after the fall of the Old City, its Moroccan sector, home to more than 200 Palestinians who had lived there for generations, was razed to create what was essentially a parade ground in front of the Wailing Wall. When asked at the time whether it had been a good idea to so transform an area sanctified for prayer, Mayor Teddy Kollek is reported to have said that the old place had been tarred with the atmosphere of the *galut* (exile): "It was a place for wailing."[107] His remarks show just how much—psychically, as well as politically—was at stake. No more yearning, no more Diaspora. Lament gives way to the forward march of history. There must be no sorrow. Not for the Palestinians, clearly; but equally and no less significantly, not, or rather no longer, for the Jews.

Although Israel's victory in the war was far more than rhetorical, the triumph of rhetoric over reality would be one way of describing both how that victory unfolded and its long-term effects. According to Amos Elon, who fought in the war, the morning after the fall of the Old City, newspapers envisioned the Messiah walking behind advancing Israeli tanks. A few days later, David Ben-Gurion called for the Old City walls to be torn down because they had been built by Ottomans, not Jews (they remained in place). By August, Moshe Dayan was insisting that Israel must never return to her former borders, citing Ben-Gurion, who had once said, again according to Elon, that the borders of 1948 were a cause to "lament for generations" because they had not included the West Bank.[108] In his book *The Blood-Dimmed Tide*, Elon describes the mounting euphoria, the creeping sense that these freshly acquired lands represented a new stage in the fulfillment of the nation's biblical destiny. (Dayan described it as "the dream of a nation come true.")[109] The pre-1967 territory had embraced, not the land of the ancient Hebrews, but that of their enemies. It was low in monuments bearing witness to the Jewish past. Hebron, Jericho, and Anathot, newly conquered, were instead, in Dayan's words, the "cradle" of our history.[110] Standing by the Wailing Wall on June 7, he declared: "We have returned to our holiest places, we have returned in order not to part from them ever again."[111]

Although the official policy was that Israel did not seek territorial gain, slowly but surely, more and more parts of the occupied territories were declared to be inseparable and then unalienable parts of Israel's ancient heritage. (In speeches after the war, Dayan described the territories as "part of the State of Israel's new territorial map.")[112] According to Elon, this mounting conviction, which he witnessed in the making, possessed such "primeval force" that one may well ask "whether any government would dare oppose it."[113] The 1967 war was not, then, just the start of what has become one of the longest-running occupations of modern history. It was also the moment when a new form of language would bind the soldier-citizen to the state and when the newly expanded borders of the nation became sacred. In the words of Darwish, "The Israelis have to distinguish between the boundary of the Old Testament and reality." (He was talking in 2000, when the Occupation had lasted over three decades.)[114]

In this context, the idea that poetry speaks the unspoken acquires a new force and a new political edge. When rhetoric has played such a key role in establishing a new reality on the ground, then to challenge that rhetoric is to unravel political conviction at its source. Amichai's poetry has been described as "one monumental argument with the Almighty."[115] Raised by Orthodox parents in the German town of Würzburg, Amichai has described the rupture with a loved father with whom, as with God, he remained throughout his life in permanent dialogue. Amichai was a member of the Jewish fighting force, the Haganah, spending a year in Arab countries illegally smuggling arms and munitions to the fledgling state. With the exception of the Lebanese offensive of 1982 (which will be central to the final chapter of this book), he fought in each of Israel's wars: 1948, 1967, and the "Yom Kippur" war of 1973. It is all the more important, therefore, that, in Amichai's searing vision of his country, God is absent, has failed, or asks too much. If these statements might seem to cancel each other out, then it can only be said that Amichai turns to radical poetic and political effect what Freud famously described as the kettle logic of the unconscious (the neighbor returning a damaged kettle who insists it is not damaged, that it was damaged when he borrowed it, and that he never borrowed it in the first place). Amichai's God offers no sanction to this world, to this nation. He takes the nearest prophet and "as if with a wooden spoon, he stirs and stirs" ("I Lived for Two Months in Quiet Abu Tor").[116] Israel's people are caught in a "homeland trap," speaking a weary language "that was torn from its sleep in the Bible":

> Dazzled.
> it wobbles from mouth to mouth. In a language that once
>   described
> miracles and God, to say car, bomb, God.

The poem from which these lines are taken is called "National Thoughts."[117]

Amichai's famous poem "Jerusalem 1967" begins:

> This year I travelled a long way
> to view the silence of my city.
> A baby calms down when you rock it, a city calms down
> from the distance. I dwelled in longing. I played the game
> of the four strict squares of Yehuda Ha-Levi:
> *My heart. Myself. East. West.*

He chooses to evoke his return to the city in the language of the famous medieval "singer of Zion," Yehuda Halevi, whose poem "Between East and West" opens with one of the most famous lines in Hebrew poetry: "My heart is in the East, and I myself am on the western edge." From Grenada in Spain, Halevi travels in his mind to Zion. (At the end of his life, he set off for Palestine, but it is a mystery whether he died en route or arrived.) In his 1927 commentary on Halevi, Franz Rosenzweig describes the poet's lonely yearning for Zion as the "first beacon" of the new movement. In the millennium at the start of which the poet was born, "Jewish life begins to flow back into the ancient land."[118] To describe one's "self" as in the west, one's "heart" in the east is to encapsulate, we could say, the trajectory of the Zionist project which had just been fulfilled for so many, euphorically as spiritual destiny, by the victory of the 1967 war, the conquest, at last, of the east of the city.

Into this sacred combinatory, Amichai pours a new poetic language that leaves none of its elements in their proper place, as the four "strict" or "severe" squares of Halevi are turned into a game ("Sikhati bemiskhak"—the expression in Hebrew has the connotation both of a formal game like hopscotch, which is Stephen Mitchell's translation, or something closer to a mental game). In the process, self and heart each lose their bearings, their unequivocal bond to west and east: "*My heart. Myself. East. West.*" In this opening stanza, Amichai subjects the words of his poetic ancestor, and the longing of which they have become the emblem, to the most radical destabilization. Nor is this a harmonization of the different parts (a new unity of the city, as was being so forcefully claimed). Rather, it is a collapse of one of Zionism's most cherished historical and spiritual distinctions.

Amichai reenters the city in fear. "Now that I've come back, I'm screaming again." His is the melancholic, at moments terrified, counterpart to the dominant drift of his nation. In his account of 1967, historian Tom Segev recounts how, in the year prior to the war, Israel was close to despair—in response to an upsurge of emigration and a severe economic recession, the nation had suffered a profound loss of faith in its vision and convinced itself it faced the prospect of defeat and total destruction in the coming war: "There was indeed no justification for the panic that preceded the war, nor for the euphoria that took hold after it."[119] Across that euphoria, Amichai casts his poetic shadow, refusing his nation's oscillations of the heart. He does not present himself as immune from the sense of a new beginning. (He never presents himself as immune from anything.)

> I'm beginning to believe again
> in all the little things that will fill
> the holes left by the shells: soil, a bit of grass,
> perhaps, after the rains, small insects of every kind.

But he does so "In this summer of wide-open-eyed hatred and blind love." The love of the people is blind; their hatred is tearing open their eyes. ("Sin'ah keruat einayim lirvakhah," which can mean scales falling from the eyes, also carries this more violent connotation.)

This is unquestionably a return:

> A man who comes back to Jerusalem is aware that the places
> that used to hurt don't hurt anymore.

But this is a return undeceived by conquest. It offers no redemption, its own brightest moments of optimism a cause of dread. There is something ominous in the air. Everything is illuminated—the Tower of David, the Church of Maria, the patriarchs sleeping in their burial cave. Bodies, faces, stones turn translucent. A glow can also be a warning in the dark: "a light warning remains in everything,/ like a movement of a light veil: warning."

By the end of the third section of this long, plangent poem, the writing is on the wall:

> terrible, true X-ray writing
> in letters of bones, in white and lightning: *MENE MENE TEKEL UPHARSIN.*

In the Bible, the exiled Daniel is alone capable of deciphering the deathly warning for Balthazar, which appears as he drinks from vessels his father tore from the Jewish temple: "God has numbered thy kingdom the days of your reign and [it is] given to the Medes and Persians" (Daniel 5:26–28). Balthazar would die the same night, and Daniel becomes the third in rank in the kingdom. It is a story of the vindication of the Jews. But no victor is immutable. And what has become of Jerusalem today that the poet compares it with Babel? What is the destiny here being foretold for the Jews? In this shocking analogy, today's triumphant Jewish nation is being compared with the Jews' former conquerors who sat carousing with looted vessels beside a wall marked with a prophecy of destruction that no one could understand. (Amichai, like Daniel, becomes the prophet.) It is a celebration of the blind ("wide-open-eyed-hatred and blind love.") To write like this about 1967 was counterintuitive to say the least. Amichai is calling on his Biblical heritage to subdue the conquering pride of his own people.[120]

At the time of the victory, Na'omi Shemer's song "Jerusalem of Gold," originally commissioned for the Israeli Song Festival in May to be performed on Independence Day, which fell that year on May 15, became something like a national anthem of the war—it was sung by soldiers, entering the Old City two days after the outbreak of the war, as they reached the Wailing Wall:

> Jerusalem of Gold . . .
> How the water cisterns have dried out
> The marketplace is empty,
> And no one visits the Holy Mount
> In the Old City . . .
> And no one goes down to the Dead Sea
> By way of Jericho.

As more than one commentator has pointed out, this is to empty the city in verse of its Arab inhabitants.[121] Return, then, becomes an act of mercy, which revives and replenishes an essentially derelict space. These lines were added to the poem after the conquest of the City:

> Jerusalem of Gold . . .
> We have returned to the water cisterns, to the marketplace and
>   the square.
> A ram's horn [*shofar*] calls out on the Holy Mount
> In the Old City.

"Jerusalem 1967" strikes a dramatically different chord. On the night of Yom Kippur 1967—"The Year of Forgetting"—the speaker walks to the Old City. Spelling out the word "Forgetting" from the Hebrew year (תשכ״ח) is of course to go against the whole tradition and purpose of Yom Kippur as a festival of atonement and remembrance—*yom zikaron* (as is putting on his "dark holiday clothes," since white is worn in the synagogue on this day). Standing for a long time in front of an Arab's shop not far from the Damascus Gate, he tells him why he is here: "my father's shop was burned there and he is buried here." In fact, that "he" of "he is buried here" is ambiguous—it could be the father, it could be the Arab, buried as in oppressed (*kavur* also carries the political meaning) in the newly conquered city. But for Amichai, the historical record, the past presence of his own family, and his buried father offer no sense of entitlement. Amichai knows how to hold the intense ambivalence of this moment. "I told him in my heart that my father had a shop like this":

> a shop like this, a shop with threads and buttons
> buttons and zippers and spools of thread
> in every colour and snaps and buckles.
> A rare light and many colors, like an open Ark.

Amichai can only bring his father to life by evoking, no less vividly, the fabric of life of his enemy. *"Belibi,"* in my heart, returns us to the first stanza's evocation of Halevi—as he enters the east of the city, what resides in the Jew's heart today is an internal dialogue with an Arab. For a moment, the two shops, with their bloodily divergent histories, subsist on the same page. It is watching the Arab shop that summons in the mind of the Jewish observer the rare light of the Ark—this is a holiness that knows no racial or ethnic bounds. The poet leaves when it is time "for the Closing of the Gates prayer" (the final prayer of Yom Kippur and the most spiritual moment of the entire Jewish year), and the Arab lowers the shutters and locks the gate of his shop. The Jewish holy moment, therefore, chimes with the quotidian gesture of the Arab. (*Ne'ila*, the closing, as a noun is derived from the verb *na'al*, to lock or close down.) Amichai is dissolving boundaries. It is the borders that are most suspect. Not because, as Ben-Gurion believed, they had not in 1948 taken enough land—Israel often claims that better borders would make the nation safe—but because they are an illusion:

> Loneliness is always in the middle
> protected and fortified. People were supposed
> to feel secure in that, and they don't.

Or, to refer again to the lines of the opening epigraph, you can only pretend to be happy, only pretend to be safe, behind a wall.

In "The Redress of Poetry," Seamus Heaney talks of those poets for whom the struggle of an individual consciousness toward affirmation merges with a collective straining for self-definition.[122] Mahmoud Darwish is the very model of such a poet whose poetry yearns toward an identity that is never achieved or complete ("struggle," "towards," and "straining" being key to Heaney's description). Not only or always a political poet, yet Darwish saw the link between poetry and politics as unbreakable. "No Palestinian poet or writer," he stated in an interview in 2000, "can enjoy the luxury of severing ties with this level of national work, which is politics."[123] Uncompromising in his political vision, Darwish's crafting of a homeland in language has been one of the strongest rejoinders to dispossession. He is also at every level a poet who crosses borders. This was true literally in that originary flight and return that left his status so eloquent of a people's predicament:

> absence piling up its chosen objects
> and pitching its eternal tent around us.
> "The Owl's Night"[124]

It was also true in the multiple forms of exile that characterized his life. (He left in 1970 for Beirut, then lived across the cities of the world, before returning to live in the Palestinian town of Ramallah in 1995.) "I still suffer from doubts concerning my first departure from Palestine," he said in a 2002 conversation with Palestinian legal activist and writer Raja Shehadeh. "I continue to ask myself, Was it right to leave?"[125]

But Darwish's borders are also poetic, formal, and linguistic as well as personal and intimate. As a young boy, he was taught by a Jewish woman teacher to understand the Old Testament as a literary work. "Like a mother," she saved him from "the fire of distrust . . . a symbol of the good work a Jew does for his people." (His only other contact with a Jew had been the Israeli military governor who had threatened to stop his father's quarry work if the son did not stop writing poetry.)[126] For Darwish, the poetic response to 1948 had to involve a revolution of forms—it was the Palestinian conservatives, cooperating with the Israelis, he said, whose poets clung to traditional verse.[127] For Darwish, the *nakba* propelled Palestinian poetry into a new era. In his poetry, he is constantly testing poetic boundaries, crossing in language and fantasy the borders laid down by the new nation. "You created two people from a single stalk," he laments to God in one poem. (As for Amichai, Darwish's God has failed.)[128]

It is crucial that we do not simplify Darwish. He challenged Amichai: "We write about the same place. . . . Who is the owner of the language of this land? Who loves it more?" But he was also one of Amichai's most fervent admirers and saw him as Israel's greatest poet whose aim was to create a new Israel.[129] Darwish was also capable of entering at the deepest level into the spirit of Jewish history, writing a poem on the death of Paul

Celan in which he sends himself in exile from Sodom to Baby-
lon. (His political judgment does not stand in the way of the
profoundest identification.)[130] Writing of Darwish's traversing
of this boundary in his 2007 book *In Spite of Partition*, Gil Z.
Hochberg cites this letter from Darwish to Palestinian-Israeli
poet Samih al-Qāsim: "[So many texts] convey to us that no
individual could today carry within him the two: the Arab and
the Jew. But why? why? Is it because writing about such dual-
ity as finds itself in a time of conflict and a place of war needs
another time? [And] after the wound of identity heals, will [we]
have the right to be Arab and Jewish, without symbols, betrayals,
defeat?"[131] Darwish's language has, in his own words, "a part in
the Book of Genesis . . . a part in the book of Job . . . a part in
the anemones of the *wadis* in the poems of the ancient lovers, a
part in the wisdom of the lovers demanding to love the face of
the Beloved when killed by her." The lines are taken from the
1992 "Eleven Stars at the End of the Andalusian Scene," one of
a sequence of love poems to his Israeli lover, whom he names
Rita, which scandalously translates the biblical Song of Songs
into the longing of these two lovers across enemy lines.[132] In an
article on Darwish, Arabic literature specialist Angelika Neuwirth suggests that it was the loss of this lover that first unsettled
the more confident Palestinian self-affirmation of his earlier
poetry. In conversation with translator and critic Mohammed
Shaheen, Darwish fleshed out the context of the poems: after
the 1967 war, when the Israeli lover of a Palestinian became an
object of contempt, and the public sphere destroyed the space
of intimacy. "Rita and the Gun," the most famous poem of this
extraordinary cycle, is a lament that brings the latent political
violence of his love affair, whether actual or metaphoric, to the
surface (needless to say, it intensifies rather than reduces the
passion):

> Between Rita and my eyes is a gun
>
> . . . .
>
> ah Rita
> between us are a million sparrows and a picture
> and countless promises.

She fired a gun at them.
Rita's name was a festival [*Eid*] in my mouth.
Rita's body was a wedding feast in my blood
And I sunk into Rita for two years.[133]

In Shaheen's translation, the line "She fired a gun at them" reads "A rifle fired at her!"[134] It is impossible to convey in translation the radical ambiguity of the Arabic ("atlaqat nārun 'alayhā . . . bunduqiyya")—*'alayhā* can refer to Rita or to everything (birds, images, promises) of the preceding lines, and *Bunduqiyya*, coming after ellipses that halt the reader and heighten the poetic tension, to Rita or the gun. It is a mistake, therefore, to try and establish, as indeed I did on first reading, whether the Israelis or Rita alone are the agents of violence (as if the poem could be resolved by answering the question: Who is shooting at whom?). Rather, it is the gun—the war of 1967—that is destroying their love, firing at all they had before. This is a love that plunges into a past when Arab and Jewish children could mingle—"I kissed Rita when she was young"—and into a form of memory now crafted into the natural world—"I remember Rita / as a sparrow remembers its lake." (Against the drift of most of Darwish's poetry, this is to make Rita, an Israeli woman, rather than Palestine, his long lost home.) All of this the war has destroyed. A sexual boundary between the two peoples is being brutally redrawn. The poem caused a scandal when it was first published in Damascus in 1968 (although it also provided the lyrics for a song by the famous Lebanese singer Marcel Khalife, who sang it at a memorial for Darwish at the University of Jordan in 2008).

Like the Rita poems, like Amichai's "Jerusalem 1967," Darwish's "A Soldier Dreams of White Tulips" was also written in the aftermath of the war.[135] Like Amichai's poem, it offers a moment of dialogue in a landscape where the possibility of dialogue, or any form of meaningful contact, was being ruthlessly and violently undone. The poem stages an encounter between an Israeli soldier and a Palestinian, named as Mahmoud, drawing on a real moment of the poet's life in the days following Israel's victory.[136] The Palestinian interrogates the soldier on his love for the land. The soldier replies:

All my attachment to the land is no more than a story or a fiery speech!
They taught me to love it but I never felt it in my heart.
I never knew its roots and branches, or the scent of its grass.

This might seem shocking and peremptory. How can Darwish claim to speak for the Israeli, undo his felt connection to the land? The Arabic, *uhibbu hubbahā*, literally, "they taught me to love its love," turns the concrete love (roots, branches, grass) which the soldier lacks into an abstraction. In fact, the Arabic word *muhādara* is not so much "story" as "lecture" or "essay," there is, therefore, no implication that the attachment is fictive. At moments, the translation has intensified the critique. Here the soldier is speaking:

I love it with my gun,
And by unearthing feasts in the garbage of the past
and a deaf-mute idol whose age and meaning are unknown.

The Arabic, *kharā'ib*, is more "ruins" than "garbage," and "whose age and meaning are unknown" is closer to "lost in time and identity." As if Darwish were recognizing the force of, entering—at least partly if precariously—into the relics, lore, and memory of the Jews.

As the poem proceeds, it becomes increasingly clear that Darwish is offering a gift to the young soldier who might have no cause to identify blindly with the reason of state. He is granting his enemy a form of humanity with the power to resist the official clamor, and the capacity to claim as a better birthright a life without war. The soldier describes his mother weeping as they led him to the front:

How her anguished voice gave birth to a new hope in his flesh
that doves might flock through the ministry of war.

In the Arabic, "a new hope in his flesh" is more visceral, "a new wish digging under his skin" (yahfuru tahta jildihi).

What would happen if birds flocked into the ministry of war? In the original, "that doves might flock" is repeated, suspended on its own on the next line. "When will peace," he asks in another poem, "open our citadel doors to the doves?"[137] It is, of course, a cliché to have birds fly across national frontiers, although, in fact, in both these cases the birds are rather storming the citadels of power. I see them somewhat like the red balloon in Elia Suleiman's 2002 film *Divine Intervention*—which I discuss in the last chapter—which drifts over the checkpoints and across the border as the Palestinian lovers, unable to get through, sit clutching each other's hands in their blocked, unmoving car.

In his dreams, the soldier sees white tulips, an olive branch, and a bird embracing the dawn. As a soldier, he is drowning in rhetoric: "I need a bright day, not a mad fascist moment of triumph." The order of the Arabic: "I need a bright day, not a mad moment of triumph . . . fascist" makes the controversial word "fascist" a faltering, hesitant, as much as a decisive, conclusion to the line. (Darwish also condemned the flights of rhetoric on the Arab side to which some Palestinians attribute their defeat in 1967.)[138] Above all, the soldier is living in a world that allows no place for the sorrow of war:

> *Did you feel sad?* I asked.
> Cutting me off, he said, *Mahmoud my friend,*
> *sadness is a white bird that does not come near a battlefield.*
> *Soldiers commit a sin when they feel sad.*

Not everyone, of course, will appreciate Darwish ascribing to the soldier such profound disillusionment with his nation's self-affirmation. But this is 1967, a time when the language of triumph was wiping out the possibility of justice. In "A Soldier Dreams of White Tulips," Darwish performs an act of extraordinary poetic and political generosity by granting this one soldier an unusual, unprecedented knowledge of the grave damage that his nation, in the throes of victory, was doing and would go on doing, both to the Palestinians and to itself.

"She was in the peculiar situation of knowing and at the same time not knowing," Freud writes of Fraulein Elizabeth von R in *Studies on Hysteria*, "a situation, that is, in which a psychical group [of ideas] was cut off [from her conscious thoughts]."[139] As this chapter has tried to suggest, there are ways of being and forms of writing—Freud, Proust, these poets—that allow something to rise to the surface, unsettling the surface boundaries of the world. My next question is, Why is it so hard for nations and for people to remember what they have done?

The House of Memory

We speak so much of memory because there is so little of it left.
«PIERRE NORA, "Entre mémoire et histoire"[1]»

Behold, O my people, I will open your graves
And cause you to come out of your graves
And bring you into the land of Israel.
«Ezekiel 37, inscribed on Nathan Rapaport's *Scroll of Fire*, Martyrs' Forest, outside Jerusalem[2]»

The participants [in my works] keep the memory of their own participation in the work's procedure, which also bears witness to their responsibility to their own times.
«ESTHER SHALEV-GERZ, "The Perpetual Movement of Memory"[3]»

The Art of Memory

The opening story in Frances Yates's famous book *The Art of Memory* tells of the Greek poet Simonides who lived in Ceos around 400 BC.[4] According to Cicero, he was invited to a banquet where his task was to sing in praise of his host, Scopas, a nobleman of Thessaly. Annoyed by the fact that his ode paid equal tribute to the twin gods Castor and Pollux, Scopas only paid him half the promised fee. In the midst of the banquet, Simonides was summoned by a messenger who told him that two young men—we assume these are the two gods—had come to see him. Outside, he found no one, but during his brief absence, the roof of the hall fell in, crushing everyone inside. The bodies were so mangled that not even relatives could identify them. But Simonides remembered the places where they had been sitting and therefore could identify them each and every one. From this experience, the art of memory is said to have derived. (The story, told by Cicero, is recorded in the anonymous *Ad Herennium* of 264 BC.) No doubt relieved at his own escape—the gods' payment for his ode—Simonides understood that attaching memory to places and images was the best way of preserving it in the mind. But the art of memory has a bloody genesis. If only unconsciously, Simonides appears to have been storing his memories against the disaster to come. Although Yates does not comment on this aspect of the story, it suggests that memory's most urgent task is to keep a record of people about to be mangled beyond recognition by a violent, unanticipated death.

The title of this third chapter is "The House of Memory." I start with Yates not only because of the story but also because she suggests that there is the closest link between the understanding of memory and houses, both actual and metaphorical, between the buildings on the streets and the places in our minds. "Architectural memories," she writes, "were in ancient times of a precision, vividness, and extent impossible for us to conceive." Roman orators used architectural memory as a way of memorizing speeches. In a famous passage from the *Institutio oratoria*, Quintilian issues a set of instructions about memory conceived as the movement around "a spacious house divided into a number of rooms":

> Everything of note therein is diligently imprinted on the mind. . . . Then what has been written down, or thought of, is noted by a sign to remind of it. . . . These signs are then arranged as follows. The first notion is placed, as it were, in the forecourt; the second, let us say, in the atrium; the remainder are placed in order all around the impluvium, and committed not only to bedrooms and parlours, but even to statues and the like. This done, when it is required to revive the memory, one begins from the first place to run through all, demanding what has been entrusted to them, of which one will be reminded by the image.[5]

He then adds reassuringly—assuming this is all crystal clear and of course bound to succeed: "What I have spoken of as being done in a house can also be done in public buildings, or on a long journey, or in going through a city."[6]

Today, Yates insists, the value and possibility of such mnemonics have been all but wiped out by the advance of printing and other technologies in effortlessly preserving whatever we need to retain (as well as a great deal, I would add, we neither need, nor wish to, retain). Yet Quintillian's image still resonates. In a poignant evocation of the process, distinguished historian Tony Judt, whose writing on European memory will also figure prominently in this chapter, describes in an interview how he had recourse to a similar technique since being suddenly and brutally struck down with a rare form of motor neuron disease: "During the night he builds a Chinese memory palace—or in his case a modern Swiss house—and into each of its rooms he imagines placing a paragraph or theme of the piece he is composing. The next day he recalls each room in sequence, unloading its contents by dictating it to his assistant."[7] In a world he saw as having lost the vision of a shared social purpose, Judt was writing a book on how to encourage the young to think collectively again.

Memory, I take from these moments, has a special intimate relationship to the physical spaces, notably the houses, in which we move. We secure ourselves and our minds—our sense of who we are and have been—according to the paths we tread along corridors and walls. The artist Rachel Whiteread—whose work includes the famous cement-filled house in London's East End (it was about to be demolished) and more recently a collection of dolls houses poised on craters as if they were about to be carted away—talks of the childhood memory which set her on her path. Sitting inside a wardrobe, she wanted to create, to solidify, its internal—Freud would call it *heimlich* (intimate familiar)— black space.[8] A later work, *Ghost*, is the cast of a room in a house in Archway, similar to one she had grown up in, which makes the viewer a property of its architectural space: "I realise I had made something quite extraordinary, quite other . . . something in which you the viewer were the wall."[9]

Asking herself whether buildings might lend themselves more readily to visual memory than other classes of object, Yates cites the refrain: "I remember, I remember the house where I was born."[10] Its childlike rhythm carries us back to a moment which, presumably, if we are remembering it, we have in fact left behind—as if in the moment of remembering, we lose all distance and become the child we once were. But if memory is inhabited by physical, domestic space, as well as the reverse—our houses are filled with our memories—Simonides's story suggests that there is also something more sinister at play. The house may be about to collapse, and the home turn into a grave. According to *Ad Herennium*, exceptional beauty or singular ugliness is the best aid to memory: "if we ornament them, as with crowns or purple cloaks, so that the similitude may be more distinct to us; or if we somehow disfigure them, as by introducing one stained with blood."[11] In this chapter, I will be suggesting that these bloody images, Simonides ghastly story, are not incidental to the problem of memory. Rather, they might offer one way of approaching the relationship between memory and violence in the modern world.

To say something strange and disturbing has been happening in the world of memory today is an understatement. In a *Guardian* report on the eve of the 2008 Italian elections, Federico Moneta, an Italian voter, explained why he would not be voting for Silvio Berlusconi's rival, Walter Veltroni, leader of the center-left Democratic Party and former Communist: "I can't forget the history of communism in Europe."[12] Even before the election that chillingly ushered in the most right-wing, protofascist, government in Italy since the war, it seems fair to ask: How come no memory of fascism? He may well, of course, have been too young to have such a living memory. Even so, the blitheness of his response, his apparently complete oblivion to Italy's fascist history, especially given this appeal to memory as guarantee, was sinister. When, shortly after the election, Rome Mayor Gianni Alemanno announced his plan to purge the capital of twenty thousand illegal immigrants, Amos Luzzato, former head of the

Union of Jewish Communities, commented: "Italy is a country that has lost its memory."[13]

In a 2008 article in the *New York Review of Books* entitled "What Have We Learned, If Anything?" Tony Judt argued that the world is rapidly forgetting the worst of the twentieth century.[14] This became his theme. The epilogue on postwar memory to his 2005 *Postwar: A History of Europe since 1945*, has the title "From the House of the Dead: An Essay on Modern European Memory."[15] Above all, he argued, what is being forgotten, notably in the United States, is the meaning of war—the damage to life and limb, the disfigurements and destruction. Another way of putting this would be to say that we are involved in the continuous eviction of dead bodies from our homes (the modern Western dream of war with smart bombs and no home casualties). Today death falls out of the skies, at once random and precise, rather as it did in the 400 BC story from Ceos. When Walter Benjamin said that we have pushed death from the center of our experience, he was not writing specifically about war, but the inability to countenance death which he attributes to modernity takes on a new resonance in the context of the twentieth century violence that he did not live fully to see.[16] It is, Freud wrote, impossible to imagine one's own death (which is why we like to attribute death to accident or disaster, as if it were something we might, if we are lucky, be spared). Today, we are witnessing a technocratic perfection of violence, together with a flood of images of disaster on our screens, whose paradoxical consequence seems to be the idea that death is history. Death—above all, death in war—is being forgotten.

In this forgetting, the United States is not, of course, alone. Indeed, as Judt stresses, the United States at least has the excuse of not having experienced the full ravages of either of the twentieth century's two world wars. Europe, however, did have that experience, and while that may have protected Europe from the neoconservative glorification of military prowess under the Bush administration, this has not stopped the fascist resurgence in Italy (and not just in Italy) any more than it prevented the

U.K. government from joining in the carnage in Afghanistan and Iraq. For Judt, the ease with which we in Europe have engaged in a seemingly morally unimpeachable war against terror—and against the "extremists" or "Islamofascists" who are meant to be its chief agents—is "a sure sign that we have forgotten *the* lesson of the twentieth century: the ease with which war and fear and dogma can bring us to demonize others, deny them a common humanity or the protection of our laws, and do unspeakable things to them."[17] Our collective failure of memory allows us to do the worst we have already done—over and over again.

It is a central part of Judt's argument that this forgetting has been accompanied by, and indeed facilitated by, a false memorialization of the past. In his introduction to *Lieux de mémoire*, the monumental documentation of modern French memory carried out under his direction in the 1980s, Pierre Nora describes how memory today is delegating itself to the archive, where it sheds its responsibilities "as a snake sheds its skin."[18] For Nora, a superstitious veneration of the trace covers for the true, lost art of remembering. (In a note, Nora ascribes the origin of his whole project to Yates's *The Art of Memory*.) Memory ossifies inside its objects as a way for people to avoid the disturbance that memory, if left to its own devices, might provoke. Nora is writing specifically about France, where national, state-sanctioned memory—for which he coins the term *"mémoire-nation"*—has promoted a unitary vision of the nation all the more energetically, and indeed desperately, in proportion to such a vision having been lost. In this context, memory becomes the chief custodian of a false national consciousness clinging to itself for dear life. "Today," he writes, "memory has become the only springboard which allows '*la France*' to find once more, as will and representation, the unity and the legitimacy which it has only ever enjoyed through its identification with the state."[19] Crucially, he locates the beginnings of this form of national memory to the defeat of 1870 by Prussia which played such a central role in unleashing the hatreds of the Dreyfus Affair. Remember Julien Benda in his essay "The Dreyfus Affair and the Principle of Authority" in *La revue blanche*, criticizing the nationalists for harboring a metaphysical idea of "*la France*"—"feminine, with a heart, arms, children and a past," believed in, in exactly the same way, "as the salons believe in High Society."[20]

For Judt, as we turn into the twenty-first century, a new archive of European memory is yet again allowing us to shed responsibility for our history, camouflaging the most disturbing aspects of the past. "The Western solution to the problem of Europe's troublesome memories," Judt observes in "The House of the Dead," "has been to fix them, quite literally, in stone."[21] The twentieth century is in danger of becoming a "moral memory palace: a pedagogically serviceable Chamber of Historical Horrors whose way stations are labelled 'Munich' or 'Auschwitz.'"[22] As if on cue, in the same week as the article about the Italian elections, the *Guardian* newspaper carried a story about a German "remembrance train."[23] The organizers of a traveling exhibition on the deportations by rail of thousands of children to Nazi concentration camps had been told by the authorities that they could not stop the train at Berlin central station. If the banning of the train spoke volumes of a desire to forget, at the same time this "remembrance train" seemed an almost surreal image of the way stations Judt was warning against. (Without casting doubt on the intentions of this citizens' project, we can still ask what it means to bring the train to life and turn such an exhibition into a traveling show.) In relation to the crimes of history, modern memory, it seems, is at once too little and too much. In this chapter I will be arguing that tracking the process of memory in the psyche might be one way of trying to understand how and why.

Memory, notably memory of the dead, is the place where our intimate and social selves are joined, where fantasy and history are irrevocably intertwined. In the same month as Judt's article, one more example of memory, at once grotesquely private and public, disgorged itself from the basement of a house. The story of the Fritzl family of Amstetten, in northeastern Austria, offered its hideous confirmation of the tie between memory, history, and a childhood home. Josef Fritzl, a convicted rapist, had imprisoned, raped, and fathered seven children with his daughter Elizabeth over twenty-four years in a cellar underneath his house, without his wife or anyone else in the community suspecting a thing. The mother was told that her daughter had run away, but it remains a question whether she could possibly *not* have known—the Austrian social services also insisted they could not have been aware of anything. According to the report of expert witness, engineer Peter Kopecky, the soundproofing of the cellar was imperfect and the sounds from the cellar would have been audible in the house above ground. Already this resonates with the nation's history—the famous claim of the bystanders that they did not know.

How can we fail to see in this steeled-off bunker the last stand of Austria's past? A young woman gives birth in darkness, not once but seven times, to a mutant future. (One of the children died.) Her father thereby fulfills the National Socialist edict of pure interbreeding to the letter—the call to ethnic purity always being somewhere a call to incest. Judging from his threat to gas the children in the bunker, it seems that his daughter, as well as representing National Socialist Woman, was also, in his mind, a Jew. In his confession to his lawyer, Fritzl made the link to Nazism: "I grew up in the Nazi times and that meant the need to be controlled and the respect of authority. I suppose I took on some of these old values. It was all subconscious of course."[24] In their study of the case, Stefanie Marsh and Bojan Pancevski rightly insist that this attempt to shed blame should not be taken seriously. The links are, however, unavoidable. Fritzl was born into an Austria rife with racist sentiment. Hans Höller, mayor of Amstetten at the time, was chairman of the anti-Semitic league. Hitler was given a rapturous welcome when he visited the town on 15 March 1938, three days after the Anschluss. (Fritzl would have been three.) When Nazi Wolfgang Mitterdorfer took over from Höller, he announced plans to turn Amstetten into a "fortress town," a *Führerstadt*, the honorable title conferred on special cities of the Third Reich. Mauthausen, the notorious death camp, was thirty miles away, with two of its satellites just outside the town. It was the Nazi's biggest death camp, based on the twin principles: *Vernichtung durch Arbeit* (extermination through work) and *Rückkehr* (return undesirable). For refusing to take refugees into her house during the war, Fritzl's mother was incarcerated there for several months. It is just one of the ironies of the case that, as Amstetten was subjected to intense bombardment—more bombs were dropped on the town than there were inhabitants—she would bundle Fritzl off into the network of underground bunkers built through the hills on the edge of town, while she sat in the house preferring to face death than the prospect of emerging from underground to find her house obliterated. Fritzl's town was a Nazi fortress. His childhood was one of camps, fortifications, and bunkers. (Today the Austrian Jewish community refer to far-right politicians who make a public display of condemning Nazism as "cellar Nazis.")[25] His perversion can therefore be read as a form of remembering, but also not remembering—repeating a history while burying it under the ground.[26]

"Austria is not the perpetrator," Austria's then chancellor, Alfred Gusenbauer insisted within days of the discovery. "This is an unfathomable criminal case. . . . We will not allow our country to be held hostage by one man"; Natasha Kampusch, who was similarly held in a cellar for eight years in Austria before escaping in 2006, had other ideas: "I think this exists worldwide, but I also think it is a ramification of the Second World War when the suppression of women was propagated and authoritarian education was very important."[27] No investigation into the role of the police or social services in the Fritzl case was instigated by the Austrian government. "What is undoubtable," state Marsh and Pancevski in the foreword to their book, "is that, still now, Austria itself has yet to face its past, or analyse with any seriousness its impact on the present."[28] In a bizarre twist, Kampusch eventually bought the house where she had been held. She did not want to see it vandalized or demolished: "It's not as threatening as it was back then. But it is still a house of horrors."[29]

The first public commemoration of the Holocaust in Austria was Simon Rattle conducting the Viennese Philharmonic at Mauthausen in 2000. (It was also the year when Jörg Haider's far-right Freedom Party entered a coalition government.) Four years previously, the Austrian Republic had initiated an international competition for a monument to pay homage to Austrian resistance to Nazism. The successful artists, Esther Shalev-Gerz and Jochen Gerz, proposed an intervention at the site of Feliferhof, one of the most important shooting grounds of the military, to be called *The Geese of Feliferhof.* It would have consisted of four white flags with four red sentences emblazoned upon them: *"Courage is punished with death"*; *"Betraying the country is honoured"*; *"The soldier's fiancée is barbarism"*; *"We too, are called soldiers."* Having approved the project, the Austrian army retracted it. The past returns to a nation which had been foremost in trying to forget. The nation is "not the perpetrator." "After Germany was defeated," Judt writes in *Postwar*, "Austria fell into the Western camp and was assigned the status of Hitler's 'first victim.'" This was a "stroke of doubly unmerited good fortune," as he puts it, because it authorized exorcism of the past.[30] One editor responded to the Austrian chancellor: "It would make sense to start looking for answers—many of which are slumbering deep within us—instead of reacting in a patriotic knee-jerk way."[31] When a nation so visibly attempts to control its memories, you can be sure that there is something wrong.

Our Mental Home

When we go to bed at night, we all like to think we are safe in our homes. We like to think that our homes are where we are. "When I woke thus," writes Proust in the first pages of *Combray*, which opens *À la recherche*, "my mind restlessly attempting, without success, to discover where I was, everything revolved around me in the darkness, things, countries, years."[32] In this twilight state, with his body too numb to move, the narrator tries to locate the position of his limbs "in order to deduce from this the direction of the wall, the location of the furniture, in order to reconstruct and name the dwelling in which it found itself."[33] It is hard not to read the whole passage as a modern-day rendering, not to say parody, of Quintilian:

Its memory, the memory of its ribs, its knees, its shoulders, offered in succession several of the rooms in which it had slept, while around it the invisible walls, changing place according to the shape of the imagined room, spun through the shadows. And even before my mind, which hesitated on the threshold of times and shapes, had identified the house by reassembling the circumstances, it—my body—would recall the kind of bed in each one, the location of the doors, the angle at which the light came in through the windows, the existence of a hallway, along with the thought I had had as I fell asleep and that I had recovered upon waking.[34]

This is a mind asleep, or rather, barely awakening, that spins in the shadows and falters in the face of ghostly, unidentified times and shapes. Struggling to place itself, to find itself inside its own room, it trusts to the location of ribs, knees, and shoulders, only to discover that each one contains the memory of other rooms and worlds: "everything revolved around me in the darkness: things, countries, years." Far from grounding us, memory dislocates. It is too full of itself. "From the honeycombs of memory," Benjamin wrote in his essay on Proust, "he built a house for the swarm of his thoughts."[35] The original art of memory aimed to fix images securely in the mind. In the story of Simonides, it was the counter to a disaster in which it did not partake. The house may have been about to fall in, but the walls of memory were safe. At the time, there was no conception of the way memory deposits its traces in the body—the body as a palimpsest housing memory upon memory—nor an idea that memory might reside at the precarious threshold between conscious and unconscious, between waking and sleeping life, or that memory, precisely because it is your most precious belonging, might be a place where you can lose yourself. "He lay on his bed," writes Benjamin, "wracked with homesickness, homesick for the world distorted in the state of resemblance, a world in which the true surrealist face of existence breaks through."[36]

It is crucial for Proust—and for Freud, as I will discuss shortly—that the mind cannot control its memories. "If I can have, in me and around me, so many memories that I do not

remember," Proust muses in *Sodom and Gomorrah*, "this forgetting may apply to a life that I have lived in the body of another
man, or even on another planet. A same forgetting wipes out
everything"—the French is "*oubli*," translated both by Scott
Moncrieff and John Sturrock as "oblivion," which somewhat
domesticates or reduces, I think, the surreal quality of this moment.[37] In his essay "Proust: The Music of Memory," critic Michael Wood characterizes this passage as comic or mischievous, a
mere pastiche of Henri Bergson, on whose version of time Proust
is known to have drawn.[38] Instead, I suggest we might see this
as the unsettling but logical consequence of recognizing that the
mind is not master in its own home. If we do not know our own
minds, then how can we know not just what, but *who* is inside
them? For Proust, the dead live on in the mind of the living,
as more than ghosts. In a famous passage in *Time Regained*, he
describes a book, indeed, the book he has just written, as "a huge
cemetery in which on the majority of the tombs the names are
effaced and can no longer be read."[39] He is reproaching himself
for the way he has exploited his dead grandmother and Albertine
after her death as tools for his art. But much earlier—here it is
important that the first and last volumes were completed more
or less together before anything else—he spins the onset of his
creativity, which we have already seen plunging its roots into the
night, out of the belief that the living might be summoned back
to life, called out of eternal sleep, by the dead. The passage comes
at the end of *Combray* right before the far better-known madeleine episode which it inaugurates:

> I feel that there is much to be said for the Celtic belief that the
> souls of those whom we have lost are held captive in some inferior
> being, in an animal, in a plant, in some inanimate object, and thus
> effectively lost to us until the day (which to many never comes) when
> we happen to pass by the tree or to obtain possession of the object
> which forms their prison. Then they start and tremble, they call us
> by our name, and as soon as we have recognised them the spell is
> broken. Delivered by us, they have overcome death and return to
> share our life.[40]

It is, we might say, a strange, ghostly extension of what psycho-analysis will later term object-relations theory, which also says that, without recognition by the other, the infant will not come to be. Except that in these lines from Proust, the act of recognition has been carried across the threshold between life and death, as if all the dead need to return to life, all they are waiting for, is to be seen. Or to be remembered. "Perhaps," Proust muses much later in *The Guermantes Way*, "the resurrection of the soul after death is to be conceived as a phenomenon of memory."[41] "The dead annex the quick," writes Beckett in his essay on Proust, "as surely as the kingdom of France annexes the Duchy of Orleans."[42] The dead are colonizers, grabbing the living like a piece of land. Beckett's analogy simply picks up how Proust's most intimate, personal insights so often bring with them, as we have already seen, their own inexorable political gloss. (Beckett's essay opens the final chapter of this book.)

"And so it is," the passage from *Combray* continues, "with our own past."[43] If Proust's great work shows us, in a way no writer has before or since, the irreducible, unsettling, mobility of memory, here he is also suggesting that the act of memory is inextricably, and ethically, bound to our recollection of the dead. Together, these two insights may seem to cancel each other out. If we cannot find our way in the house of memory, how can we possibly, with any degree of sureness, call to life those we have lost? I want now to suggest on the contrary that only if we rec-ognize what Esther Shalev-Gerz calls (in the third of this chap-ter's epigraphs) "the perpetual movement of memory,"[44] is there any chance whatsoever of a responsible reckoning with both our personal and historical past. "Memory," writes Nora in "Between Memory and History," "is a perpetually actual phenomenon"— "open to the dialectic of remembering and forgetting, uncon-scious of its successive deformations."[45] If memory is perma-nently on the move, it is because of its proclivity to distort itself. To put it more simply, the house of memory is not a comfortable place. If we are to follow Nora's and Judt's important reflections on memory and history, we need to acknowledge the anguish of memory. We need to travel once again into the darkest corridors of the mind, to look more closely this time at how memories are made and undone.

The Ghost of Memory—Freud

Memory, of course, is not always possible. There is a resistance to memory inside memory itself. Psychoanalysis, as I described in the first chapter, starts here. The hysteric suffers mainly from reminiscences. In fact, this is a somewhat misleading statement, since the hysteric is the one who precisely cannot reminisce. She is fighting against unwanted, unconscious, memories which at once crowd and slip from her mind. As I described in chapter 2, psychoanalysis is about the divisions of our mental space (or splitting of the ego, in Freud's strongest late terms). There are things housed inside the mind that the mind cannot bear. The house of memory—to take our central metaphor for this chapter—has many closed doors. If memory came easily, there would be no call for psychoanalysis. Seen in this light, our contemporary surfeit of memory is a decoy. "We speak so much of memory," writes Nora in my opening epigraph, "because there is so little of it left."[46] We only bathe ourselves in memory, because we have hidden memory away.

As early as "The Project for a Scientific Psychology" of 1895, Freud was trying to understand the power of painful memories to disrupt the integrity of the psyche. When thought alights on a memory that generates too much unpleasure, it stalls and interrupts itself. Even when the unpleasure is gradually "tamed" by the ego, the very process of subjugation leaves its mark, blocking the pathways of thought—our freedom of thought, as one might say. (His expression for this blockage is "thought-defence," one of the earliest appearances of a term that will have a rich afterlife in the work of his daughter, Anna Freud.)[47] Nor can we assume that a painful memory will be subdued by the passage of time: "What is it, then," he asks, "that happens to *memories* capable of affect till they are *tamed*? It cannot be supposed that 'time,' repetition, weakens their capacity for affect, since ordinarily that factor [repetition] actually contributes to strengthening an association."[48] Time does not always and invariably diminish the pain of remembrance. It can increase it. The idea of demonic repetition, or the death drive, which will be central to Freud's later thinking also makes its first faint appearance here. The struggle of the ego to tame our memories leaves a permanent scar on the mind.

At this stage of his work, Freud believed the symptom could be traced to a lost experience which was the primary source of pain—not necessarily a single traumatic event but something more diffuse, which he refers to in his 1893 paper "On the Psychical Mechanism of Hysterical Phenomena" as "a whole story of suffering."[49] Slowly this idea stretches its limits to include the suffering that the mind inflicts on itself. Freud would come to discard the idea of trauma as the sole etiology of hysteria in favor of the idea that the mind was troubled as much by its internal processes—no experience, not even a traumatic experience, has meaning without being subjected to the complex, often perverse, pathways of our unconscious thoughts and desires. In this moment, which could be said to inaugurate psychoanalysis proper, Freud's critics have seen a downgrading of memory and a denial of the impact of history on the mind. In fact, the problem of memory does not diminish—far from it—when it is no longer an event or experience, but guilty fantasies and lost pleasures that are at play. In fact, one way of describing the famous shift in Freud's thinking from event to fantasy as the cause of neurosis would be to say that our most hidden, secret pleasures—what we do not wish to remember about ourselves—now become one of our chief mental obstacles and one of the most powerful sources of psychic pain. If it is the task of civilization to control those impulses, it is one of Freud's most radical insights, that civilization is hopelessly unequal to this task. The law knows no limit in its capacity to make our pleasure intolerable to our judgment. But the law also reeks of the pleasures it would ideally subdue (which is why it so often fails). In Freud's account, the violence of the law mimics, draws on, and taps into the untamed aggression of the psyche. Our attachment to pain has plunged its roots ineradicably into the unconscious. Some will argue that in the process, psychoanalysis has lost its reference to the contingencies of a hostile world. You could, however, say the opposite, as the latent violence in all of us rises progressively to the surface of Freud's work. We are still prey to a "whole story of suffering." But now we are tormented not only by a harsh reality but equally by the perverse cruelty of our own minds. What we cannot bear to remember is the worst of who we are.

In that first traumatic etiology of hysteria, suffering could only ever be something inflicted by somebody else (hence its limit and temptation). By discarding that theory, Freud does not, therefore, relinquish his responsibility to history; on the contrary, he makes history the responsibility of everyone. Today, the enormous resonance of that shift could not be clearer. By enshrining the memory of suffering in stone, Judt argues, "indulging to excess the cult of commemoration," we veil the issue of the perpetrator, displace murderers with victims, and shed our own responsibility for our times.[50] We become innocent for the rest of our days. The ethics of memory requires a Freudian turn.

If the traces of demonic repetition in Freud's thought are already present in the 1890s—something pacing inside the mind that we cannot control—Freud's first fully recognizable reference to the repetition compulsion or death drive does not come until 1914 at the outbreak of the war. Freud's famous paper on technique, "Remembering, Repeating and Working-Through," has become crucial to recent theorization of memory.[51] It is often read as offering a straight path or sequence to mental health, as well as a blueprint for psychoanalytic practice—instead of repeating, or repeatedly enacting, what you are most profoundly in flight from, you remember, take hold of the memory, and work it through. The ordering of the title is, however, misleading. "Remembering" should logically not be at the beginning but in the middle as the transitional term, the instance that brings about the decisive passage from repetition to working-through. In fact, both of these two are forms of remembering. In the first, repetition, the patient remembers without knowing it, unconsciously reenacting for the analyst the worst of his past, everything he once was and still is; in the second, working-through, his conscious retrieval of that same past allows him to lay it to rest. It is, however, the idea of "work" that I think has made this paper so persuasive for those trying to theorize the memory of twentieth-century horror— the idea of memory as submitting to a work ethic, something we can confront and face down, precisely work on.[52] Viewed in this light, Freud's text offers a get-out clause in relation to the idea that history repeats itself. (It was Santayana who coined the expression in 1905 that those who do not remember history are condemned to repeat it.) You resist, and then, with analytic help, you remember and move on. Deployed in the service of historical progress, the concept of working-through becomes the path to a better future for us all.

But is that quite what Freud is saying? Is not the idea of the repetition compulsion as a stepping stone or stage on the path to something else, something better, a contradiction in terms? Or to put it another way, is working-through the strongest principle at play, or as strong as the wished-for sequence the title suggests? Repetition is itself; it precisely repeats. Hence its demonic nature and its increasing association from this point on in Freud's thinking with death. It is 1914, at the outbreak of the war which will give birth to Freud's texts on war, melancholia, and transience, as well as leading to the complete overhaul of his mental topography. From this moment on, the death drive will become one of the most compelling forces, if not the most compelling force, of the mind—hence, repetition *compulsion*. (Eros is given no such gloss of inexorable fate.) In his paper, Freud goes to great lengths to describe the battle of the analyst in combating the patient's resistance to analytic work—an "arduous task," "a trial of patience for the analyst," faced with the "armoury," the "weapons" (this word twice) with which the patient's resistance confronts him. If the analyst cannot place the "reins of transference" on the "untamed instincts"—remember "tamed" of 1895—or if the "bonds" that attach the patient to the treatment are broken, then the analysis will fail.[53] Thus, while remembering is the goal of the treatment—the "awakening of the memories, which appear without difficulty, as it were, after the resistance has been overcome"[54]—the overriding impression of this paper is of a war that is only with immense difficulty, indeed if ever, fully won. If we are to pursue the path of memory into the unconscious, issue a type of injunction to memory, then it is crucial not to underestimate the forces it is up against.[55] In this account of just how hard it is to bring memory alive, indeed, one might say in his entire theorization of the death drive after the war, Freud is in a way predicting the will to forgetfulness that Judt so brilliantly describes as casting its shadow over the past century. There is a deathly occupant in the house of memory. It is because something lethal has entered that we turn away.

This is another of those moments where Proust's vocabulary is strikingly resonant of Freud's. "When these resurrections [of the past] took place," he writes in *Time Regained*, the distant scene, surfacing from the past, "grappled like a wrestler with the present," but the past invariably loses the fight: "If the present scene had not very quickly been victorious, I believe that I should have lost consciousness."[56] For Proust, the struggle of the past to reach consciousness is so difficult that, in order to avoid it, the mind will readily forgo consciousness itself.

The repetition compulsion is the ghost in the machine. It lingers in Freud's paper, creating havoc as it goes. In a note added by the editors to the last lines, they suggest that the concept of working-through is inextricably linked to that of psychic inertia, the obstacle to psychoanalytic progress in Freud's last works (notably in the posthumously published "Analysis Terminable and Interminable" of 1937 to which they refer the reader). But this deathly insight would seem to be barely tolerable to the editors themselves. On the previous page, they append a note to the following sentence which perhaps best encapsulates and summarizes the project's progressive dimension and the whole concept of working-through: "One must allow the patient time to become more conversant with this resistance, with which he has now become acquainted, to *work through it.*[57] The only problem with this translation, however, is that it is drawn, as they explain, from the first edition of the text: "sich in den ihm nun bekannten Widerstand zu vertiefen." All subsequent German editions, following Freud's alteration, have corrected "nun bekannten" to "unbekannten" which would translate as "this resistance that is unknown to him." The difference speaks volumes. Resistance is not something you get acquainted with (*nun bekannten*). It remains unknown (*unbekannten*). Beautifully the translators encapsulate and repeat the problem that Freud, that the whole of psychoanalysis, addresses—of what is fundamentally unreachable in the mind. "In my analysis," wrote Joan Rivière in a personal reminiscence of 1958, "[Freud] one day made some interpretation, and I responded to it by an objection. He then said: 'It is *un-conscious.*' I was overwhelmed then by the realisation that I knew nothing about it—I knew nothing about it.... I have never forgotten this reminder of what the unconscious means."[58] "She was in the peculiar situation of knowing and at the same time not knowing." Now things have got considerably more difficult. For if it is true—it is indeed the basic premise of psychoanalysis—that only the patient has somewhere the knowledge he or she most needs to own, it is also the case that the whole progression of Freud's thinking can be measured in terms of the increasing obstacles which we all, as human subjects, lay in the path of that knowledge.

"Remembering, Repeating and Working-Through," this key text of Freud, wills a psychic progress it cannot deliver. Our resistance, our struggle with memory is interminable. Written at the outbreak of the war, Freud's text is a child of its times. I see him as arguing with himself: "Things have never been this bad. The world will not get better. It will." We need, therefore, to add another dimension to the essential instability and movement of memory captured so vividly by Proust. Memory, like Freud's writing, fails to settle, because somewhere we are always in flight from the unbearable violence of history and of our own minds.

In response to the First World War, Freud recasts his topography of the mind. He dies at the outbreak of the Second. Much later, fiction will bring its own confirmation to the struggles he describes, at once deeply personal but now spread to all corners of the nation, in ways he does not exactly predict but which seem to give the cruelest historical embodiment to his thinking. Walter Abish's 1982 novel, *How German Is It (Wie Deutsch Ist Es)*, is the story of postwar Germany in the throes of repudiating its history. (The first part is called "The Edge of Forgetfulness.") A pristine new nation driving itself to perfection—an impulse which has the fullest collaboration of the international community after the war—wants to know nothing of its own past: "But how reliable is this evidence, these articles by former inmates or by writers who specialise in the sensational, the outrageous? . . . Did this really occur or have these photographs been carefully doctored, ingeniously concocted simply in order to denigrate everything German?" (Holocaust denial appears first in Germany.) When a mass grave is uncovered outside the new city of Brumhold- stein, built over the remains of Durst concentration camp, no one wants to recognize that these are the bodies of Jews: "They should have immediately covered it with a ton of cement." (The locals refer to Durst as a "*so-called* extermination camp.") "There are no books to be found on Durst. And Durst, accordingly, has no official history." A creeping new racism, directed at Turks, Greeks, and Arabs, insists that no one can be truly German or fully enter into the spirit of the nation unless they "speak, read and think in our mother tongue."[59]

At a key point in the novel, the teacher Anna Heller instructs her class in the concept of the "familiar." As the earth throws up the buried history of the nation, Anna evokes the house of memory as a way of beating back this unwelcome eruption of Germany's past:

> When we wake up in the morning, said Anna Heller, as soon as we open our eyes, they come to rest on the familiar outlines of our possessions, our furniture, our wall posters and drawings, our shut- ters and windows, and everything that we can see as we stand at the window. . . . Everything is familiar. We get up and walk to the

bathroom, where we brush our teeth and wash our hands and face
and look in the mirror and comb our hair. All that is familiar. We
say good morning to our parents. We are in a sense establishing and
reaffirming our sense of the familiar. . . . Now if we think about the
past, if we think about anything that happened in the past: yesterday,
the day before, a week ago, aren't we to some extent thinking about
something that we consider familiar?[60]

"But why," asks the narrator, "would Miss Anna Heller spend so
much time discussing the familiar, unless she had some doubts,
some reservations, regarding the familiar, day-to-day events of
her life."[61] The question, lacking an interrogative sign, turns into a
statement. Likewise with the book's title, *How German Is It: Wie
Deutsch Ist Es,* which then becomes not "how far can we say it
is (was) German?" but something closer to "Look how German
this is!" The title alone thus becomes Abish's way of demanding
that Germany take responsibility for the past. What does the
"familiar" mean, what on earth can the walls, shutters, windows
of a house do, when a mass grave is being excavated on the edges
of your hometown?

Memory and Nation

For Proust, a book is a cemetery because we so ruthlessly deposit
between its covers the lives on which we have drawn. This is a
profanation. He knows that his readers will do no less to his
work. They will violate its sanctity by projecting their own lives
and loves into his characters, casually disposing of their unique-
ness, transfiguring them beyond recognition. He cannot object,
however, because he is guilty of the same crime. If he has suffered
successively for Gilberte, Mme de Guermantes, and Albertine,
he has also forgotten each and every one, only his love—the so-
lipsistic residue of his own being—outliving them all. Horrified
by this truth, he then makes this extraordinary analogy: "I felt
something near to horror at myself, the self-horror that some
nationalist party might come to feel after a long war fought in its
name, from which it alone had profited and in which many noble

victims had suffered and succumbed without ever knowing . . . what the outcome of the struggle would be."[62]

This is only one of the moments when Proust veers, with what can seem like startling promiscuity, between the private and public realms. (The opening exordium of *Sodom and Gomorrah* discussed in the previous chapter would simply be the most striking, finely orchestrated example.) For me, however, these lines stand out, perhaps because there is something not quite right about them. What nationalist party, victorious in war, is appalled at being the sole beneficiary of the struggle (oh dear, we won) and mourns its victims? It would hardly survive as nationalism, surely, if it did. All nations, as Ernest Renan famously remarked, rely on historical forgetting. ("Forgetfulness grew thicker by the day," wrote Reinach of France's early oblivion to the fate of Dreyfus.[63]) Today the new century is in danger of losing the memory of war and with it our responsibility for our own history—"displacing murderers with victims," in Judt's phrase. In this, nationalism can fairly be designated the chief culprit. "Only rarely," James Young writes in his 1993 *The Texture of Memory*, "does a nation call upon itself to remember the victims of crimes it has perpetrated."[64] What nationalist party—Proust says "party," note, not even "nation"—feels horror at itself? Horror can be the propaganda of no party, not at least in its own cause. As everything in our most recent history attests, nationalism is the place where a people enshrine their most passionate and intractable self-love (which is why Hannah Arendt, in her famous letter to Gershom Scholem, said she could not love her own people).

The French, which is almost untranslatable, reads: "Je n'étais pas loin de me faire horreur," which reads literally, "I was not far from giving myself a horror" (as in "se faire peur," "give oneself a fright"). It then continues, "comme se le ferait peut-être à lui-même quelque parti nationaliste": "as perhaps"—Ian Patterson's recent translation includes the "perhaps," omitted by Scott Moncrieff, which at least allows Proust a moment's hesitation—"as *perhaps* some nationalist party might do to itself." "Se le ferait à lui-même"—"would do to oneself." "Do" rather than "feel," as

both translations have it—the French conveys less of a sentiment, something closer to a self-inflicted wound—"se le ferait
à lui-même." However we translate it, Proust has created the
profoundest link between the abuses of the heart—what we do
to each other in our most intimate personal lives—and war: "in
which many noble victims had suffered and succumbed." Barely a
few lines later, the narrator offers his celebrated image of his book
as a graveyard "in which on the majority of tombs, the names are
effaced and can no longer be read." Casting its shadow down the
page, Proust's analogy turns his graveyard into a war cemetery.

In Judt's argument, as the violence of war fades from memory,
so does historical accountability, which is veiled in a shroud of
suffering. Viewed in these terms, Israel is something of a test
case—not least because the Jewish people can claim with justification to have been the repeated victims of history. Hence the
second epigraph to this paper, cited by James Young in his chapter on Israel and Holocaust memory—the lines from Ezekiel
etched onto Nathan Rapaport's *Scroll of Fire*, outside Jerusalem
in the Martyrs' Forest, which is composed of six million trees:

> Behold, O my people, I will open your graves
> And cause you to come out of your graves
> And bring you to the land of Israel.[65]

Think back to the lines from Combray where the dead are summoned by our memory into life. In Israel, the dead are summoned to create a nation. "Like any other state," writes Young,
"Israel remembers its past according to its national myths. . . .
Unlike that of other states, however, Israel's overarching national
ideology and religion . . . may be memory itself."[66] In a special
commemorative issue of the *Jewish Chronicle* for the sixtieth anniversary of the founding of Israel, Ehud Olmert remembered
1948: "Surrounded and outnumbered by hostile neighbours, the
nascent Israel was forced to defend itself against invasion and
certain destruction." No hint of a suggestion that the founding of the nation entailed violence against another people. (The
piece was entitled "A Very Happy Birthday.") This, he said, was

the history of Zionism: "The history of the Zionist enterprise is well known."[67] Israel finds it almost impossible to think of itself as a perpetrator even when, as today, it is armed with the full panoply and might of the state. Even when, by its own account and choosing, the ethos of the perpetrator has also been urgently inscribed into the nation's self-fashioning as the historic response to what is felt to have been the former weakness of the Jewish people. In 2004, Esther Shalev-Gerz curated a video installation of found Holocaust objects and the curators who had handled them, *Menschendinge*, or *The Human Aspect of Objects*, at the Buchenwald Memorial. "I know that for many people it sounds shocking," comments curator Naomi Tereza Salmon, one of those working with the objects, formerly a curator at Yad Vashem, "but a part of the . . . how should I say it . . . the conclusion of the educational programme I grew up with, in Israel, when you ask what the lesson of the *Shoah* is, would be: 'Rather be stronger than weak.' And in that sense: 'Rather be the perpetrator than the victim.' Being the victim is not a good state, we saw that, rather be stronger, rather be harder. And personally I can't live with that conclusion. I think it's the wrong conclusion."[68]

In Israel-Palestine, the struggle over national memory shows no sign of diminishing with time. In February 2010, Benjamin Netanyahu decided to include two sites on the West Bank—the Tomb of the Patriarchs in Hebron, known to Palestinians as the Ibrahimi Mosque, and Rachel's Tomb near Bethlehem—in a new national heritage list. "Our existence here in our country depends not only on the strength of the IDF and our economic and technological might," he told the cabinet. "It is anchored first and foremost, in our national and emotional legacy, which we instil in our youth and in the coming generations."[69] Simultaneously, the government is planning to invest in restoring hundreds of historic sites, museums, and archives and in building two trails between archaeological sites and landmark stations from the era of the Yishuv, the pre-state Jewish community. (As the reporter observed, Arabs will have no share in this cultural heritage.)[70] Time erases nothing—past affect is stubborn it leeches on to the present. At once enacting and forgetting its own violence, Israel is a nation that cannot live without this endlessly renewed version of the past.

Remembering for a People—S Yizhar

We can, I believe, remember differently. In the final part of this chapter, two figures from the world of literature and art might help us to imagine how. S Yizhar (Yizhar Smilansky), little known outside Israel, is considered inside the country to be the godfather of Israeli letters: "There is some of Yizhar," writes Amos Oz, "in every writer who has come after him."[71] Esther Shalev-Gerz, an artist who was born in Lithuania, lived in Jerusalem from 1957 to 1980 and has lived and worked in Paris since 1981. If Yizhar's link to this history and conflict could not be closer—he was a member of the Knesset in the ruling party Mapai from 1949 to 1966—Shalev-Gerz's relationship is at once intense and oblique. One of her earliest works is a permanent installation at Tel Hai, forged in the middle of the first Lebanese war of 1982 (see fig. 1). The shape of a soldier sculpted out of a piece of Jerusalem stone casts its shadow, when you move to one side of it, as fragments on the ground. Tel Hai, as already indicated, was the site of the isolated Jewish farm where, in a clash with Arabs in 1920, the national hero, Trumpeldor, fell in battle, his death becoming a legend. He is famously credited with the dying words "It is worth dying for the land of Israel."[72] Against such fossilizing of history, Shalev-Gerz creates what might be described as memory "at the time," that is, a memory already forming itself around the knowledge of, and responsibility for, its own future. In the same instant that the soldier rises up out of the rock against the horizon of this historically saturated site of national remembrance, he crumbles into fragments, laying his ruinous shadow over the land, as if a soldier could take responsibility for his own violent, unfolding destiny. (Bombs were dropping in the 1982 war as the sculpture was carved.) Nations, unlike national parties, can of course feel horror at wars being fought in their name. The mass protests against the 2003 war in Iraq would be a case in point. For many inside Israel, the 1982 invasion of Lebanon (which will be central to this book's final chapter) was the breaking point, the first for which no defensive motive could be claimed.

Yizhar is the dissident chronicler of 1948. In *Sacred Landscape: The Buried History of the Holy Land since 1948*, Meron Benvenisti significantly links him to Mahmoud Darwish because of their profound, shared acknowledgement of the trauma inflicted on the earth by the creation of Israel as a nation. Something in the land, Yizhar writes, "knows and does not forget, cannot forget": "Only one who knows how to listen to the unforgetting silence of this agonised land, this land 'from which we begin and to which we return'—Jews and Arabs alike—only that person is worthy of calling it a homeland."[73]

Yizhar's most famous story, *Khirbet Khizeh*, was written in the course of the 1948 war. (The first full translation into English, by Nicholas de Lange and Yaacob Dweck, appeared in 2008.) The only published story to narrate the expulsions of the Palestinians, *Khirbet Khizeh* provoked a crisis of national remembrance that in many ways has never ceased. Anita Shapira's lengthy article of 2000 on its reception is called "Hirbet Hizah: Between Remembrance and Forgetting." According to Shapira, no soldier of the *sabra* generation, the native-born Israelis who fought in the war, seems to have actively participated in the controversy unleashed by the story on its publication almost immediately after the war: "They were weary, eager to forget the war's events as quickly as possible—and especially to forget its most inglorious, perplexing, oppressive chapter: the Arab expulsion."[74]

The story Shapira tells is a tribute to the disingenuity of national forgetting, a tale of different forms of denial which range from outright rejection of the story's truth to its inclusion in the school curriculum from 1964 seemingly on condition of its being transported out of history and into a universal moral tale—a story of the "struggle for truth" or of mental distress, human grief, and suffering with no need of any reference to the founding mo-

ment in which it was set. (A proposal that it be included in the
new civics class in the 1970s, which would have ensured its discussion as history, was never implemented.)[75] In the first debates
of the 1950s, the issue was whether the story was representative of
the army's conduct and then whether the expulsion, and its violence, could be historically justified. (For one detractor, the problem with the story was the apathy of a new generation, which did
not hate the Arab enemy enough.) By the time of the election
of the first right-wing government under Menachim Begin in
1977, the moral compass had been dropped, the issue had become
more clearly political. Reference to 1948 was now seen as a dele-
gitimation of the state, a problem that persists to this day. A new
focus on Israel's international image required a sanitized version
of history. Shapira calls it the "high noon of self-righteousness":
"a kind of local anaesthetic for those stretches in national memory that remained unpleasant to recall."[76] The expulsion of the
Palestinians was on its way to becoming something close to a
state secret. Despite the best efforts of the new historians of the
1970s and 1980s, who had access to the newly opened archives
and who devoted much of their efforts to uncovering this history, nobody wanted to talk about it anymore.[77] (*Khirbet Khizeh*
anticipates their findings by decades.)

In response to this shift, as well as to the 1977 temporary banning of the film version on Israeli TV, Yizhar himself stated more
clearly than he had before that the story, while not necessarily
representing a "totality of events," was true—"reality, black on
white": "Everything there is reported with great accuracy, meticulously documented, beginning with the operation order on a
certain date right down to all the details."[78] Former 1948 veteran
Ephraim Kleiman, writing in 1978 when he was professor of eco-
nomics at the Hebrew University of Jerusalem, was more willing
to generalize: "In general, there are many in this country who
repress their memories, each Israeli soldier has his own private
Hirbet Hizah." (His article has Hirbet Hizah in the plural.)[79]
At the time of her article, and indeed in many ways her reason
for writing it, Shapira can still insist that this history has not

sunk into public consciousness, that it has no salience in Israel's collective memory ("this past is not present"). Significantly for this study, she compares this willed forgetting to the French inability to confront Vichy.[80] France's "tortured, long-denied and serially incomplete" memory of the war, writes Judt, has "backshadowed" all of Europe's postwar efforts to come to terms with what happened. Not, he adds crucially, that France behaved the worst: "It is that France mattered most."[81]

Before the full translation of *Khirbet Khizeh*, the only pages translated into English came from that part of the story when the soldier is recounting the evacuation by the Israeli army of the Arab village in 1948—shocking enough since it was unambiguous that the soldiers entered the Arab fields "in order to dispossess them."[82] The fragment has become famous for the scandalous affinity it proposes between the plight of the Arab and the history of the Jews. (Shapira's reference to Vichy can be read as the intensifier of that connection.) In the face of an Arab woman—"stern, self-controlled, austere in her sorrow"—the narrator lowers his eyes and is shamed into remembering the exile of his own people. The following famous passage is worth quoting at length:

> Something struck me like lightning. All at once everything seemed to mean something different, more precisely exile. This was exile. This was what exile was like. This was what exile looked like. . . .
>
> I have never been in the Diaspora—I said to myself—I had never known what it was like . . . but people had spoken to me, told me, taught me, and repeatedly recited to me, from every direction, in books and newspapers, everywhere: exile. Our nation's protest to the world: exile! It had entered me, apparently, with my mother's milk. What, in fact, had we perpetrated here today?[83]

In the Hebrew, the tense of exile is the present tense: "This is how exile is" (hineh ze galut). This is memory in the here and now. And the binding of the past into the present is tighter—"Diaspora" is again exile/*galut*. We are being told far more clearly that the two experiences are one and the same. In later editions, there is also a

sentence at the end of the passage in which the responsibility of
the soldier *as a Jew* is underlined: "Anakhnu yehudim higleynu
galut"—"We Jews have exiled an exile."[84] Perhaps even more important, the lines "but people had spoken to me, told me, taught
me, and repeatedly recited to me" echo the *Shema*, the central
Jewish prayer in which God instructs his chosen people to take
his words into their heart: "And you shall rehearse them to your
sons and speak of them when you sit in your house and when
you go on the way and when you lie down and when you rise."
Yizhar's "repeatedly recited" (*shinen*) echoes Deuteronomy's "rehearse," which Robert Alter construes as a variant of *shanah*, to
repeat.[85] Deuteronomic law, writes Frank Crüseman, "is about
the unity of God and totality of the love for him which is required of Israel, 'with all your heart, with all your soul and with
all your strength,' throughout all activities of life."[86] As David
Shulman remarks in his afterword to the English translation of
Khirbet Khizeh, Yizhar is famous for this type of Biblical allusion.
There is, however, something almost sacrilegious here. Israel has
inscribed its national plaint into the minds of it subjects in the
same way that God issues his spiritual injunction to his people.
(The prayer is described by one commentator as "Judaism's greatest contribution to the religious thought of mankind.")[87]

Yizhar, it must be said, was never an outspoken critic of the
Israeli government in which he played an active role. During
the war, he had been actively engaged in the offensive against
Egypt—another famous story, "Midnight Convoy," his tribute
to the soldiers, enters exuberantly into the drama of trying to
get supplies past the enemy to an army under siege.[88] But in
1967, in response to the euphoria of that victory, Yizhar returns
once more to the analogy between the Jews and the Arabs at the
center of *Khirbet Khizeh*. Now, if anything, the lesson is clearer.
What the Jews should take from their history of dispossession
is the principle of justice: "Being a refugee is a question that
touches and binds every Jew. Or dispossession. If there is indeed
a 'Jewish consciousness,' it must pause here to ponder our own
selves." And of nonbelligerence: "What does victory by armed

force actually bestow upon the victors? . . . Because you don't get
a country by means of weapons. Any such acquisition is unjust."[89]
This is to say far more than that the Palestinians have been the
objects of a historic injustice. It is to bind that recognition—
and the principle of justice it entails—into the very core of what
it means to be a Jew ("a question that touches and binds every
Jew"). Remember Léon Blum looking back at the Dreyfus Affair:
"Justice is the religion of the Jews."[90]

Yizhar then becomes one of the writers—Amichai is another—who at once narrate and predict the dangers of a military
triumph that places not just the people it subjugates but also the
victorious nation in peril. There is something more—even more
important for the argument of this chapter. You cannot tell from
the earlier published extract or indeed from any of the commen-
taries I have read, that the whole story is offered as a reluctant,
unwilling memory, one from which not only the soldier but the
whole nation has taken flight. "True, it all happened a long time
ago, but it has haunted me ever since."[91] Yizhar's opening lines
tell us even before we have begun that the memory of what is
about to be told will be unwelcome. The passage continues: "I
sought to drown it out with the din of passing time, to diminish
its value, to blunt its edge with the rush of early life, and I even,
occasionally, managed a sober shrug, managed to see that the
whole thing had not been so bad [*nor'a*] after all." (The Hebrew,
closer to "awful," carries a religious or spiritual charge.)[92] In his
discussion of the story, Gabriel Piterberg describes it as Yizhar's
lieu de mémoire.[93] Alongside the painful trawling of history, the
denial is there, unmistakably, from the start: "I even, occasionally, . . . managed to see that the whole thing had not been so
bad after all." Written in the midst of the war, before the war
had even begun to succumb to the erasures of memory, *Khirbet
Khizeh* becomes a diagnosis of the nation's future (quite literally
an instance of "memory at the time").

Yizhar's parents were the pioneers of the new nation—his
father, Ze'ev Smilansky had arrived from Europe to become one

of the early settlers centrally involved in what they saw as the "redemption" of the land. To remember 1948 like this could already be read as a form of treachery (of which Yizhar was indeed accused). But to remember himself as the child of the founding ideal was, it seems, harder. Yizhar's monumental account of the fading ideals of Zionism—*Days of Tziklag*—was published in 1958. Then in 1961 he fell silent as a writer for thirty years, publishing his three-part semiautobiographical novel between 1992 and 1996, six years before he died. The first volume, *Preliminaries*, was translated into English for the first time in 2007.[94] Although the translator, Nicholas de Lange, says the reasons for the delay both in this case and that of *Khirbet Khizeh* have been contingent, it is hard not to see the appearance of the two works in 2007 and 2008 as offering the melancholic counterpoint to Israel's two effusive but stricken commemorations: of the 1967 war and of the founding of the nation in 1948. Like *Khirbet Khizeh*, *Preliminaries* is an act of remembrance. For the Jews who had arrived—fragile, demoralized, often barely surviving—from Europe, the first native-born Jews in Palestine—the *sabras*—carried the nation's dreams. As he casts his mind back, Yizhar knows that to decompose the ideal in the mind of a growing child is to strangle at birth the faith of the new nation. The boy around whom the narrative turns does not, cannot, belong. In prose at once broken and seamless, the language paces his torment:

> Because even when they are all together there is always one who is left on his own. And even when he is surrounded by them there is always one who is left on his own. And even when they all belong there is always one who does not entirely belong. Or let's say he belongs yet doesn't belong, or not wholly, or not all the time, even if he is with them all the time. And not because he likes it like this but because that's the way it is. And even though it's sad being on your own there is always one who doesn't entirely join in, who doesn't entirely belong, who is always slightly not. And how can someone like that rebuild the Land when you all have to rebuild the Land together, and one on his own cannot build anything? Or it's as though

he's only there to watch, from the sidelines, watching, seeing, saying nothing, but writing it down as it were in a notebook that doesn't exist yet, and, since it's so, it's as though all the time he is required to explain something about himself, to make excuses or apologise, instead of admitting, leave me alone, friends, let me be and don't wait for me. Even though, at the same time, strangely enough, wait for me, I'm coming too. A single lamp and everyone in the dark room around the pit of light, and beyond the lamp there is nothing and nothing can be seen and beyond the house there is nothing and even if you want to you cannot see anything because there is nothing, the darkness has closed in.[95]

A house which he enters reluctantly and to which he does not belong. A house with a single point of light beyond which there is nothing. Darkness closes in. A whole tradition of finding oneself safe, of securing one's memories, inside the walls of a house seems to be extinguished in these lines. Although he was a member of the Knesset, Yizhar remembers himself as a child who could find no solace inside the nation's walls. "How can someone like that rebuild the Land?"—the Hebrew is *yivneh*, or "build," rather than "rebuild," which has none of the politically loaded connotation of reclaiming the land or a return.[96] And "when you all have to rebuild the land together" is stronger: "when you can build a land *only* with everyone together" (rak 'im kulam yakhad), implying that if even one withdraws, the project, the creation of the nation, will fail.[97] All he can do is write everything down in a notebook that doesn't yet exist. In this passage—and in many more—Yizhar runs a straight line between his place as outsider child to the Zionist ideal and the ethical task of the writer. Like *À la recherche*, this is a work that describes its own genesis. (For his devotion to the craft of memory as well as the intense sensuousness of his prose, Yizhar has indeed been compared with Proust.) Out of such moments, therefore, not only *Preliminaries* but all his other writing, including *Khirbet Khizeh*, will be born. These stories will have to be written. As if to say, the nation will have to remember what it cannot bear to remember. It will have to listen to the voice of the one who stood on the side watching.

The Movement of Memory—Esther Shalev-Gerz

On a lead-covered column installed in the German town of Harburg in 1986, Esther Shalev-Gerz and Jochen Gerz inscribed these already quoted words:

> We invite the citizens of Harburg and visitors to the town, to add their names here to ours. In doing so, we commit ourselves to remain vigilant. As more and more names cover this 12 meter high lead column, it will gradually be lowered into the ground. One day it will have disappeared completely and the site of the Harburg monument against fascism will be empty.
>
> In the long run, it is only we ourselves who can stand up against injustice.[98]

Engraving their signatures on this disappearing monument, each citizen immediately becomes part of the history they are protesting against; they become agents in a process whose future will depend on them alone. It is the powerful ambiguity of the demand being made on them by the artists, that in writing their names, they become at once the bearers of a hideous past and those who can, who might (the question is of course open), make it disappear. Hence the importance of the title of this famous piece—"Monument against Fascism"—crucially no antimonument, as it has sometimes been termed, since it is the monumentality of history and of our accountability for it that is being inscribed here. "My approach invites an enactment of agency," writes Shalev-Gerz in "Reflecting Spaces/Deflecting Spaces," "creating a memory, a remembrance (the 'I was there') signifying the commitment of people to the(ir) world."[99] The fragment of memory is written in the minds of the participants even as they will its occasion to disappear. Finally, only a plaque—template to the work's own history—remains visible on the ground. The aim, writes James Young in his discussion of the monument, is "not to accept graciously the burden of history, but to throw it back at the town's feet."[100]

Crucially, this does not signal the absence or unrepresentability of the event. On the contrary. "The memory of the horror, and the resolve to stop it returning," Jacques Rancière comments in an essay on Esther Gerz's later Buchenwald project *Menschendinge*, "only have their monument in the wills of those who exist in the here and now."[101] This is, if you like, memory arguing with itself in the moment of its formation. It is memory as a process whose historical and political consequences are not clear.

Above all, it is not memory as sacred word or object. In *Menschendinge*, or *The Human Aspect of Objects*, the found objects had been retrieved against a second forgetting from the trash dumps around the memorials of the 1960s and 1970s. The objects bore witness to a dual impulse, in the words of Rancière: "to tear them out of their universe of night and fog [a reference to Alan Resnais's famous 1955 holocaust documentary, *Nuit et Brouillard*], and deprive them of all sacred-object status at the same time." It was crucial to the project that each one bore witness to the craft devoted to them by the inmates and that the exhibition's curators should be shown talking about their experience in video installations as they turned the objects in their hands. "We are not in front of these images," writes Rancière, "we are in the middle of them, just as they are in the middle of us." You do not gaze at these objects and despair, consoled by your own compassion—"the objects here are not testifying to a condition, they are not telling us what they have lived through, but what they have done." Like the monument—like history itself—the object is not a fetish. It is a piece of work—Rancière's essay is called "Die Arbeit des Bildes/The Work of the Image"—with the important difference from Freud's working through, as it is often read, that the process is never complete. "The question," writes Rancière, "is to know what the people of the present make of them." Again this is a question of memory: "The memory of the horror and the resolve to stop it from returning only have their monument in the wills of those who exist in the here and now."[102]

In "The Perpetual Movement of Memory," Shalev-Gerz explains how the success of the Harburg monument led to a run of demands from German towns asking for memorials that would likewise evoke Nazism and bear the names of the lost Jewish inhabitants. Each and every time, she has insisted that any such monuments should bear the names of the executioners too. "Compassion for the victims tends to rely on the comfort provided by historical distance," she writes. "Humanizing and personalizing only those who suffered from a purposeful, wilful destruction would be to exterminate them more efficiently."[103] In 2001, Shalev-Gerz proposed a monument, "The Judgement"— a "philosophical walk"—for the victims of the Nazi military tribunal in Murellenberg to consist of a walkway, guiding the visitors to the former execution site, consisting of luminous flags of Plexiglas, one of whose sides would be dedicated to the story of the condemned and the other to that of the judge (the tie between the two being irreducible). We cannot endlessly postpone our encounter with judgment. "The only ones that were not judged," she comments, "were the judges themselves."[104] This was a "purposeful, wilful" destruction. What possible historical reckoning can there be if we silently bury the will and the purpose, if we lament the horror while innocently uncoupling ourselves from its cause? It is, she writes, "about giving human destinies to history and overcoming repression." "Each one of us is encouraged to encounter judgement—as an active appropriation of the social process of commemoration and as a taking on of democratic responsibility."[105] (This project was also unrealized.)

To align Yizhar and Shalev-Gerz is not to equate Nazism with the war of 1948. I could not sign a letter to the *Guardian* protesting the anniversary celebrations in May 2008, because it seemed to me that this was precisely what it did. (The one I did sign instead just noted Israel's continuing oppression of the Palestinians as a reason not to celebrate.)[106] But I am suggesting that the history of the Jewish people makes it perhaps uniquely hard for Israel as a nation to see itself ever as the agent of the violence of its own history. Although Shalev-Gerz left Israel, and none of her commentators, she tells me, have ever discussed the monument at Tel Hai, her work has the abiding importance of having made the difficult journey between the two worlds. Another unrealized project in Israel, "Tower (without Wall)," proposed in 1997, would have built a tower offering sight in all directions, beyond the given boundaries, floating free from the wall that is normally its justification and support. "As history shows," she writes in the proposal, "walls in general have been erected by foreign people who settle in a conquered territory . . . to indicate their own right of belonging in a place they did not belong."[107] (Proposed before today's wall tearing through Palestinian land gave it such renewed relevance, this project was also never made.)

For me, what links Yizhar and Shalev-Gerz is the idea of something intolerable to thought, something that requires a particular form of willed attention which the mind will precisely resist with all its force (as Freud came increasingly to recognize). When Shalev-Gerz filmed camp survivors talking of their memories, she moved the camera in on their faces to convey what Rancière describes as "the movement of attentive thought calling for attention." Not, he insists, "simply a vehicle for transmitting testimony."[108] It is with the barriers to such thought that this chapter has been above all concerned, walls inside and outside the mind.

To return then, finally, to houses. Shalev-Gerz's 2003 *Daedel(us)* project in Dublin took photographs of houses and projected them onto other facades across one run-down area of the northeast inner city, rife with drugs while also undergoing a certain gentrification.[109] The extraordinary effect was to create houses that you recognized but also no longer know. (See figures 2, 3, and 4.) It also put parts of the area that were furiously differentiating themselves from each other—drugs and rising new properties, old residents and new—in touch, through luminous nighttime images of which they became the bearers. It was a tripartite structure involving the consent of those whose houses would be photographed, those whose houses would host the projectors, and those whose houses would have the images of other houses projected onto them. (A concern that drug dealers fearful of being recorded would sabotage the whole thing turned out to be baseless.) Houses upon houses. Memory layered upon

FIGURE 2. Esther Shalev-Gerz, *Daedel(us)* (2003).

FIGURE 3. Esther Shalev-Gerz, *Daedel(us)* (2003).

FIGURE 4. Esther Shalev-Gerz, *Daedel(us)* (2003).

memory. Quintilian, I imagine, would be turning in his grave. The project is representative of a new strand of Shalev-Gerz's work in which cross-border participation is proposed not as the response to trauma but as the preemptive fabric of daily, endlessly mobile life, a way of negotiating the margins of citizens and of identity in the modern world. The continuity with the earlier work is nonetheless clear. Memory must be kept moving, and links must continue to be forged between people with no reason to—with every reason not to—recognize themselves in each other.

The final image of this chapter comes from another house, *Blind Light*, by British sculptor Anthony Gormley, the title work of his exhibition at the Hayward Gallery in London in 2007. Gormley has always been interested in pushing our familiar spaces to the limits of the strange. ("Uncanny Sculpture" was the title of Anthony Vidler's essay in the catalog.) In this case he went one step further. *Blind Light* is a house filled with steam— you enter and immediately lose anyone else who might have entered with you and, more importantly, yourself. If you put your hands out before you, you are most likely to touch semitranslucent outer surfaces which you know, from the time you have spent waiting outside to go in, will be transmitting the shadow of your hands, almost like an X-ray, to the space outside. It is impossible to describe how deeply disorientating this is. This is the inverse of Rachel Whiteread's project, in which she alienated the space by filling it in. Gormley describes how he sees it: "Architecture is supposed to be the location of security and certainty about where you are. It is supposed to protect you from the weather, from darkness, from uncertainty. And *Blind Light* undermines all of that. You enter this interior space that is the equivalent of being at the top of a mountain or at the bottom of the sea.... It is very important for me that *Blind Light* is a room that has been dissociated from its room-ness so that inside you find the outside."[110]

Blind Light offers a perfect model for what we might need to do to ourselves in order to give memory another shape. The message of this chapter is finally simple. Our responsibility for our history—past and future—depends on how much we can bear to house inside our minds.

4

Endgame: Beckett and Genet in the Middle East

Memories are killing.
«SAMUEL BECKETT, "The Expelled"[1]»

Strictly speaking, we can only remember what has been registered by our extreme inattention and stored in that ultimate and inaccessible dungeon of our being to which Habit does not possess the key, and does not need to because it contains none of the hideous and useful paraphernalia of war.
«SAMUEL BECKETT, "Proust"[2]»

I might as well admit that by staying with [the Palestinians], I was staying—I don't know how, how else to put it—inside my own memory.
«JEAN GENET, *Un captif amoureux*[3]»

Beckett, Genet and Proust

When Beckett writes about Proust, something explosive enters his prose. Involuntary memory is an "immediate, total and delicious conflagration."[4] Rising from the dead, the past object returns as a Lazarus "charmed or tortured." It is as if Beckett can only evoke the force of involuntary memory by producing its combustion of the mind on the page. "In its flame, [involuntary memory] has consumed Habit and all its works." While Habit—that "minister of dullness," our false agent of security—concludes its countless treaties with the world, involuntary memory opens up a domain intolerable to thought: "the perilous zones in the life of the individual, dangerous, precarious, painful, mysterious and fertile, when for a moment the boredom of living is replaced by the suffering of being." This is, for Beckett, the real: "what the mock reality never can and never will reveal—the real." Confronting it is a "disaster" which consciousness struggles "feverishly," at the "extreme limit of its intensity," to avert. "The old ego dies hard" and disappears with "wailing and gnashing of teeth."[5] In Beckett's hands, the Proustian life of the mind is ushered into a world of catastrophe.

To say that Beckett has raised the mental pitch is something of an understatement (even though the line about conflagration is given as Proust's own). After all, in Proust, involuntary memory is an epiphany, and the struggle of memory, at least at the end of that first famous "madeleine" section of Combray, is to retrieve its object rather than push it away. Even if, as discussed in the last chapter, involuntary memory calls up the dead and therefore brushes against the shades, it is also a source of joy—precisely through its powers of resuscitation, its ability to bring what is lost back to life. In Beckett's reading, habit is a form of violence that contains, as in the second epigraph, its own deadly paraphernalia. But the mind will only be made to shed its debris and break its false treaties with the world by something akin to war.

In Beckett's vision, there are no limits to the lengths to which consciousness will go to avert the disaster of having to look suffering in the face. At the same time, suffering is a form of freedom that opens the mind to its fullest potential powers: "The suffering of being: that is, the free play of every faculty."[6] Without suffering, life is constricted and mundane. When the "boredom of living" is replaced "by the suffering of being," life becomes fertile again. (Likewise, Freud argued that life only regains its full interest when its highest stake, life itself, may be lost.)[7] As well as presenting a threat, suffering also has a beauty; habit tries to empty the world of both beauty and threat. But that does not make it any easier for us to contemplate.

Although Beckett insists on the utter amorality of Proust and is positively scathing about the moral tone that he detects in his actual depiction of war, nonetheless, in this stress on suffering, there is, I would suggest, an ethical strain, something like an impulse which I will be arguing can be identified in each of the writers that bring this study to its end. Perhaps habit's deadliest alchemy is to transform "the individual capable of suffering into a stranger for whom the motives of that suffering are an idle tale."[8] Proust's narrator dreads losing touch with his own grief at the loss of Gilberte and then Albertine. (In this as in so much else, he considers he has abused them for his art.) Suffering slips away. We cannot hold on to the memory of our own suffering, let alone the suffering of anybody else. (It is of course a question whether "other people" exist at all in Proust's work.) Suffering becomes a stranger. Even if it once was our own, it ends up looking like the paltry property of another as it dwindles into insignificance over time. In this context, "idle tale" is important ("a stranger for whom the motives of that suffering are an idle tale"). One of the chief ways we turn our back on suffering is through the language with which we tame it, toy with it, and brush it away. To attempt anything else, Beckett suggests via Proust, is to risk a mental meltdown.

In Beckett's rendering of Proust, involuntary memory acquires the meaning not just of something unanticipated or unwilled, but of a fervent—indeed "feverish"—rejection, the mind kicking and screaming (or wailing and gnashing its teeth); it becomes the unwelcome harbinger of suffering that is unbearable and untold. When Freud described the phenomenon of "de-realisation," which involves the psyche not just repressing but blotting out parts of itself (as a term, he used "de-realisation" sparingly and therefore with some dramatic effect), he took as his example the fifteenth-century Moorish King Boabdil: on receiving news of the fall of his beloved city of Alhama, he kills the messenger and throws the letters in the fire. Needing to "combat a feeling of powerlessness," Freud writes, "he was still trying to show his absolute power."[9] (The issue of suffering is inseparable from that of power.) Enraged by the insufferable, the mind stops at nothing, violently erases reality, and defaults on itself. Out of Proust's writing—as his greatest tribute to him—Beckett conjures the areas of the mind that the mind cannot bear and which it will destroy at any price.

Beckett is not, of course, writing "about" suffering. To suggest that he is would be to make nonsense of the radical challenge he presents to any conception of representational art. "An unreconciled reality," Adorno writes in his famous essay on *Endgame*, "tolerates no reconciliation with the object in art."[10] If reality is intolerable, then it would not just be smug, but the crassest violation, as well as a contradiction in terms, to claim, or even aim, to give it satisfactory representation. But in this short essay on Proust, Beckett might be offering us one indication as to why suffering will never be something that we can simply represent or talk about. He might also be suggesting how his antirepresentational project (if that is the right expression) and the suffering of being to which his work bears some kind of testimony are linked. This is far from the relentless focus on suffering—crucially, the suffering of others—whose Western genealogy from iconic painting to war photography Susan Sontag has recently traced.[11] The worst torment—what Beckett refers to in *The Unnameable* as "labyrinthine torment"—cannot be "grasped, or limited, or felt, or suffered, no, not even suffered."[12] Or, in the words of Clov in *Endgame*, "You must learn to suffer better"[13]—a demand as palpably absurd as it is urgent.

What the mind cannot tolerate has already been my theme in these pages, together with the strategies it employs either in expelling unwanted contents (partition) or in refusing to harbor the worst memories of what it has been, once did, or was before. In both cases, I have suggested that the strategy fails—necessarily—but that this does not stop it from being deployed, both in the mind and in the world, to increasingly devastating effect. Israel-Palestine has been my focus first, because the state of Israel arises out of one of the twentieth century's most brutal acts of partition, whose consequences are with us to this day. But Israel, as I have shown, also carries a specific historic relation to the problem of memory. From Ernest Renan onward, how a nation remembers or misremembers its own beginnings has come to be seen as constitutive of modern nationhood. At moments, as discussed in the last chapter, it has seemed that forgetting has been Israel's condition of survival. It is not news of a fallen city that leads Israel to kill the messenger and throw the letters in the fire—apart from the second Lebanese war of 2006, Israel has been the victor in all its conflicts—but news of what, in the name of that survival, it has been capable of.

In May 2010, the Knesset passed a law—widely termed the "Nakba" Law—that withdraws funding from any group judged to be "acting against the principles of the country," which includes commemoration of the nakba. In March of that year, the month of the law's preliminary reading, Netanyahu designated the Tomb of the Patriarchs in the West Bank city of Hebron (and Rachel's tomb in Bethlehem) as national heritage sites. Thousands of Israelis gathered in Hebron to celebrate : "Hebron," said M. K. Tzipi Hotovely of Likud, "is four thousand years old." (Israel's claim is ancestral; there is no Palestinian history.)[14] Memory becomes more, not less, of an imperative when part of memory must be got rid of at any cost.

If Beckett and Genet are at the core of this final chapter, it is because each of them in their very different ways presents us with the mind and body *in extremis*. Both push the problem of how to represent the intolerable to new lengths. Scandalous, they force us to the limits of what can be spoken and thought. They each have something to teach us, therefore, about the radical kernel of being, what Beckett presents in his essay on Proust as the "suffering of being" alongside which everything else that goes by the name of reality is mere dross: "The point of departure of the Proustian exposition," he insists, "is not the crystalline agglomeration but its kernel—the crystallised."[15] It is something precious and insufferable that Beckett finds at the heart of Proust's work, which becomes in these moments forerunner and model of his own. It is something precious and insufferable that Genet finds in Palestine. His famous report on the Sabra and Chatila massacres of 1982, "Quatre heures à Chatila," breaks a writing block that had lasted sixteen years.[16] The experience will lead to his final memoir, *Un captif amoureux*, which is barely complete when he dies; he was working on the proofs in his last hours. (It might not be going too far to describe it as Genet's "endgame.")[17]

These may seem worlds apart, the transition shocking, but there is a crucial historical link between them. When Adorno reads *Endgame* as the exemplary text after Auschwitz, he lays on it the burden of a moment of suffering that will lead more or less directly in time to the creation of Israel as a nation-state; more or less directly to the trauma—the second trauma as we might call it—of the Palestinian people that rises, with a type of awful tragic necessity, on the back of the first and which Genet's final writing makes its own cause. (If the role of the camps in the creation of Israel can be argued, the temporal sequence is unmistakable.) In their historical moment and destination, Beckett and Genet thus face each other at either end of the taut wire that binds Europe to Palestine.

Suffering is, of course, the property of no one. "There is," wrote Edward Said in one of his at once most obvious and boldest statements, "suffering and injustice enough for everyone."[18] After all, suffering reduces man and woman, whoever they may be, to the barest limits of life. "Subjects thrown back on their own resources" is how Adorno describes the players of *Endgame*, "worldlessness become flesh, they consist of nothing but the wretched realities of their world, which has shrivelled to bare necessity." (The German "Fleisch gewordenen Akosmismus" is stronger, not just not of the world, but not of this universe.)[19] This is Adorno in anticipation of Giorgio Agamben's "bare life." Said is talking of the legacy of suffering that was carried by Israel from Europe and whose aftereffects were then laid on the indigenous Arabs of Palestine. ("Why should the Palestinians pay for the crimes of Europe?" being the angry, militant form of this recognition). Suffering shunts its way across the globe. This is not, it should hardly need stressing once more, to suggest an equivalence between the two histories. It is, rather, their most intimate implication with each other—although this link would appear to make it harder, rather than easier, for each of the two peoples to see the suffering on the other side.[20]

And given this mutual implication, these powerful, uncanny transpositions of time and place, it should come as no surprise— although I was in fact surprised—to find something of Beckett's lugubrious rendering of horror making its way into the representation of Palestinian lives in what has come to be known as the signature film, *Divine Intervention*, of the Palestinian director Elia Suleiman. (The film, released in 2002, is subtitled "A Chronicle of Love and Pain.") "How does one measure a man's suffering," he asked in a 1998 interview. "How can we take responsibility for defining sorrow or suffering?"[21] Or to discover Genet's text on Chatila appearing as a type of key witness in the 1998 Palestinian epic *Bab el Shams*, or *Gate of the Sun*, by Lebanese novelist Elias Khoury.[22] For better and worse, the question of Europe's cultural legacy in the Middle East is not closed. Like Amichai and Darwish in the second chapter, or Yizhar and Shalev-Gerz in the third, Suleiman and Khoury will appear at the end of this book as artists—crucially, in this case, Palestinian and Lebanese—who subject an intolerable, often seemingly hopeless, reality to the most radical cultural metamorphosis. But by starting with Beckett and Genet, I am also asking another question, perhaps the most important for a critic from Europe writing about the Middle East: What can a European bear and not bear to see—bear and not bear to take responsibility for—faced with the bleakness that is present-day Israel-Palestine?

Proust hovers over both, a shared object of passion. According to Edmund White, Genet's biographer, Proust was Genet's most important literary influence. In *Un captif amoureux*, the allusions to Proust are loving and explicit—the whole book is an act of memory, its two sections entitled "Souvenirs I" and "Souvenirs II." In his essay on Genet's late work, Said suggests that Genet's struggle with the Palestinian question in *Un captif amoureux* throws light retrospectively on *Les Paravents*, his play on the Algerian war, "in an almost Proustian way."[23] In a self-penned biographical note of 1931, Beckett, writing of himself in the third person, refers to the deepening of his lyrical impulse through the influence of Proust. (For one Beckett critic, each of the heroes of his five novels are parodic versions of either Proust or Joyce: "aging invalids who lie in bed, obsessively writing inventories of their past, or vagrant derelicts who wander from place to place.")[24] Proust allows both Beckett and Genet to orient themselves, albeit in some strange dislocating way. Together with Proust, who has been at the heart of this study, they thus take up the final staging posts on the pathway I have been tracing from the heart of Europe to the Middle East.

There is another connection that binds Beckett and Genet into the story told in this book. In their different ways, both complete the history of France that began with Dreyfus in chapter 1. Against the advice of his friends, Beckett insisted on returning to Paris at the outbreak of the Second World War, where he remained throughout the Nazi occupation, joining the Resistance in 1940 and then serving at the end of the war as a medical orderly in the Normandy town of Saint-Lô. (Devastated by Allied bombing, it was known as the "capital in ruins.") Even if, as Marjorie Perloff points out, the word "war" appears nowhere in Beckett's writing, his work is no less saturated by war: Saint-Lô is the subject of one of his most haunting poems; the actions of Clov in *Endgame*, storekeeper of painkillers, echo the gestures of a field-hospital nurse; the landscape of *Godot* can be read as the countryside of a devastated, occupied country; and one early name for Estragon was apparently Levi.[25] "I'm in a ditch," Beckett commented on writing *Endgame*, "somewhere near the last stretch and would like to crawl up on it."[26]

For his part, Genet, as well as writing about Palestine, provoked one of the strongest theatrical scandals of his career by his merciless anticolonialist parody of the French military in Algeria in his 1961 play *The Screens*. Its opening run in April 1966 was greeted with right-wing riots, commandos and military cadets invaded the stage and assaulted the actors. One among those blocking the theater entrance was the young Jean-Marie Le Pen, who had militated against French withdrawal from Algeria. (Genet refused to allow the play to be performed in France again until 1983 and kept it out of print until 1975.)[27] Thus, *The Screens* plays its part in bringing to its end, we could say, the military self-aggrandizement so central to the Dreyfus Affair (in Said's formula, "France as empire, as power, as history").[28] "As a ward of the army, he'll enter the Military Academy," the General observes of his eleven-year-old son in one scene. "But he won't have a career in the Colonial Troops.... *(Sadly)* There won't be any Colonial Troops since there won't be any colonies, won't be any Foreign Legion since there won't be any Foreigners."[29] "In the image of its rotting warriors," the Lieutenant announces without the pathos, "France will be able to watch itself rot."[30] A stage direction at the end of the play states simply: "The Europeans wake up and leave."[31]

Remember that some of the worst practices of the French army toward its disciplined soldiers, exposed by the *Revue Blanche* at the time of Dreyfus, took place after the conquest of Algeria. French colonialism was the only partly hidden underside of the Affair. Remember Urban Gohier in "Le Péril," published in the *Revue Blanche* in 1898: "To prove our indomitable courage, we go off and kill defenceless negroes ... prey to the murderous insanity that fatally seizes a man with weapons."[32] "Our leaders have always encouraged us to regard ourselves as perfect objects," the General states in *The Screens* "in a severe tone," "ever more perfect, hence more insensitive, wonderful death-dealing machines."[33] As Herr wrote to Barrès: "Scrape beneath your national patriotism ... you will find haughty, brutal, conquering France, pig-headed chauvinism ... the native hatred of everything that is other."[34] After Vichy, after Algeria, both Beckett and Genet attest, France will never see itself the same way again.

"Corpsed": Beckett

From the opening moments of *Endgame*, we are presented with a drama that turns on the "without." Beckett could have translated "le dehors" of his stage direction in French by the more familiar "the outside," choosing instead to make use of an archaism that evokes the outside world, not so much as designated place but as something missing, a type of reified dereliction. As Clov shuffles back and forth with his ladder in the opening wordless sequence, drawing back the curtain on each of the two small windows, looking out—"Brief laugh"—he sets the stage for a play that will focus, at key moments, on this missing world. He is the only one of the four characters who, by means of a telescope, can see it. The "without" is therefore also beyond; it has to be magnified in order to be seen. It is also an object of violent contestation between Hamm and Clov:

HAMM [*violently*]: But you have the glass!
CLOV [*halting violently*]: No, I haven't the glass![35]

When he points the telescope at the auditorium, he sees a "multitude ... in transports ... of joy." (The joke is, of course, on the audience.) When he directs it back to the "without," he sees "Zero," or something close:

HAMM: Nothing stirs. All is—
CLOV: Zer—
HAMM [*violently*]: Wait till you're spoken to!
   [*Normal voice*]: All is ... all is ... all is what?
   [*Violently*]: All is what?
CLOV: What all is? in a word? Is that what you want to know? Just a
   moment.
   [*He turns the telescope on the without, looks, lowers the telescope, turns
   toward Hamm*]
   Corpsed[36]

"Corpsed" then becomes something of a refrain: "The whole place stinks of corpses."

Later Clov tells Hamm about the madman he used to visit in his asylum whom he would drag protesting to the window. Again Clov is the gatekeeper and the drama hinges on a radical clash of vision:

CLOV: Look! Look there! All that rising corn! And there! Look! The sails of the herring fleet! All that loveliness!
[*Pause*]
He'd snatch away his hand and go back into his corner.
Appalled. All he had seen was ashes.
[*Pause*]
He alone had been spared.[37]

This time it is Clov who is in the place of the auditorium: in transports of joy, blind to the death all around. But that is not typical. More often, his own vision is in tune with that of the madman from whom, in this brief instant, he so lyrically seems to distinguish himself: "If I open my eyes and between my legs a little trail of black dust. I say to myself that the earth is extinguished, although I never saw it lit."[38] "The madman's perception," writes Adorno, "coincides with that of Clov, who peers out of the window on command."[39] In the earlier exchange with Hamm, he is ruthless:

HAMM: And the horizon? Nothing on the horizon?
CLOV [*lowering the telescope, turning toward Hamm, exasperated*]: What in God's name could there be on the horizon?[40]

Moments like these allow Adorno to read *Endgame* as testimony to a world in ashes.[41] It is the Nazis who have transformed the natural connection between the living into "organic garbage." The madman becomes the last witness of the camps, the only one who can still bear to see a reality no one wants to see and for which he is locked away. (Like the audience, the rest of us prefer to be transported by joy.) "After the Second World War," Adorno writes, "everything, including a resurrected culture, has been destroyed without realising it; humankind continues to vegetate, creeping along after events that even the survivor cannot really survive."[42] The allusions to the camps are scattered—garbage heaps, trashcans, insecticide, the extermination of rats. "Everything," Adorno writes, "waits to be carted off to the dump" (from which, in Esther Shalev-Gerz's *Menschendinge*, they will be retrieved).[43] The worst remains "without": "All he had seen was ashes." "Outside of here it's death." This is why, in Adorno's reading, Beckett goes one step further than Proust, who still belongs to a subterranean mystical tradition, clinging to what Adorno calls a "physiognomy," a belief that, by means of involuntary memory, we can strip back to the "secret language of things."[44] In Beckett, "that becomes the physiognomy of what is no longer human."[45] In an early note on *Endgame*, Beckett himself described the play as "more inhuman than *Godot*," depending mostly on the "power of the text to claw."[46]

But if *Endgame* is a testimony, it is crucially a testimony that fails, since both the world and the ability of words to name the world unravel and lose their way in the very act of speech. Clov's "Corpsed" arrives in a moment of intense exasperation: "What all is? in a word? Is that what you want to know? Just a moment." "All in a word"—it is worth pausing at this formula. You cannot get all, indeed anything, into a word. (Language leaves "the thing" behind.) Hamm's demand would mean the death of language. "Corpsed" is Clov's offering, which he throws like a dummy or dead weight onto the stage. "The fact that all human beings are dead," Adorno comments, "is smuggled in on the sly."[47] Beckett's war fictions, writes Perloff, combine "a curious literalism with the Mallarmean principle that to name is to destroy."[48] It is a delusion to believe that reality can be captured in words.

We need, therefore, to be cautious. In Beckett, it is language that is above all destitute, shorn of its capacity to represent.[49] His genius is to produce literature out of such acknowledged failing. Commenting on the painter Bram Van Velde, to whom he attributed a new form of art, Beckett spoke of making "this admission, this fidelity to failure, a new occasion, a new term of relation, and of the act which, unable to act, obliged to act, he makes an expressive act, even if only of itself, of its impossibility, of its obligation."[50] Writing is an obligation, an ethical task. In her recent study, Pascale Casanova argues on this basis that Beckett could not be further from the existentialism and theater of the absurd with which he is so routinely associated. (There is no generalized or generalizable angst in Beckett, but a precisely focused engagement with the limits of literary language and form.) With reference to *Worstword Ho!* she comments: "How to say the worst and how to work incessantly to worsen the worst? If by definition, 'said is missaid,' whatever one says, how, stylistically, can one convey the idea of the worst, and say it ever worse? How can one win the incredible wager of a 'better' that would be a successful statement of the worst?"[51] Seen in these terms, Beckett can only be understood with reference to a post–World War Two literary and pictorial avant-garde. Against what he saw as the "paralysingly holy," "vicious" nature of the word, his self-consciously crafted project was to strip out meaning and thereby to drag into modernity a literary language that was dangerously lagging behind the other arts. (The aim could not, then, as he insisted, have been further from Joyce's apotheosis of the word.)[52]

Seen in these terms, death, corpses, and ashes do not signal a final, transcendent reality, or rather, they can do so only by issuing at the same time a warning or challenge to the hubris of speech. "There'll be no more speech," drips inside Hamm's head.[53] "I ask the words that remain," Clov states at the end. "They have nothing to say."[54] "Speak no more."[55] Far from being moments of pathos—along the lines of "and the rest is silence"—these utterances should be taken at their word. The alternative to knowing the limits of language is to see loveliness everywhere: "All that rising corn! The sails of the herring fleet." Rising corn and herring fleets might then be taken as metaphors for language's false claims to plenitude, as well as being part of a scathing critique of theater that makes its audience comfortable—lifts them to transports of joy—by offering the delusion that the world is passing in front of their eyes. To say this is not, however, to weaken but to increase the play's historical density. Adorno is referring to totalitarianism. It is because "the power of a superior apparatus" has rendered humans "interchangeable or superfluous" that the meaning of language has been destroyed.[56]

Endgame requires us to be skeptical about our access to the world. In Adorno's reading, it becomes the play that best transcribes the trauma inflicted not just on the world post-Auschwitz but equally, or more so, on our ability to conceptualize that world anymore. If the worst has truly come to pass, then it can hardly be present, ready to be plucked for our—even anguished—delectation. As has often been commented, there is something wrong or even contradictory in insisting on the unprecedented destruction of the Second World War while assuming that our ability to register it as conscious, cognizant subjects has somehow remained perfectly intact. To that extent, Adorno's famous comment about the impossibility of poetry after Auschwitz is not a lament for the lost lyricism of the world, but a demand that we at least ask what Auschwitz has done to our minds and hence to our relationship to words. It is the central characteristic of consciousness today to be so "bombed out"—Adorno's term—that it no longer has a place from which to reflect. This is not the same, crucially, as bestowing on the camps some kind of ineffable sacralization, since it is a historical point. If history is outside, it is because history itself "has dried up consciousness's power to conceive it, the power to remember" (die Kraft zur Erinnerung).[57] Nor should this be taken to signal the end of thought, because it is this snow-blanketing of our thinking that consciousness, indeed art, has to struggle against. We are not—in the tradition Casanova scathingly traces to Maurice Blanchot—talking about a transcendent, eternal limit of language that the camps had the dubious privilege of having reached.[58]

We are not, therefore, outside time. (As well as stressing the strict formal permutations of Beckett's writing that for her make him a revolutionary writer, Casanova is meticulous in situating him within his historical moment.) Adorno's own references to the "incommensurable" are in fact saturated with historical reference. The unspeakable is not beyond. Rather, it is grounded, beneath our feet. It is something we have to reckon with even while we acknowledge, as historical subjects, our inability fully to do so ("unable to act, obliged to act, an expressive act, even if only of its impossibility, its obligation"). "About what is incommensurable with experience as such," he writes, "one can speak only in euphemisms;" he then continues: "the way one speaks in Germany of the murder of the Jews."[59] The Germans are guilty of evasion. They will not name the Jews. In refusing to do so, they are also revealing (without knowing it) the mental destruction that Nazism would have wreaked on the whole world.

"It would be ridiculous," Adorno writes, "to put Beckett on the stand as a star historical witness."[60] *Witness*, as we have seen, is not the right word. But his prototypes are historical because they "hold up as typical of human beings only the deformations inflicted upon them by the form of their society."[61] Deformation is irreversible even if, as Adorno also insists, the endurance of the characters in *Endgame* testifies to their wish, and the will of consciousness, to survive. Again this is more or less exactly where Beckett takes Proust. "Deformation," he writes in his essay, "has taken place": "There is no escape from yesterday, because yesterday has deformed us, or been deformed by us. . . . We are no longer what we were before the calamity of yesterday."[62] In Beckett's reading, Proust is construed as sentient of the worst, dipped in the colors of a trauma barely commencing when the young Beckett wrote his essay in 1931. But was the prescience Proust's alone? Or was Beckett in fact projecting back onto his mentor horrors waiting in the wings to be unleashed onto the modern world? (Hitler would not become chancellor until 1933, but, in a shock 1930 election result, his party had become the second largest in the country.) This may be laying on him too much. But certainly by the time Proust had combusted in Beckett's hands in 1931, one could no longer say—as T. J. Clark can say with reference to Matisse's *La femme au chapeau* of 1905—that "the face burns underneath the flummery with a livid, unstoppable flame."[63] A shadow is already passing over the world, blotting out any such jubilant incandescence.

Genet, Proust, and Palestine

Reading Proust changed Genet's life. It made him a writer. He read *A l'ombre des jeunes filles en fleurs* in prison during the war (in the late 1930s and early 1940s), coming across it in the prison yard, where the prisoners were trading books on the sly. Because he wasn't, as he puts it, very concerned about books, he took one of the last volumes on offer, convinced—on sight of the title it would seem—that it would be "a pain in the butt." On finishing the first sentence—"a very long sentence"—he closed the book and said to himself: "Now I'm calm, I know I'm going to go from one marvel to another." The sentence was "so dense, so beautiful that this adventure was the first big flame that told of a blaze to come."[64] It is the opening of "Madame Swann at Home," which forms part 1 of *A l'ombre de jeunes filles en fleurs:*

> My mother, when it was a question of our having M. de Norpois to dinner for the first time, having expressed her regret that Professor Cottard was away from home and that she herself had quite ceased to see anything of Swann, since either of these might have helped to entertain the ex-ambassador, my father replied that so eminent a guest, so distinguished a man of science as Cottard could never be out of place at a dinner-table, but that Swann, with his ostentation, his habit of crying aloud from the house-tops the name of everyone he knew, however slightly, was a vulgar show-off whom the Marquis de Norpois would be sure to dismiss as—to use his own epithet—a "pestilent" fellow.[65]

Genet's initiation into Proust does not, therefore, come, as one might expect or indeed hope, via *Sodom and Gomorrah*. It is not scandal or sexual impropriety that draws him into the work. It is not homosexuality, of which there is no trace in these lines unless we choose to detect it in the flurry of excitement with which the men anxiously police the distinctions that bind them to, and divide them from, each other. (Mme Swann, for whom the whole section is named, rapidly concedes her opening position in the sentence to the men.) The sentence that blows Genet's mind, his induction into the world of Proust, is a sentence about social caste. What it reveals beneath, or rather through, the social veneer is perfectly vicious. It is the first intimation of the drawing room whose ugly partitions were traced in the second chapter of this book. Swann is dumped twice if not three times, first by the narrator's mother, who confesses to having "ceased to frequent him entirely," and then by her husband, as well as by Norpois since the husband attributes to him with such total confidence the opinion that Swann "stinks." (The French *"puant"* is translated by Scott Moncrieff as "pestilent," by James Grieve in the new Penguin translation as "rank outsider," both of which considerably weakens its force.) Clearly from what Genet says, it is the form of the sentence that dazzles him—we might also note again, as with Beckett's essay on Proust, Genet's vocabulary of fire, the flame, and the blaze. But what the sentence contains, what it slowly but surely glides toward through the twists and turns of Proust's famous syntax, is the stench of the Jew. (*"Puant"* is the last word.) Genet most likely will not have registered Swann's Jewishness from these lines, but he will undoubtedly have picked up the whiff of the social outsider, since the whole of his life and writing was dedicated to the outcast, of which he himself, of course, was one. In the words of Edmund White, Genet was the "Proust of the criminal class."[66] "I was thirty years old when I began to write," he states in a 1983 interview. "And thirty-four or thirty-five when I stopped. But it was a dream, in any event a daydream. I wrote in prison. Once free I was lost."[67]

Accompanied by Palestinian militant Leila Shahid, who had also been his companion in Lebanon, Genet only reluctantly gave the 1983 interview from which that last quote is taken; it was published in the *Revue d'études palestiniennes* as "Une Rencontre avec Jean Genet." As a witness to Sabra and Chatila, he was in Vienna for a massive demonstration against the massacre organized by the International Progress Organisation, an NGO affiliated to the United Nations. He agreed on condition that he would only be asked questions about the Palestinians. As the editor comments in his opening remarks, it is impossible to record the silences with which Genet punctuated his words. (Describing a meeting with Genet in 1972 in Beirut, Said writes of his "long, puzzling, yet compellingly impressive silences.")[68] Genet does not want to speak. He knows how easy it is for violence, of the kind he has just witnessed so concretely, to be travestied by words. He impatiently rejects the interviewer's suggestion that the European is merely a spectator for whom news of the conflict in Palestine arrives decked in an aura of the unreal: "It is you who makes everything unreal . . . , you who accept the massacres and transform them into massacres that are unreal."[69] There is, Genet insists, no similarity whatsoever between his own report and the government inquiry, known as the Kahan Commission, whose aims could not be further apart. Published in February 1983, the government inquiry assigned "indirect responsibility" for the massacre to Israel. (Under pressure, then defense minister Ariel Sharon resigned, but he remained in the cabinet to become prime minister of Israel two decades later.) "To my mind, [Israel's] investigation is part and parcel of the massacre," Genet states in the interview. "Let me explain. There was the massacre that tarnished an image, and then there is the investigation that wipes out the massacre. Have I made myself clear?"[70]

In fact, Genet is scrupulous in his accusations: "To say the Israelis wanted this massacre," he states, "is difficult. In fact I am not sure about that. But they let it take place. It took place under—in a way—their protection. Because they lit up the camps."[71] In this he is far more cautious than many Israelis at the time. When the Kahan Commission absolved the government of all but indirect responsibility, Yizhar Smilansky, unhesitant as in 1948 and 1967, commented: "We have released famished lions into the arena. They devoured the people; therefore, the lions are the guilty party who devoured the men, aren't they? Who could have foreseen, when we opened the door and let them in, that these lions would devour the people?"[72] He was responding to the remark by Yosef Burg, Israel's interior minister: "Christians killed Muslims; how are the Jews responsible?"[73] Prime Minister Menachim Begin's comment, "Goyim kill goyim, and they come to hang the Jews," is the epigraph to Genet's "Four Hours in Shatila."[74]

I take Yizhar's quote from the report of Amnon Kapeliouk, the French-Israeli campaigning journalist, a consistently outspoken critic of the Occupation, and since the 1950s a rare chronicler in Israel of the Arab world. His *Enquête sur un Massacre* was published more or less at the same time as the Kahan Commission and Genet's report.[75] His remarkable document appears again in this chapter in relation to Elias Khoury's *Gate of the Sun*—a final instance of the ceaseless traffic between politics and literature that has been a repeated theme of this study.

Sabra and Chatila, which took place on 16–18 September 1982, was the massacre of between 3,000 and 3,500 Palestinians by the Lebanese Christian Phalange militia, who had been let into the refugee camps by the Israeli army. It will become another event in Israeli history that the nation will try to forget. At the time, it provoked the largest antigovernment demonstration in Israel's history, reinforcing for many Israelis their sense that something had radically changed, that it was impossible to ascribe the invasion of Lebanon and the violence it had unleashed to the rubric of national self-defense (unlike 1948 and 1967, so the argument ran). The massacre came in response to the assassination two days before of Bashir Gemayel, Lebanese president-elect, on whom Israel was relying to secure its position in Lebanon; Gameyal's adversaries called him "the President supported by Israeli bayonets."[76] Israel had invaded Lebanon in June 1982 in order to flush out the Palestinians. (Yasser Arafat was driven by the invasion from Beirut to Tunis.) By September, the increasing toll of the war—18,000 dead and 30,000 injured according to Lebanese statistics—was leading to growing international condemnation, including from Israel's unfailing ally, the United States. In the face of such criticism, the election of Gemayel was seen by Ariel Sharon, the increasingly beleaguered defense minister, as a personal triumph. Gemayel was the sworn enemy of the Palestinians, declaring in an interview published in *Le Nouvel Observateur* in June 1982 that in the Middle East, "there is one people too many: the Palestinian people."[77]

In response to Gemayel's assassination on 14 September, Sharon, with the agreement of Prime Minister Begin but with no consultation with the government, immediately sent his forces into West Beirut. From the outset of the war, he had wanted to seize the western part of the city. (The operation, code-named Iron Brain, had already been mapped in Tel Aviv.) "Had I been convinced that we had to enter Beirut, nobody in the world would have stopped me," Sharon had remarked in an interview two weeks before with the famous Italian journalist Oriana Fallaci. "Democracy or not, I would have entered even if my Government didn't like [it]."[78] Later, he would deny having made the remarks. The occupation of the city provoked unanimous global protest. When Reagan's special envoy, Morris Draper, visited Begin on 15 September, he stated that his objective was to maintain order in the city. The Israeli newspaper *Ma'ariv* reported him as saying, "With the situation created by the assassination of Bashir Gemayel, pogroms could occur."[79] In the meantime, the international community had intervened and secured the withdrawal of all PLO forces and Palestinian leaders from Beirut under the protection of a multinational force. It is generally agreed that by mid-September there was no armed presence left in Sabra and Chatila. As Kapeliouk observes, if there had been heavily armed Palestinian fighters in the camps, "no one would have dared send in a unit of one hundred and fifty Phalangists of mediocre fighting ability."[80] The Kahan Commission recognized, finally, that there had been in fact no terrorists in the camps.[81]

Begin's allusion to the pogroms would return to haunt him. On 20 September, the day after the massacre was announced, the headline article in *Ha'aretz*, by military correspondent Ze'ev Schiff with the title "War Crime in Beirut," opened:

> A war crime has been committed in the refugee camps of Beirut. The Phalangists have killed hundreds, if not more, of elderly people, women and children, exactly in the same fashion pogroms were carried out against Jews. It is not true, as claimed by official spokes-

men that we didn't learn of this crime until Saturday at noon after receiving reports filed by foreign correspondents stationed in Beirut. I personally heard about it on Friday morning. I brought all my information to the attention of a senior official who took immediate action. In other words, the massacre began Thursday evening, and what I learned on Friday morning was certainly known to others before me.[82]

An eyewitness like Genet, Schiff also describes his attempt to pass on the reports of a *dabah* (Arabic for "massacre") from a contact in the General Staff to other General Staff officers and how they either "denied any knowledge of the rumour or belittled its veracity."[83]

"Until this day," wrote Isaac Bashevis Singer, "the word 'pogrom' had a connotation which directly concerned us, Jews, as victims. Prime Minister Begin has 'extended' the scope of the term: there was Babi-Yar, Lidice, Oradour, and now there is Sabra and Shatila."[84] The Kahan Commission itself made the same analogy—the pogroms have taught the Jewish people that the bystander must be condemned. And they appeal to the "outlook of the ancestors" to make the point: "It is said in Deuteronomy [21:6–7] that the elders of the city who were near the slain victim who has been found (and it is not known who struck him down) 'will wash their hands over the beheaded heifer in the valley and reply: our hands did not shed this blood and our eyes did not see.'" They then cite Sforno, a later commentator on Deuteronomy: "There should not be spectators at the place, for if there were spectators there, they would protest and speak out."[85] The acknowledgment does not, however, come without a price, as Israel's failure accrues to its own moral superiority: "All those concerned were well aware that combat morality among the various combat groups in Lebanon differs from the norms in the IDF, that the combatants in Lebanon belittle the value of human life beyond what is accepted and necessary between civilised peoples."[86]

Others went further in their associations. Novelist Yitzhak Orpaz wrote: "I shall never forgive you for leading the country which I love into a dreadful debauchery of blunders and death.

In the camps of Sabra and Shatila my father and mother, whom I lost in the Holocaust, were murdered for the second time."[87] In his response to the assertions of Israeli officers who stated before the Kahan Commission that they did not witness the massacre, prominent Israeli writer A. B. Yehoshua wrote: "Even if I believed that Israeli soldiers stationed a few hundred meters from the camps did not know what was happening, this would be the same type of ignorance as that of the Germans stationed near Buchenwald and Treblinka who did not want to know what was transpiring. We also did not want to know. When we talk of 'liquidation' and 'purification,' and when we label the Palestinians as 'two-legged animals,' then we must not be shocked that a soldier allows such horrors to be committed nearby."[88] According to Kapeliouk, the Israelis, equipped with telescopes and binoculars with night vision, were able to observe the operations from the seventh-floor roof of the three Lebanese buildings they had occupied since 3 September (two hundred meters away from the major location of the carnage).[89] He also quotes on Israeli soldier who described it as being like watching "from the front row of a theater."[90] Despite going to some lengths to insist that the events were not visible to the army, the Kahan Commission also states: "Major General Drori was at the forward command post from approximately 7.30 [16 September] and followed the fighting, as it was visible from the roof of the forward command post."[91]

As a scar in Israeli's memory, Sabra and Chatila raises in especially acute form all the questions of national memory that have been the focus here. From the first moments of its becoming known, the official impulse was, in the words of Ze'ev Schiff, "to pass the blame as far as it would go." "If there is a moral to the painful episode of Sabra and Shatila," he wrote at the time, "it is yet to be acknowledged."[92] At the same time, this first war in Lebanon also provoked some of the most powerful writing from inside the conflict, notably Mahmoud Darwish's prose poem and meditation *Memory for Forgetfulness*, written in Beirut under siege.[93] When I was preparing this book, however, it did not seem that the moment was anything near the forefront of the nation's consciousness. An ugly episode which one could understand the impulse to forget, it also seemed to be another instance of Israel's failure to reckon with its own violence. Then, in what felt like a strange coincidence, in 2008, as I was starting to write on these events, Ari Folman's film *Waltz with Bashir* was released onto Israeli screens, provoking something of a crisis—and catharsis (which could be seen as the film's main intent)—among its public. *Waltz with Bashir* tells the story from the point of view of a soldier who was present at the time of the massacre, and who—with psychic effects that are only just catching up with him—has blotted it from his mind. This is not Yizhar's *Khirbet Khizeh*, which was written in the midst of the 1948 war—*Waltz with Bashir* returns to the event decades later. Instead of predicting a national amnesia, it tries to unravel such amnesia from the other end.

That the film constitutes—and indeed stages—a breakthrough of national memory cannot be disputed.[94] And yet, we can still ask: What kind of memory, indeed, whose memory, is being privileged by this film? Genet, as I will soon discuss, lived with the Palestinians. In doing so, he made their story his own, while constantly alerting us to the fraudulent nature of any such claim. He was of course an outsider—that was the point. It was as a European observer of the Palestinian predicament that he indicted himself. (The problem of how to reach the "other" is therefore engraved into the heart of his work.) For Folman, as an Israeli, the difficulty was something else—how to draw up from the forgotten past a moment of cruel self-reckoning. Yet if this is the strength of the film, it is also its weakness. *Waltz with Bashir* is the story of the perpetrator who suffers. Until the final sequence, which shows the devastated Palestinians in the camps in real footage, it is told from the point of view of the soldier, the trauma is his trauma. (The rest of the film is animation transformed from an original live-action documentary.) And in the subtitled version of the film, the words of the Palestinians are not translated.

"My film," commented one Israeli combat soldier in a discussion of the film. "It was done from my viewpoint, exactly."[95] In one scene, a young Israeli soldier hides behind a rock on the beach after escaping an enemy ambush and then swims out to sea and along the coast where he miraculously rejoins his unit. He is the sole survivor of his crew. As the spectator lives the episode through him (survival as the Israeli soldier's tale), so the Arab as enemy is grafted into the very structure of identification within the film, the place from which it lets us see. "At that moment, as I watched the film," comments Melamed, another combat soldier taking part in the discussion, nineteen at the time of the war, "I felt myself merge with the rock. . . . I returned to the moment when I . . . felt that it was the only thing that could protect me, that I was liable to be shot at any moment, that I was waiting for the moment when a bullet would kill me."[96] In another episode, the Folman character in the film is encouraged by a friend partly taking on the role of therapist to remember Auschwitz (he is the child of survivors), in order to persuade him that he has simply projected onto Sabra and Chatila the traumatized memory of his own people: "Your interest in those camps is actually about the 'other' camps. . . . Unwillingly you took on the role of the Nazi. . . . You were firing flares but didn't carry out the massacre." It is a deeply flawed distinction. The case against the Israeli army rests not just on having let the Phalange into the camps but on the fact that its soldiers fired flares from nearby rooftops to illuminate the camps, thus playing a part in allowing the massacre to take place. Combat soldier Melamed was part of the unit that secured the front command for the senior officers of the IDF: "We saw the illumination flares that were fired, and in my estimation, looking back on it, the forward command could have understood what was going on."[97] "We understood that it had been going on for three days," Shahid remembers being there with Genet, "under the watch of the Israeli army, who sent up flares throughout the night."[98]

Witnessing

Genet's involvement with the Palestinians dated back to the early 1970s, when he had spent six months living with the fedayeen in Jordan. (This is the topic of *Un captif amoureux*.) It was a passion. He was, by his own account, in love with them, hence the title, *A Captive in Love*. The title's translation as *Prisoner of Love* dilutes the meaning of a "captive in love with his captors," implying far more blandly, like the title of a bad romance, someone "captivated" by love. In the interview with the *Revue d'études palestiniennes*, he describes how the Palestinians, together with Black Panthers (to whom he had also given his fervent support), changed his life.[99] "I didn't really find myself, find myself in the real world, until these revolutionary movements." He is, however, keen to turn the discussion away from the personal history that drew him to these movements: "If you want to know any more, you simply have to read my books." He is also, at this point, dismissive of Proust: "To create is always to speak about childhood." "You know as well as I do," he elaborates, "probably better than I do that the first sentence of the entire work of Proust begins: '*For a long time I went to bed early.*' And then he recounts his whole childhood, which lasts fifteen hundred, over two thousand pages in fact."[100] Proust is, therefore, evoked, for the moment at least, as the counterexample (spinning two thousand pages out of childhood as a flight from the real world, disappearing into the void of oneself).

The experience of Sabra and Chatila has not, therefore, just unblocked Genet's writing. It has also, and in the same gesture, made him wary about language, as well as about the whole of his past writing life, which he now characterizes as mere "dream or daydream": "It was a dream. Or in any case a daydream."[101] There is no limit to what you can do to your own daydreams (the whole point of a daydream being that it is yours to do with as you will), but there is a limit to what you can do to the real. The discipline required of him in relation to the Palestinians is of a different order, not "grammatical," not a question of the order of words. This gives another meaning to the word *captive* of his title: "I had to submit myself to the real world."[102]

On the Sunday afternoon after the massacre, Genet was interrogated at gunpoint by three Lebanese soldiers in a jeep: "'Have you just been there?' He pointed to Shatila. 'Yes.' 'And did you see?' 'Yes.' 'And you are going to write about it?' 'Yes.'"[103] There could be no clearer ethical writing imperative than this. Genet will be precise. This is writing in alleyways: "From Paris, if one knows nothing of the lay-out of the camps, one might doubt the whole thing."[104] His supreme duty is to be the recorder of horrors. (Only reading the text can convey these horrors, whose effect I will not attempt to reproduce here.) They are designed to push the reader to the limit. Leila Shahid was convinced that what he had seen was so appalling that he would not survive.[105] Timeless—these things happen everywhere—they also belong to their time. (The exact number of days, the silence, the days it took for the news to emerge—all are a crucial part of the story.) Language must be bent to the unrepresentable. In the context of Sabra and Chatila, this carries an additional responsibility because, as already noted, these were acts which the Israeli army insisted its officers, on the seventh floor of an adjacent building, meters away from the carnage, could not see.

Later in the 1983 interview, he goes further. There is something inherently treacherous about words: "As soon as I speak, I am betrayed by the situation. I am betrayed by the person who is listening to me, quite simply because of the communication. I am betrayed by my choice of words."[106] If there is a corruption endemic to language, it is not, therefore, one from which Genet wishes to exempt himself. In his essay on Genet's late style, Said writes of his "unceasing search for the silence that reduces all language to empty posturing." (You cannot print silence on a page.)[107] Like Beckett, in Perloff's formula, he fuses literalism with the "Mallarmean principle that to name is to destroy." (He is, we could say, as self-effacing as he is precise.) It is a crisis of representation that Palestine provokes. "There is no doubt," he writes in *Un captif amoureux*, "that the Palestinians precipitated a breakdown of my vocabulary."[108] Faced with the extremity of Chatila, it becomes the duty of language to pare itself back to bare life. Genet is ceding his power: "In my books I was master of my imagination. Now I am no longer master of what I have seen."[109]

At the same time as we register the weight of this obligation (this submission), it is impossible not to be struck by the aura of hesitation, the frailty, with which Genet surrounds his presence as writer in Palestine. The essay on Sabra and Chatila begins: "No one, nothing, no narrative technique, could say what were the six months, and especially the first weeks, which the fedayeen spent in the mountains of Jerash and Aljoun in Jordan."[110] "No one, nothing, no narrative technique, could say . . ." These are the first words of the report. Language fails. Partly this is marvel, as in "No words can capture." Genet is enchanted by the beauty, a term he does not hesitate to use, he discovers in the lives of the fedayeen. His opening is therefore an act of political defiance and a type of magic. Before arriving at the worst, Genet veers away, returns to the fedayeen in the mountains, as he will in *Un captif amoureux*, bringing them to life against the death on the pages to come. As Adorno put it in relation to Beckett, consciousness has the will to survive. In the very last days of writing, Genet added this opening to *Un captif amoureux*:

> The page that was blank to begin with is now crossed from top to bottom with tiny black characters—letters, words, commas, exclamation marks—and it's because of them that the page is said to be legible. But a kind of uneasiness, a feeling close to nausea, an irresolution that stays my hand—these make me wonder: do these black marks add up to reality? The white of the paper is an artifice that's replaced the translucency of parchment and the ochre surface of clay tablets; but the ochre and the translucency and the whiteness may all possess more reality than the signs that mar them.[111]

Language induces nausea (like witnessing horror). A disfigurement—the French for "mar" is *défigurent*, or "violation"; it bleeds across the purity of the page. Right to the end, Genet is struggling with the issue posed to him as a writer by the Palestinians—as by no others—the obligation of language to a reality that it also betrays. "I got goose flesh," Shahid comments as she recalls first reading these lines, "because Jean was already a corpse and yet I heard in these words something stronger than death . . . for they interrogate the author and the reader: what is more real, more true? The white or the black on the page? What we see or what we do not see of reality, what will escape us forever?"[112]

In this faltering relation to what can be said, there is also another dimension, the European acknowledging at once his deepest implication in, and his cruel detachment from, the events: "By bringing the war back to Europe," he wrote in 1972 of images of Palestinian "terrorists" on French TV screens, "they have brought it back to its true terrain ... [they] are returning with perfect logic to the source of their misfortunes."[113] And yet as a European, he is alone in Palestine: "Doubtless I was alone, I mean the only European."[114] It is because Genet is the supreme outsider, because he lays down or cedes his authority that, for anyone trying to approach the Middle East from the outside, he speaks with such authority for all of us. "This sort of little account I wrote, it was not with my own ideas. The words were mine, but in order to speak of a reality that was not."[115] Genet will bear witness while knowing that at every turn there is the threat of losing touch, that every utterance he emits, every page he writes about Palestine, risks contamination simply by dint of the place from which he writes and speaks. "Let no one touch the spectacle I am looking at," he had written in relation to the Palestinians in 1972. "If the landscape is only looked at [by the Westerner or Westernized person], he who looks has a reassuring if somewhat sadistic feeling of peace, since he neither is the landscape nor is he in the landscape."[116] In response to Sabra and Chatila, he goes further. We are the "spectators of revolutions up to our necks in the plush velvet of Italian-style theatre boxes. If these are wars of liberation, from where else could we be watching? Who are they—the ones over there—meant to be to liberating themselves from?"[117] No European, he comments wryly at one point in *Un captif amoureux*, "will ever read this book."[118]

Genet knows that his vision, if not tainted, is inflected and probably distorted by his point of origin in the French metropolis that the Palestinians, and the Black Panthers before them, allowed him so definitively to flee. (He was never at home like this in France.)[119] However much he tries to convey the reality in front of him, he knows that it is the fate of the European, finally, to watch from the outside as if in a dream: "That city lying in smithereens which I saw or thought I saw, which I walked through, felt, and whose death stench I wore, had all that taken place?"[120] "This whole escapade should have been subtitled *A Midsummer Night's Dream.*"[121] In *Un captif amoureux* he writes, "By agreeing to go first with the Panthers and then with the Palestinians, by playing my role as a dreamer inside a dream, wasn't I just one more element making for the unreality of these Movements? Wasn't I the European saying to the dream: 'You are a dream—above all, don't wake the sleeper'?"[122] When he taunted the journalist in Vienna for being the one who makes the massacres unreal, the one he is really accusing is thus himself (as strictly must be the case). If this is writing that holds onto the real, it does so, therefore, a little like a man falling from a building who clutches onto a windowsill with his nails. Or to put it another way, Genet is making a confession—the dreamer who knows he is in a dream. What would it mean to make a stronger, more confident claim? Such radical disorientation is, I would suggest, Genet's way of keeping faith—with the otherness, as well as with the insufferable nature, of what he has witnessed. But he has also added to Beckett's struggle to represent what can barely be spoken a further political dimension—the impropriety, for any colonizing presence or, more simply, of one who does not strictly belong, of believing he or she can fully represent what he or she has seen.

It would be wrong, therefore, to think that Genet's acute ear for the real does not bring with it its own dimension of the dream, wrong too to think that he does not, finally, if perhaps surprisingly, bring Proust to Palestine. "Of course," he concedes in the 1983 interview on Chatila, "if you push the analysis further, we know only too well that reverie is part of the real world. Dreams are also realities."[123] Genet is in Palestine out of his own need. "Sometimes I wonder whether I didn't live that life especially so that I might arrange its episodes in the same seeming disorder as the images in a dream."[124] Sometimes, even more radically perhaps, he wonders "if our brain's only purpose is to dream our lives."[125] The more he records the reality of the fedayeen, the more conscious he becomes of his own desire (which does not mean sexual desire, as he insists more than once). You do not choose the people you are born into; but if you choose to make another community your own, your attachment will be "non raisonnée" (not reasoned), but "sensible, sensuel," sentimental, sensual, palpable.[126] The translation of "sensible, sensuel" as "emotional, intuitive" loses the unmistakable Proustian quality, the allusion to an affect that, running through the body, takes on sensual, physical, shape. "It would be," he writes, as pointless to try to "think" the revolution as, waking up, to try and "see the logic in a dream."[127] Now Genet assigns his own tryst with the Palestinians to that half-waking life with which Proust ushers in the two thousand pages of his story, the very moment he cited only to dismiss in the interview of 1983: "I would fall asleep again, and thereafter reawaken for short snatches only," Proust writes in the first pages of *Du côté de chez Swann*, "just long enough ... to stare at the shifting kaleidoscope of the darkness." "When, half awake," writes Genet, "I think about the revolution."[128]

Like any love, Genet's passion for the Palestinian cause, he recognizes, will diminish. Should they achieve their aims, become a people, or indeed a nation, like any other, he will lose interest (it is the struggle, not its aims, with which he identifies): "Listen," he says to the interviewer in 1983, "the day the Palestinians become institutionalised, I will no longer be on their side. The day the Palestinians become a nation like other nations, I will no longer be there. ... I believe it will be at that moment that I will betray them."[129] Likewise Elia Suleiman, to whom we next turn, has recently said: "I will fight to raise the Palestinian flag; once it is going to rise, I will fight to lower it."[130] Genet is cautious about the future of the struggle to which he devotes himself. Above all, what, or who, the Palestinians have allowed him to find is himself. (Here again, the affinity with Proust is profound.) He loves the Palestinians because of what they have allowed him to be: "The Palestinian revolution has established new kinds of relations which have changed me," he observed in 1972, "and in this sense the Palestinian revolution is my revolution."[131]

Fifteen years after living with the fedayeen, *Un captif amoureux* is the last thing he writes before he dies. The book emerges from the depths of his unconscious like an unbidden guest: "Perhaps this book came out of me without my being able to control it. . . . After fifteen years, despite my holding back, my sealed mouth, the repressed has leaked out of the cracks."[132] "What if this book," he asks, "were only a memoir-mirror for me alone?"[133] Of course, for Proust, memory, above all involuntary memory like this, has the character of an epiphany. To make the Palestinians part of his memory is to preserve them, as the most precious objects, in the deepest recesses of his mind. And as with Proust, such memory, if it can be plumbed, will break false treaties, shatter mundane cliché and bad habits, and answer the hapless distortions of the world: "They were so opposite from what they were said to be that their radiance, their very existence, derived from that ne-gation. . . . I might as well admit that by staying with them, I was staying—I don't know how, how else to put it—in my own memory."[134]

In his essay in the *Revue d'études palestiniennes* devoted to Genet, Félix Guattari suggests that what the uneven paving stones in the courtyard of the Guermantes are to Proust in *Time Regained*—boldly making a link perhaps more shocking than any I have made here—the devastated camps of Sabra and Chatila are to Genet, the stimulus for the ultimate self-discovery and outpouring of the past. (Remember, *À la recherche* was created like a fan, the first and last volumes written before anything else.)[135] "By that rather childish expression," Genet continues the lines just cited, "I am saying as clearly as I can that the Palestinian revolt was among my oldest memories."[136] Making the Palestin-ians the core of his inner landscape is to give them, then, amongst other things, a literary status that in French culture veers close to the sacred (although Genet, who can always be relied on to scandalize, combines this unmistakably Proustian moment with a reference to the Qur'an). Nonetheless, by claiming for the Pal-estinians the status of ancient memories, Genet brings Palestine into the heart of European culture, makes of the Palestinians in some sense its forgotten core: "Is that enough to reveal the importance I ascribe to memories?"[137]

When Proust trips on the paving stones in *Time Regained*, that last volume of his work, he is on his way into a soiree at the Duchesse de Guermantes's where, faced with figures he has not seen for years, he believes at first that they are all sporting the false signs of age, like a mask in which he refuses to see prefigured his own death. The death in this final moment, therefore, circles back to the beginning at Combray, where the first involuntary memory was linked by the narrator to the shades of the dead. Genet's encounter with Palestine also came at the end. Certainly it gave him a new lease of life—according to Shahid, he had been "a corpse for several years," until his meeting with the Palestinians seemed to bring him back to life: "I felt that he was returning to life, to creation." (On the eve of their departure for Lebanon in 1982, he had announced that he no longer wished to live.)[138] All of this suggests another reason for seeing the Palestinian writing as a type of endgame (hence its place in Said's essays on *Late Style*). "Perhaps," Genet muses, "the memories I record are mere draperies with which my corpse is still being decked."[139]

For Guattari, Genet goes one further than Proust in allowing his memories to be transformed, blasted even, by what he encounters in Palestine: "He never encloses himself in the universe of memory. On the contrary, the process is endlessly exposed to the encounter with heterogeneous realities capable of inflecting it, of upsetting its pre-existent equilibrium, or even of turning it upside down."[140] Genet finds himself, but he does not *know himself*, in Palestine. It is in this sense that Said can suggest that the choice of Palestine for Genet in the 1970s and 1980s was "the scariest journey of all."[141] Proust's world, Guattari suggests, is like *The Well-Tempered Clavier*. In Genet, there is something more, which might also be something less: "an opening up of a vaster space, the insistent presence of death, of finiteness, and the risk of total and definitive incomprehension."[142]

Beckett and Genet face each other across an abyss. It is the abyss between Europe after the Second World War and Palestine. But it is also for both of them, in their different ways, the abyss that opens up in the mind when confronted with the insufferable, the dying of language, the empty posturing of speech.

Daily Life, Daily Death: Elia Suleiman

In an early sequence of Elia Suleiman's 2002 film *Divine Intervention*, a man stands interminably at a bus stop; when another comes out of his house twice to tell him there will be no bus, he first ignores him and then replies that he knows. Another man goes up and down a ladder onto the roof of a home, where he lays out empty bottles in seemingly interminable rows. Two old men sit on a wall watching. A child's bouncing a ball appears along the top of the wall on which they sit. Every moment feels suspended and slowed down, as the pace of daily life crawls almost to a halt. (Daily life has none of the redemptive power here that we see in some Palestinian writing.) These people are not identified. Like characters in a Beckett play, they seem wedded to a futile reality with no end. When violence erupts, it does so randomly, like an afterthought. The man on the roof starts smashing the bottles and is taken off, after a struggle, by police, pausing with chest pains on the side of the road before being driven away. When he returns, he takes a club to an already shattered pavement, disappears back into his house, knifes the bouncing ball when it lands on his roof, and is then, we assume from noises off, beaten up by his neighbor, who crosses the road to enter his home. Another man rips the license plate off a neighbor's car and throws it onto the street when, having asked him to move it, the neighbor responds with a set of increasingly insane questions about the car's identity. The camera pauses endlessly on a corner of a house or a road. The dialogue is minimal. The characters are never given the cinematic props that would allow them to become part of a sustained story or the fabric of a fuller life. (This is their life.) It is "not daily life," as Suleiman puts it in his earlier film *Arab Dream*, "but daily death."[143]

At moments like these, *Divine Intervention* seems to be skirting a disaster it refers to obliquely—the Occupation is pervasive and glimpsed but as yet unnamed. Something dreadful has happened offstage, before the story and the filming begins. "Deformation," as Beckett puts it in his essay on Proust, "has taken place. . . . We are no longer what we were before the calamity of yesterday." These lives appear to be deprived of even the frailest capacity to understand or even notice themselves. They are no joke, even if Suleiman manages to make them unwittingly, or so it seems, comic. "I can tell you one thing that is as close as possible to some memory that I have," Suleiman has said in interview. "I had the capacity to make people giggle very fast. I knew how to get the gag in the story telling, and I knew how to make them cry."[144]

In my earlier discussion of Beckett, I did not focus on, or indeed even mention, his comedy. A key part of his writing, Beckett's comic strain is, of course, a kind of gallows humor, as well as a demand for a particular form of attention. When Freud wrote of humor—as opposed to jokes—he ascribed its agency to the superego making light of the dangers of the world. The Arab mother in Genet's *The Screens* defines her life as belonging to the nettles, shards, and ruins of the world. "Hello! I'm laughter," she announces, "not just any laughter, but the kind that appears when all goes wrong."[145] In Beckett's hands, humor may do this, but it also moves in the opposite direction—making things larger than they normally seem, pushing pain to a limit where the body erupts at its own capacity to take delight, against all odds, in what it cannot, or should be unable to, tolerate (side-splitting, as one might say). Humor in Beckett always has for me the quality at once of release, but also of an eraser screeching as it is wiped back-to-front against a blackboard. "The laughter it arouses," Adorno writes of Beckett's drama, "ought to suffocate the one who laughs. . . . This is what has become of humour . . . without a place of reconciliation from which one could laugh, and without anything harmless on the face of the earth that would allow itself to be laughed at."[146] It is as if we were being forced to ask: What is there, what is there not, to laugh about?

It is the scandal of Elia Suleiman's cinema to bring a comic dimension to the suffering of the Palestinians. "In Suleiman's cinema," writes critic Hamid Dabashi, "absurdity remembers the dark dread at the heart of its own memory of the terror, it must and cannot but, remember." (He has also been described as a "depressive clown.")[147] "We dissimulate our dark side," he has also observed, "because this dark side is the darkest of all."[148] Only via something that verges on the ridiculous can the memory of an unbearable history creep back into life. Suleiman's films rearrange these forsaken memories, Dabashi continues, "as if with Tourette's syndrome, where the subconscious begins to speak its anxieties out loud, with no control. . . . What emerges is a new register of absurdity."[149] Comedy is, therefore, perhaps as always, anxious (remember that for Freud jokes always skirted on the socially unspeakable or repressed), a form of unsolicited memory— again this takes us back to Proust—bringing something to the surface, to the point of eruption before, momentarily, calming it back down. In the last scene, after the father's death, mother and son sit dourly watching a pressure cooker—"That's enough. Stop it now." Tongue-in-cheek, these words offer themselves as the too obvious allegory for the predicament of the Palestinians and are the last words of the film.

In Suleiman's case, such a register may result, at least partly, from his split vision. Born in Nazareth in 1960, he left Israel and went into voluntary exile in the United States in 1981, where he remained until 1993, when he relocated to Paris. "I don't have a homeland," Suleiman states in an interview of 2000. "And since exile is the other side of having a homeland, I'm not in exile." (He also describes his state of exile as a choice.)[150] As Ella Shohat describes him in the preface to the new edition of her pathbreaking 1989 study *Israeli Cinema: East/West and the Politics of Representation*, he is at once an exile and a cross-border artist. In *Divine*

Intervention his actors include himself as ES in the lead role; the Israeli star Menashe Noy, playing the part of a sadistic soldier at a checkpoint; and George Ibrahim, a Palestinian-Israeli TV entertainer, playing a Santa Claus who is stabbed by children in the hills of Nazareth in the first shots of the film.

Suleiman's Nazareth is a "tale of two cities," drawing both on Christian iconography and on daily Israeli-Palestinian lives. (The film can also be read as a parody of a whole romantic Christian tradition of portrayals of the Holy Land.) He is the new artist of partition which was the focus of chapter 2. Much of *Divine Intervention* takes place at an Israeli border checkpoint—in several long, drawn out sequences, Suleiman, the Palestinian-Israeli, and his West Bank Palestinian lover sit trapped in their car. Exposed for its routine humiliation and latent violence, the checkpoint is also subject to magic, comic violation. At one point, to the consternation of the Israeli soldiers, a red balloon with the face of Arafat drifts across the border. At another—based on a real episode—the Palestinian woman majestically and defiantly walks, to the amazement of the soldiers, who do nothing, straight across the border. In *The Time That Remains*, his most recent film at the time of writing, the character ES, also played by Suleiman, pole vaults over the barrier, or "security" wall.

As an exile, Suleiman has to seize his own history back from the foreign detritus with which it is packaged every day. According to Dabashi, images of Sabra and Chatila on U.S. television in 1982, the year after he arrived, had a huge effect. To paraphrase Genet, the existence of the Palestinians can only be conjured out of the negation of what they are said to be.[151] In this context, comedy is a form of defiance. Western images of the Arab are turned ludicrously against themselves: in a *Matrix Reloaded* sequence near the end of the film, a Palestinian ninja takes off into the skies and then proceeds to wipe out, against all realistic possibility, a group of Israeli soldiers at target practice in the desert. (At one moment surrounded by a crown of thorns, she also bears the keffiyeh and Islamic crescent, symbols of Palestinian national resistance.) Subversion is also a strategy for survival. "There is a death," Suleiman has commented, "in every image that I see."[152] In this, too, there is also something of Genet, who writes in his commentary on scene 6 of *The Screens*, "I believe tragedy can be described like this: a huge laugh broken by a sob which sends us back to the original laugh, that is, the thought of death."[153]

It would then make sense, as well as completing the circuit that began in this chapter with *Endgame*, that it is out of the trash can of existence that Suleiman seizes his opportunity for the future. I am not referring here to the film's moments of emancipatory violence—the man who blows up an Israeli tank with a fruit pip he throws from a passing car, or the red balloon moment (the best-known episode). Rather, to a moment from that earlier sequence which is so unremittingly, if comically, bleak. Three times a man steps out of his house and throws his rubbish over the wall into a woman's backyard. (Seemingly oblivious, another woman—possibly the same woman—is shown at work piling rubbish in her yard into a pile.) When the three plastic bags of garbage land back one after the other on the outside of her wall, the man comes back out of his house and confronts her:

–Neighbour, why do you throw your garbage into my yard? Aren't you ashamed?
–Yes, neighbour. But the garbage I throw is the garbage you throw into our garden.
–So what? It's still shameful. After all, neighbours should respect one another. Why didn't you raise the matter with me first? Isn't that why God gave us tongues?

I see this moment of strained, tentative dialogue, as a pared-back, bleaker version, more than fifty years later, of that quiet moment of reflection in the 1967 Amichai poem of the first chapter. The poet reenters the city of Jerusalem and stands in front of an Arab's button shop, remembering the shop of his father. He makes no claim. Only on that basis can any kind of dialogue commence. Garbage, of course, belongs to no one. Like shame, also named in this sequence, it is the one thing no one ever wants to own. Garbage as a creed—the formula could, of course, apply as much to

Beckett (Nell and Nag in the dustbins) as to Genet. Genet once said he had written *The Screens* to show the saving potential of "a little pile of garbage." In the trial scene, Saïd, who has betrayed the Algerian rebels to the French army, is suddenly defended by one of the village women: "Must save my little heap of garbage, since that is what inspires us . . . nothing must be protected so much as a little heap of garbage."[154]

In *Divine Intervention*, this is not the world in ashes—but, as I have argued throughout this study, it is in many ways its historic consequence or sequel. So it seems appropriate that trash should be the metaphor of transformation. As if to say, it is only out of the rubble that there might be any kind of future in Palestine.

Border Crossings (Again)

One final example of unexpected, unlikely affinities will bring the journey of this book to its end. It is taken from Elias Khoury's internationally acclaimed novel *Bab el Shams*, or *Gate of the Sun*, translated into several languages, including Hebrew, and in 2004 made into a feature film by Egyptian film director Yousry Nasrallah.[155] Khoury says that before his novel appeared, writers had only given hints of what had happened in 1948, "as if they are referring to something that everyone knows but nobody dares to say."[156] In discussion at World Literature Weekend in London in June 2010, he said it could not be spoken of by the Palestinians because it is an object of shame.[157] Suleiman's *The Time That Remains: Chronicle of a Present Absentee* is also his first foray back to 1948. (Memory, as this book has repeatedly suggested, stalls, takes time.) Palestine lacked its epic. Khoury did not realize, as he now likes to tell the story, that he would be the one to write it: "*Gate of the Sun* came to fill a gap and to open the debate on Palestinian memory. It was like a key that everyone had lost."[158]

Khoury chose to write his novel in fragments that loop back and forward between 1948, the year when Khoury himself was born, Sabra and Chatila in 1982, and today. It therefore retraces the path from the founding of Israel as a nation-state to the

now partly acknowledged massacre of 1982, which has formed
the frame for this study. Chatila—today home to around 16,000
people, half Palestinians, the rest destitute Syrians and Lebanese—provides the setting. In a makeshift Galilee hospital inside
the camp, Khaleel Ayyoub, a Palestinian medic who is a witness
and survivor of the massacre, sits beside Yunis, the comatose former Palestinian militant and legendary hero, and tries to nurse
him into consciousness by narrating the story of Yunis's life. He
has been told by the camp's midwife, Umm Hassan, that, contrary to all medical indications and advice, Yunis can hear. The
symbolism is inescapable; in the words of Raja Shehadeh, "the
comatose man—a leader of a national liberation movement, still
in exile and unable to speak."[159] Khoury has chosen to write a
novel in which the story that brings to life the memory of the
Palestinian people is mouthed into the ear of a near corpse.

My episode comes roughly halfway through the novel, when
a French theater troupe arrives in the camp to put on a play
based on Genet's "Quatre Heures à Chatila." It falls on Khaleel
to show Catherine, the actress—the sole performer—round the
camp. The experiment is more or less a disaster. When they reach
the street of the massacre described by Genet, the actress leans
against Khaleel, resting her head on his shoulder and weeping:
"I tried to move away a little, for that kind of thing is not looked
upon kindly in the camp, but she wouldn't change her pose."[160]

Despite his original intention to do so, Khaleel finds himself
incapable of telling the troupe his story. As they walk around the
camp, all the doors are closed one after another in their faces.
"When the woman heard the word *massacre*, her face fell. 'No,
son. We're not a cinema. No.'" Catherine gets the message and
decides to leave—"Nous sommes des voyeurs"—but Khaleel is
not sure that he, that they, were right: "You agree," he pleads with
the comatose Yunis, "that people took a noble stand when they
refused to talk, right? They were right not to talk. How could
they, after all? We don't tell these tales to one another, so why
should we tell them to foreigners."[161] The silence is a form of
loyalty. There are other voices in the camp: "Is it true," he asks,

"that the voices of the dead flow through the camp?"[162] And there are other memories: "The dead remember, and their memories hurt like knives." (The Arabic *mu'limah* is stronger, as in "gnaws at" or even "tortures.")[163]

We are, therefore, in a haunted world with the tightest bar on access. Once again, something insufferable refuses to pass into speech. Slowly, Khaleel's grip on his story, like Genet's before him, starts to drift into the realm of the night: "The civil war had become a long dream [*manam* is "state of sleeping" or "slumber"], as though it had never happened. I can feel it under my skin, but I don't believe it. All that remains are the pictures. Even our massacre here in the camp and the flies that hunted me down I see as though they were pictures, as though I wasn't remembering but watching. I don't get upset. I feel astonishment. Strange, isn't it? Strange that a war should pass as a dream [sleep]."[164] In the original, this is more acutely in the present: "I can feel its special taste [*nakhah*] under my skin" and "as though I am not remembering but watching," which also of course makes the massacre more hallucinatingly real, at the same time as it becomes a reality he is losing grip of. Perhaps, therefore, Genet was not only describing the problem of the outsider. Perhaps this is how the worst of history, wherever you are, inscribes itself on the mind. One of the main messages of this study would then be that the world of the sleeper is not counter to reality, but the place of reality's most acute, enduring impact (an insight of course common to both Proust and Freud, who have been the faithful companions of this work).

On the point of her departure, Catherine comes to Khaleel in a state of excitement after reading Kapeliouk's report. Thus, another extant document on the massacre, along with the Genet makes its way onto the page (blurring the lines between fiction and documentary). According to the report, nine Jewish women, married to Palestinians, also perished in the camps. Catherine wants Khaleel to help her find out who they were. His patience snaps: "You come and ask me about nine Jewish women who, you say, or your Israeli writer says, were slaughtered here in the camp.

There were more than fifteen hundred killed, and you're searching for nine."[165]

If this were the end of it, then we could say that Khoury has more or less dispatched Genet from the Middle East, opening up just about as wide a gulf as possible between the role of the voyeur and that of the witness (the gulf to which Genet himself was so attuned), and between Palestinian and Jew. But Khoury does not stop there, as the immediately following story picks up the Jewish link, which has just been discarded by Khaleel with such contempt, and runs with it. It is the fundamental structure of the book that tale leads into tale and there is no way of discussing it without reproducing something of the same effect. (The interminable form also reflects Khoury's insistence that the *nakba* is not over, that it is a mistake for it to be described as something that ended in 1948.)[166] Jamal the Libyan—famous member of the Popular Front for the Liberation of Palestine, whose "chest was torn open" when he was shot by an Israeli during the siege of Beirut—had, it turns out, a German Jewish mother.[167] Sarah Rimsky, who immigrated to Israel in 1939, was a student of German literature at the Hebrew University when she met his father, a scion of a noble Palestinian family in Jerusalem. The mother embraced Islam and came to speak Arabic with a Gaza accent. No one knew she was a Jewess. She only tells her children the truth when the bombs start falling on Gaza during the 1967 war. At the end of the episode, when she is dying of colon cancer, she has only one wish, to return to Berlin to be buried: "'She was like a girl there,' the father said, 'She took me to the places of her childhood, of which not many remained—but she was happy. It was as though the pain had gone or a miracle had occurred. . . . Three days later she died, and I buried her there.'"[168]

Khoury did not, of course, have to tell this story, but it is not the first or only time in the novel that he crosses this boundary, pushing for an identification against which the whole of the novel in some sense militates. Against any such mobility or connectedness across the divide between the two peoples, Jamal, for example, ends up concluding in prison: "There's them and there's us. We're behind bars and they guard the prison. That way there's no confusion."[169] But it is central to Khoury's vision—central to the novel as a whole—that the deadliest thing is for there to be only one version of a story. "History has dozens of versions," Khaleel says to Yunis, "and for it to ossify into one leads only to death."[170] Despite himself, we could say, the story that Jamal discovers about himself is the tale of unsolicited affinities which break with the most carefully nurtured, rigid parameters of the world. The Palestinian militant is the son of a Jewess who speaks Arabic with a Gaza accent but longs only to be buried in her own land. Reversing the journey of these pages, and of so many of her people, she travels back to Europe, to Germany no less, from Palestine.

In the end it is Khaleel, the voice of the novel, therefore, who most poignantly carries the weight of such ambiguities. What, he asks Yunis, when "the Nazi beast was exterminating the Jews of Europe," did he know about the world? "I'm not saying—no don't worry. I believe, like you, that this country must belong to its people. This Palestine, no matter how many names they give it, will always be Palestinian." "But tell me," he continues, "in the faces of those people being driven to slaughter, didn't you see something resembling your own?"[171] (He is always asking questions.) And then, in an extraordinary passage, Khaleel makes the mental journey to Nazi Europe. As he remembers 1948 in Galilee, he sees himself on the platform watching the Jews rounded up on the trains. (He knows there were no trains in Galilee.) "The whistle rings in my ears. I see the people being led towards the final trains. I see the trains and I shudder. Then I see myself loaded into a basin and carried on a woman's head."[172] It is through the prism of Jewish history that Khaleel in this moment relives his own past. As if to say: you cannot think of, still less relive, the history of 1948 without thinking of the Jews. This is far more than a plea for empathy. In a novel that tells, over and over again, the story of the Palestinian catastrophe or *nakba* of 1948, in a novel that exists in order to tell that story, Khoury has made his Palestinian narrator a time-traveler, sending him back to witness the tragedy of the European Jews. For me this moment in the novel is the strongest answer to the charge of spurious analogy. This is not a claim for symmetry of suffering, but, as Khaleel makes clear, a leap of identification and a call for historic accountability that implicates us all: "You and I and every human being on the face of this planet should have known and not stood by in silence.... Not because the victims were Jews but because their death meant the death of humanity within us."[173] To refer back to the last chapter ("The House of Memory"), this is, of course, a plea for another type of memory and, to the one before ("Proust, Partition, and Palestine"), a plea for a break with the partitions of psyche and world. "How," asks Genet in relation to the Palestinians, "can arrows that fly in different directions be tied together?"[174] In a discussion at the London Barbican cinema in May 2010 following the screening of his latest film, a Palestinian in the audience asked Suleiman whether the combined power of hopelessness and persistence in his films would one day converge to "win our case." "I am not," he replied, "the person to ask about winning or losing." "Nor," he continued, "the person to speak of 'we'" [as in Palestinian alone]. He also stated that he will "always doubt the collective institution called nation."[175] "It is a question of a moral equation we must insist on maintaining, about justice in general."[176] If we return to where this book started, these last words could have been penned by Bernard Lazare.

In *Gate of the Sun*, Genet arrives more or less empty handed and leaves in something like disgrace. Yet his difficult trajectory is also redeemed, I would suggest, by the way Khoury cuts back and forth between Europe and the Middle East, as he offers his version of the journey I have been trying to trace in this book. It is not over, of course. Khoury's call for historic accountability from Palestinian to Jew is as generous as it is unexpected. The accountability of the West toward the Palestinian people has barely begun.

Notes

INTRODUCTION

1. Alfred Dreyfus, *Cinq Années de Ma Vie 1894–1899* (Paris: Charpentier, 1901), 9; *Five Years of My Life: The Diary of Captain Dreyfus* (New York: Peebles, 1977), 95.

2. Dreyfus, *Cinq Années de Ma Vie*, 9; *Five Years of My Life*, 95.

3. Dreyfus, *Cinq Années de Ma Vie*, 9; *Five Years of My Life*, 95.

4. Dreyfus, *Cinq Années de Ma Vie*, 9; *Five Years of My Life*, 95.

5. Dreyfus, *Cinq Années de Ma Vie*, 103; *Five Years of My Life*, 130–31.

6. Sigmund Freud, *Civilisation and Its Discontents* (1930 [1929]), *The Standard Edition of the Complete Psychological Works of Sigmund Freud*, ed. James Strachey (London: Hogarth, 1961), 21:64–66.

7. Elisabeth Roudinesco, *La bataille de cent ans: Histoire de la psychanalyse en France*, vol. 1, *1885–1939* (Paris: Seuil, 1986), 191.

8. Freud, *The Interpretation of Dreams* (1900), *Standard Edition* (1953), 4:270n. In his comment, Freud does allow that altruistic impulses can find expression in dreams but that egoistic impulses, overcome in waking life, can be the instigator of the dream.

9. Malcolm Bowie, *Proust among the Stars* (London: HarperCollins, 1998).

10. Jacques Rivière, in "Freud et la psychanalyse," special issue, *Le disque vert*, 1924; cited in Tomoko Boongja Woo, "Lecture de Proust, à travers Freud, par les premiers critiques," *Bulletin de la société des amis de Marcel Proust* 58 (2008): 71.

11. Hannah Arendt, *The Origins of Totalitarianism*, 2nd ed. (New

York: Harcourt Brace Jovanovich, 1979), esp. chap. 3, "The Jews and Society," and chap. 4, "The Dreyfus Affair."

12. Marcel Proust, *Jean Santeuil* (Paris: Gallimard, 1952), 2:159; *Jean Santeuil*, trans. Gerard Hopkins (Harmondsworth: Penguin, 1985), 353; translation modified.

13. Freud, "The Moses of Michaelangelo" (1914), *Standard Edition* (1953), 13:212.

14. *Letters of Marcel Proust* (1949), ed. and trans. Minna Curtiss (New York: Helen Marx, 2006), 94.

15. The ban was passed overwhelmingly by the French parliament in July 2010 and ratified by the senate in September 2010.

16. *Letters of Marcel Proust*, 94.

17. The paper was eventually published as "Our Attitude towards Death," *Thoughts for the Time on War and Death, Standard Edition,* vol. 14. See Dennis B. Klein, *Jewish Origins of the Psychoanalytic Movement* (Chicago: University of Chicago Press, 1981), 162. The episode is also discussed in Stanley Schneider and Joseph H. Berke, "Freud's Meeting with Rabbi Alexandre Safran," *Psychoanalysis and History* 12, no. 1 (2010).

18. For another discussion of this issue see Brian Klug, *Being Jewish— Doing Justice: Bringing Argument to Life* (London: Vallentine Mitchell, 2010).

19. Jacques Rancière, *The Aesthetic Unconscious* (Paris: Galilée, 2001; Cambridge: Polity, 2009), 3.

20. Marjorie Perloff, "'In Love with Hiding': Samuel Beckett's War," *Iowa Review* 35, no. 1 (Spring 2005): 101–2.

21. Jean Genet, *Un captif amoureux* (Paris: Gallimard, 1986), 445; *Prisoner of Love*, trans. Barbara Bray (London: Picador, 1989), 272; translation occasionally modified.

22. Amos Oz, "The Power Intoxicating Us," *Guardian*, 2 June 2010. Oz was criticizing the assault by the Israeli army on the humanitarian flotilla heading to Gaza to break the blockade imposed in 2006, an assault that left nine Turkish citizens on the ship dead.

23. Alain Badiou, *L'increvable désir* (Paris: Hachette, 1995); *Badiou on Beckett*, ed. Alberto Toscano and Nina Power (Manchester: Clinamen, 2003).

24. Tom Segev, *1967: Israel, the War and the Year that Transformed the Middle East* (London: Little, Brown, 2007), 19.

25. A twelve-day march by the family of soldier Gilad Shalit in May–

June 2010, calling for the Israeli government to secure his release (in response to Benjamin Netanyahu stating he supported a prisoner exchange but not "at any price") was joined at different stages by an estimated two hundred thousand, the final Jerusalem mass rally at twenty-five thousand. Jack Khoury and Nir Hassan, "12-Day March Ends with Mass Rally in Jerusalem," *Ha'aretz*, 9 July 2010.

26. Or Kashti, "Curriculum: Jordan Peace Deal—In, Oslo Accords—Out," *Ha'aretz*, 25 June 2010.

27. See Anita Shapira, "Hirbet Hizah: Between Remembrance and Forgetting," *Jewish Social Studies* 7 (2000): 1.

28. Elias Khoury, *Gate of the Sun; Bab El Shams*, trans. Humphrey Davies (London: Harvill Secker, 2005), 275; *Bâb al-Chams* (Beirut: Dâr al-Adâb, 1998), 292.

29. Brian Hanrahan, "The Key to Memory: An Interview with Elias Khoury," *openDemocracy*, 19 April 2006.

30. Hanrahan, "Key to Memory."

31. Elias Khoury in discussion with Jeremy Harding, *World Literature Weekend*, London Review Bookshop, 18 June 2010; Edward Said, afterword to *Little Mountain*, by Elias Khoury, trans. Maia Tabet (1970; London: Collins Harvill, 1990), 146, 142.

32. Elia Suleiman, "Illusions Nécessaires," *Cahiers du cinéma*, September 2001, 54; Anne Bourlond, "A Cinema of Nowhere: An Interview with Elia Suleiman," *Journal of Palestine Studies* 29, no. 2 (Winter 2000): 95.

33. Freud, *An Autobiographical Study* (1925 [1924]), *Standard Edition* (1959), 20:72.

34. Freud, *An Autobiographical Study*, 72; Philippe Lacoue-Labarthe and Jean-Luc Nancy, "La panique politique" (1989), in *Retreating the Political*, ed. Simon Sparks, Warwick Studies in European Philosophy (London: Routledge, 1997).

35. Hannah Arendt, *The Human Condition* (Chicago: University of Chicago Press, 1958), chap. 2, "The Public and the Private Realm," 35, 37.

36. Esther Shalev-Gerz, "The Perpetual Movement of Memory," *autrement (Duty of Memory 1914–1998)*, Editions Autrement: Collection Mémoires, 54 typescript, 1.

CHAPTER 1

1. Bernard Lazare, letter to Edouard Drumont, Paris, 23 October 1895, *Contre l'Antisémitisme (Histoire d'une Polémique)* (Paris: Stock, 1896), 24.

2. Léon Blum, *Nouvelles conversations de Goethe avec Eckerman* (Paris: Gallimard, 1937), 136.

3. Marcel Proust, *Jean Santeuil*, 1952, ed. Pierre Clairac with Yves Sandre (Paris: Gallimard, Pléiade, 1971), 605.

4. Ibid., 603–4.

5. Ibid., 601.

6. Ibid.

7. Ibid., 602.

8. "Was There An Armenian Genocide?" Geoffrey Robertson QC's Opinion, Doughty Street Chambers, 9 October 2009.

9. Marcel Proust, *Du côté de chez Swann, À la recherche du temps perdu*, 3 vols. (Paris: Gallimard, 1954), 1:12; *Swann's Way, In Search of Lost Time*, trans. Scott Moncrieff and Terence Kilmartin, rev. D. J. Enright, 6 vols. (London: Chatto & Windus, 1992), 1:12.

10. Proust, *Du côté de chez Swann*, 198; *Swann's Way*, 165.

11. For a discussion of the problem of self-justification and indifference in Proust, see Ingrid Wassenaar, *Proustian Passions: The Uses of Self-Justification for À la recherche du temps perdu* (Oxford: Oxford University Press, 2000).

12. When Bernard Lazare went to see Zola in 1896 in search of support for his pamphlet *Une erreur judiciaire* of 1896, he found him sympathetic but out of touch with the Affair: "I was met with sympathy; the act pleased him, but he had no idea about the Affair and I felt that at that time it did not interest him." Bernard Lazare, unpublished note to Joseph Reinach, in *"Dreyfusards!" Souvenirs de Mathieu Dreyfus et autres inédits présentés par Robert Gauthier*, ed. Pierre Nora, Collection Archives series (Paris: Julliard, 1965), 92.

13. Émile Zola, "Lettre à M Félix Faure, Président de la République," *L'Aurore*, 13 January 1898, in *La vérité en marche*, by Zola (Paris: Charpentier, 1901), 92–93.

14. Louis Begley, *Why the Dreyfus Affair Matters* (New Haven, CT: Yale University Press, 2009), 139.

15. Proust to Reinach, January 1915, in "Sixteen Letters of Marcel Proust to Joseph Reinach," by Michael Watson, *MHRA* 63, no. 3 (July 1968). See also the letter dated by Watson around 20 May 1906, "Sixteen Letters," 595. Proust's relationship to Reinach was complex. Reinach is given an unflattering walk-on part in *Du côté de chez Guermantes*, but in a letter to Madame Straus dated around 23 August 1906, Proust describes him as having "done a great deal more than Zola" (*Letters*

of Marcel Proust, 183). His letters to Reinach also show that he deeply admired his political stance until their relationship cooled over the issue of Proust's military service, on which he asked Reinach, unsuccessfully, to intervene.

16. Joseph Reinach, *Histoire de l'Affaire Dreyfus*, vol. 3, *La Crise: Procès Esterhazy: Procès Zola* (Paris: Charpentier et Fasquelle, 1903), 341.

17. Proust, *Jean Santeuil* (Paris: Gallimard, 1952), 2:117, 2:121; *Jean Santeuil*, trans. Gerard Hopkins (Harmondsworth: Penguin, 1985), 319, 322. Unless otherwise stated, all subsequent references are to these editions. Translations have been modified.

18. Tony Judt, "What Is Living and What Is Dead in Social Democracy?" *New York Review of Books* 56, no. 20 (17 December 2009–13 January 2010).

19. Reinach, *Histoire de l'Affaire Dreyfus*, 3:473.

20. Léon Blum, *Souvenirs sur l'Affaire* (Paris: Gallimard, 1935), 92, 15.

21. Steven Lukes, *Emile Durkheim: Life and Work: A Historical and Critical Study* (London: Allen Lane, 1973), 333.

22. Reinach, *Une conscience. Le Lieutenant-Colonel Picquart* (Paris: Stock, 1898), 7.

23. Reinach, *Histoire de l'Affaire Dreyfus*, 3:244.

24. Proust to Anna de Noailles, c. mid-July 1906, *Letters of Marcel Proust*, 181.

25. Proust to his mother, "Monday half-past one," September 1899, *Letters of Marcel Proust*, 64; and probably, 10 September 1899, *Letters of Marcel Proust*, 66, 62.

26. Proust to his mother, 1 September 1899, in *Letters to His Mother*, trans., ed., and intro. by George D. Painter (London: Rider, 1956), 77; my emphasis.

27. Proust to Sydney Schiff, summer 1920, ibid., 418–19.

28. Bowie, *Proust among the Stars*, 148. Louis Begley ends his account of Dreyfus with a discussion of Proust, *Why the Dreyfus Affair Matters*.

29. Reinach, *Histoire de l'Affaire Dreyfus*, 2:208.

30. Cited in Begley, *Why the Dreyfus Affair Matters*, 103.

31. Cited in Jean-Denis Bredin, *The Affair: The Case of Alfred Dreyfus*, trans. Jeffrey Mehlman (London: Sidgwick & Jackson, 1987), 222.

32. Reinach, *Histoire de l'Affaire Dreyfus*, 3:392.

33. Francis de Pressensé, *L'Affaire Dreyfus. Un Héros. Le Colonel Picquart* (Paris: Stock, 1898), 78.

34. Maurice Barrès, *Mes Cahiers*, 1936; cited in Stephen Wilson,

Ideology and Experience: Antisemitism in France at the Time of the Dreyfus Affair (London: Littman Library of Jewish Civilization, Associated Universities Press, 1982), 77.

35. *Le procès Zola*, 2:417, cited in David Robin Watson, *Georges Clemenceau et la France* (London: Haus, 2008), 35.

36. Reinach, *Une conscience*, 34.

37. Reinach, *Histoire de l'Affaire Dreyfus*, 3:375.

38. Maurice Paléologue, *Journal de l'Affaire Dreyfus, 1894–1899* (Paris: Plon, 1955), 219–20; cited in Begley, *Why the Dreyfus Affair Matters*, 122.

39. Bernard Lazare, *Une erreur judiciare: L'Affaire Dreyfus, Deuxième Mémoire avec des Expertises d'Écriture* (Paris: Stock, 1897), 63. "The jury deliberated and made its decision in thrall to the most insane terror." Urbain Gohier, "Le Péril," *La revue blanche*, 1 June 1898, 166.

40. Lazare, *Une erreur judiciaire*, 18–19, 8.

41. Reinach, *Une conscience*, 25.

42. Reinach, *Histoire de l'Affaire Dreyfus*, 3:383.

43. Ibid.

44. "Driving a Truck through Obama's Presidency," *Guardian*, 21 January 2010. For a powerful account of the analogies between Dreyfus's treatment on Devil's Island and the U.S. treatment of political detainees at Guantanamo and Abu Ghraib, see Begley, *Why the Dreyfus Affair Matters*.

45. Proust, *Jean Santeuil*, 2:95; trans., p. 303.

46. Blum, *Souvenirs sur l'Affaire*, 30.

47. Jean Recanati, *Profils juifs de Marcel Proust* (Paris: Buchet-Chastel, 1979), 94.

48. Jean-Yves Tadié, *Marcel Proust* (Paris: Gallimard, 1996), 373.

49. Proust, *Jean Santeuil*, 2:135; trans., 334.

50. Proust, *Jean Santeuil*, 2:137; trans., 335.

51. Proust, *Jean Santeuil*, 2:135; trans., 334.

52. Proust, *Jean Santeuil*, 1971 ed., 636.

53. Proust, *Jean Santeuil*, 2:128; trans., 328.

54. Proust, *Jean Santeuil*, 2:128; trans., 329.

55. Proust, *Jean Santeuil*, 2:135, trans., 334.

56. Reinach, *Histoire de l'Affaire Dreyfus*, 3:375

57. Pressensé, *Le Colonel Picquart*, 7.

58. Cited by Marcel Thomas, *L'Affaire sans Dreyfus* (Paris: Fayard, 1961), 353.

59. Pressensé, *Le Colonel Picquart*, 8.

60. Jean-Marie Mayeur, "Une mémoire frontière: l'Alsace," in *Les lieux de mémoire,* under the direction of Pierre Nora, vol. 2, *Nation* (Paris: Gallimard, 1988), 63.

61. Julia Kristeva, *Time and Sense: Proust and the Experience of Literature* (New York: Columbia University Press, 1996).

62. Proust, *Jean Santeuil,* 2:125; trans., 326.

63. Proust, *Jean Santeuil,* 2:141; trans., 339.

64. Proust, *Du côté de chez Swann,* 1:5; *The Way by Swann's,* trans. Lydia Davis (London: Allen Lane, 2002), 9.

65. Proust, *Jean Santeuil,* 2:107; trans., 312.

66. Proust, *Jean Santeuil,* 2:142; trans., 339.

67. Proust, *Jean Santeuil,* 2:142; trans., 340.

68. Proust, *Jean Santeuil,* 2:147; trans., 343.

69. Proust, *Jean Santeuil,* 2:148; trans., 344.

70. Jean Recanati, *Profils juifs de Marcel Proust,* 90.

71. Ibid., 76; my emphasis.

72. I am grateful to Ingrid Wassenaar for this insight. See Wassenaar, *Proustian Passions.*

73. Recanati, *Profils juifs de Marcel Proust,* 82; Henri B. Stendhal, *The Red and the Black,* trans. Catherine Slater (Oxford: Oxford University Press, 1992), 391.

74. Proust, *Jean Santeuil,* 1971 edition, 636.

75. Proust to Robert de Montesquiou, probably 1898, *Letters of Marcel Proust,* 54.

76. Proust, *Jean Santeuil,* 2:72, trans., 285.

77. Ibid.

78. Proust to Kiki Bartholoni, *Correspondance,* ed. Philip Kolb (Paris: Plon, 1970), 2:243–44; cited in Annick Bouillaguet, "Marcel Proust devant L'Affaire Dreyfus," *Bulletin de la Société des amis de Marcel Proust* 48 (1998): 34.

79. Proust, *Jean Santeuil,* 2:159, trans., 352–53.

80. Bowie, *Proust among the Stars,* 141.

81. Tadié, *Marcel Proust,* 374.

82. Reinach, *Histoire de l'Affaire Dreyfus,* 3:244.

83. Ibid., 3:249.

84. Ibid., 3:350.

85. Lazare, *Une erreur judiciare,* 15.

86. Reinach, *Histoire de l'Affaire Dreyfus,* 3:350.

87. Cited in Reinach, *Histoire de l'Affaire Dreyfus,* 2:196n.

88. Zola, "Lettre à M Félix Faure," 80.

89. Reinach, *Histoire de l'Affaire Dreyfus*, vol. 1, *Le procès de 1894* (Paris: Éditions de la Revue Blanche, 1901), 468.

90. Bredin, *The Affair*, 350.

91. Ibid., 351.

92. Wilson, *Ideology and Experience*, 155, 158, 157.

93. Émile Zola, "Le Syndicat," *Le Figaro*, 1 December 1897, in *La vérité en marche*, 15.

94. Bredin, *The Affair*, 352.

95. Émile Zola, "Procès-Verbal," *Le Figaro*, 5 December 1897, in *La vérité en marche*, 31.

96. L'Archiviste, *Drumont et Dreyfus: Études sur La Libre Parole* (Paris: Stock, 1898), 10.

97. Lazare, *Une erreur judiciare*, 14–15.

98. L'Archiviste, "Drumont et Dreyfus," 20.

99. Ibid., 19.

100. *La Croix*, 7 November 1894, cited in Lazare, *Une erreur judiciare*, 16.

101. Edouard Drumont, *La france juive* (1885; popular edition, Paris: Victor Palme, 1888), 32.

102. Ibid., 33.

103. Reinach, *Histoire de l'Affaire Dreyfus*, 1:470.

104. Ibid., 1:469.

105. Drumont, *La france juive*, 28.

106. *Petit Journal*, 3 November 1894, cited in Lazare, *Une erreur judiciaire*, 20–21.

107. Lazare, *Une erreur judiciare*, 21. See also on this topic, René Girard, *Le bouc émissaire* (Paris: Grasset, 1982).

108. Blum, *Souvenirs sur l'Affaire*, 63.

109. L'Archiviste, "Drumont et Dreyfus," 6.

110. Elisabeth Roudinesco, *Retour sur la question juive* (Paris: Albin Michel, 2009), 247.

111. Robert F Byrnes, *Antisemitism in Modern France* (1950; New York: Fertig, 1969), 329.

112. Cited in Fred C. Conybeare, *The Dreyfus Case* (London: George Allen, 1898).

113. Isaiah Levaillant, *Univers Israelite*, 12 November 1897; cited in Michael M. Marrus, *The Politics of Assimilation: The French Jewish Community at the Time of the Dreyfus Affair* (Oxford: Clarendon Press, 1971), 220.

114. L'Archiviste, "Drumont et Dreyfus," 39.

115. Louis Levy, *Univers Israelite*, 25 February 1898; cited in Marrus, *Politics of Assimilation*, 223.

116. Blum, *Souvenirs sur l'Affaire*, 25.

117. Marrus, *Politics of Assimilation*, 222.

118. Blum, *Souvenirs sur l'Affaire*, 27.

119. Jacques Derrida, "Force of Law: The 'Metaphysical Foundation of Authority,'" in *Deconstruction and the Possibility of Justice*, ed. Drucilla Cornell, Michael Rosenfeld, and David Gray Carlson (London: Routledge, 1992). For example: "I shall only propose a few examples that will suppose, make explicit or perhaps produce a difficult and unstable distinction between justice and *droit*, between justice (infinite, incalculable, rebellious to rule and foreign to symmetry, heterogeneous and heterotropic) and the exercise of justice as law or right, legitimacy or legality, stabilizable and statutory, calculable, a system of regulated and coded prescriptions" (22).

120. Michael Marrus and Robert Paxton, *Vichy France and the Jews* (New York: Basic, 1981), 43, 63.

121. Ibid., 3.

122. Cited in Pierre Birnbaum, "Grégoire, Dreyfus, Drancy and the rue Copernic: Jews at the Heart of French History," in *Realms of Memory: Rethinking the French Past*, ed. Pierre Nora, vol. 1, *Conflicts and Divisions*, trans. Arthur Goldhammer (New York: Columbia University Press, 1996), 411.

123. A. B. Jackson, *La revue blanche 1889–1903: Origine, influence, bibliographie* (Paris: Minard, Lettres Modernes series, 1960). See also Teng-Yueh Hong, "*Le dréfusisme proustien:* Marcel Proust's 'La revue blanche' and the Dreyfus Affair," *Literature and Linguistics*, January 2001.

124. "Protestation," *La revue blanche*, 1 February 1898, 161. The authors and staff of the *Revue* also immediately staged a special performance of Henrik Ibsen's *An Enemy of the People*, making key changes so that the references to Zola would be unmistakeable. Joan Udersama Halperin, *Félix Fénéon: Aesthete and Anarchist in Fin-de-Siècle Paris* (New Haven, CT: Yale University Press, 1988), 319.

125. Halperin, *Félix Fénéon*, 321.

126. Tárrida del Mármol, "Un mois dans les prisons d'Espagne," *La revue blanche*, 15 October 1896.

127. See Benedict Anderson, "Jupiter Hill," *New Left Review* 29 (September–October 2004): 111; republished in B. Anderson, *Under*

Three Flags (London: Verso, 2005). Also on *La revue blanche*, see Teng-Yueh Hong, *Le dréfusisme proustien.*

128. Gustave Kahn, "Zola," *La revue blanche*, 15 February 1898; "Hommage," *La revue blanche*, 1 March 1898, 321.

129. "Protestation," 166.

130. Reinach, *Histoire de l'Affaire Dreyfus*, 3:73.

131. Alain Pagès, ed., *Émile Zola: Un Intellectuel dans l'Affaire Dreyfus* (New York: Librairie Séguier, 1991), 57; cited in Frederick Brown, *Culture Wars in the Age of Dreyfus* (New York: Knopf, 2010), 194.

132. Émile Zola, "Lettre à la jeunesse," 14 December 1897, in *La vérité en marche*; "Pour les juifs," in *Le Figaro*, 16 May 1896. In Zola's 1891 novel, *L'Argent*, the central female character, Madame Caroline, mounts a defense of the Jews against anti-Semitism: "'What a strange thing!' murmured madame Caroline, who, with her vast knowledge, practiced universal toleration" (sa tolérance universelle). "To me the Jews are men like any others. If they are apart, it is because they have been put apart" (on les y a mis). Zola, *Money,* trans. Ernest Vizetelly (London: Chatto, 1894), 412–13; *L'Argent* (Paris: Charpentier, 1891), 429.

133. Zola, "M Scheurer-Kestner," *Le Figaro*, 25 November 1897, in *La vérité en marche*, 3.

134. Zola, *La vérité en marche*, 2.

135. Julien Benda, "Le trahison des clercs," *La nouvelle revue française* 167 (August 1927), 169 (October 1927); Benda, *The Betrayal of the Intellectuals,* trans. Richard Aldington (London: Routledge, 1928).

136. Julien Benda, "L'Affaire Dreyfus et le Principe d'autorité," *La revue blanche*, 1 October 1899, 203; Lucien Herr, "A Monsieur Barrès," *La revue blanche*, 15 February 1898, 241. "Intellectual" as a term of opprobrium also appeared several times in the "Henry monument": "Out of France with the kikes and their pimps, the intellectuals"; "an academic fallen victim to the intellectuals." Cited in Bredin, *The Affair*, 351.

137. As Robin Watson points out, the modern Sartrean meaning of the term, as someone who draws their authority for the political and social causes they espouse from their education and intellectual achievements, "derives from the twist given to the meaning of the word by Zola and Clemenceau in 1898." See Robin Watson, "A Left-Wing Intellectual of the 1890s: Georges Clemenceau," in *Problems in French History,* ed. M. Cornick and C. Crossley (London: Palgrave, 2000), 175. My thanks to Robin Watson for drawing my attention to the complex history of the term.

138. Herr, "A Monsieur Barrès," 241.

139. Ibid.

140. "Protestation," 162.

141. Kahn, "Zola," 270.

142. Gauthier, *"Dreyfusards!" Souvenirs de Mathieu Dreyfus*, 17.

143. Ibid., 17.

144. Blum, *Souvenirs sur l'Affaire*, 94–95.

145. Kahn, "Zola," 269.

146. Ibid., 272.

147. "Protestation," 167.

148. Joseph Reinach, *A l'Ile du Diable* (Paris: Stock, 1898), 13.

149. See Halperin, *Félix Fénéon*, 293.

150. Cited in Bredin, *The Affair*, 476.

151. G. Dubois-Desualle, "La 'Disciplote,'" *La revue blanche*, 15 July 1900, 439.

152. Reinach, *Histoire de l'Affaire Dreyfus*, 2:190; Lazare, *Une erreur judiciare*, 63.

153. Dreyfus, *Five Years of My Life*, 134.

154. Cited in Bernard Lazare, *A Judicial Error: The Truth about the Dreyfus Case* (London: Ward, Lock, n.d. [1896]), 54.

155. Dreyfus, *Cinq Années de Ma Vie*; *Five Years of My Life*, introductory note.

156. "La 'Disciplote,'" 439.

157. Joseph Reinach, *Rapport sur les cas des Cinq Détenus des Iles de Salut (Ile Royal)* (Paris: Stock, 1899).

158. Herr, "A Monsieur Barrès."

159. Gohier, "Le Péril," 161; original emphasis.

160. Ibid., 161, 163, 164.

161. Ibid., 164.

162. Ze'ev Sternhell, *La droite revolutionnaire* (Paris: Seuil, 1971), 406; cited in Bredin, *The Affair*, 348.

163. Benda, "L'Affaire Dreyfus et le Principe d'autorité."

164. Gohier, "Le Péril," 168, 169.

165. Herr, "A Monsieur Barrès," 243.

166. Gohier, "Le Peril," 166.

167. "Protestation," 164.

168. *Le procès Zola*, cited in Watson, *Georges Clemenceau et la France*, 35.

169. Gohier, "Le Péril," 170.

170. Gustave Kahn, "L'idée nationaliste," *La revue blanche*, 15 November 1899.

171. "Protestation," 165.

172. Herr, "A Monsieur Barrès," 243.

173. Benda, "L'Affaire Dreyfus et le Principe d'autorité," 192.

174. Kahn, "L'Idée nationaliste," 404.

175. Herr, "A Monsieur Barrès," 243.

176. Ibid., 244.

177. Marcel Proust, "Études," *La revue blanche*, 26 December 1893, 379, 377.

178. Mayeur, "Une mémoire frontière: l'Alsace," 63–95.

179. Marcel Proust, "Avant la nuit," 26 September 1893, *La revue blanche*, 383–84.

180. Ibid., 384.

181. Tadié, *Marcel Proust*, 368–69.

182. Drumont, *La france juive*, 28.

183. Bernard Lazare to Trarieux, n.d.; cited in Marrus, *Politics of Assimilation*, 194.

184. Bernard Lazare, *Contre l'Antisémitisme (Histoire d'une polémique)* (Paris: Stock, 1896), 28.

185. André Fontainas, "L'antisémitisme et Bernard Lazare," *Mercure de France* 245 (1933): 51.

186. Bernard Lazare, *Job's Dungheap: Essays on Jewish Nationalism and Social Revolution* (New York: Schocken, 1948), 44.

187. Léon Blum, *Nouvelles conversations de Goethe avec Eckerman*, 136.

188. Cited in Reinach, *Histoire de l'Affaire Dreyfus*, 3:144.

189. Lazare, "Nationalism and Jewish Emancipation," in *Job's Dungheap*, 97.

190. Lazare, *Une erreur judiciaire*, 63–64.

191. Bernard Lazare, unpublished reply to a critic, Nimes (1899?); cited in Fontainas, "L'antisémitisme et Bernard Lazare," 57–58.

192. Bernard Lazare, *Comment on condamne un innocent* (Paris: Stock, 1898), 2.

193. Cited in Jacques Viard, "Proust, Bernard Lazare, Péguy et Romain Rolland," *Bulletin de la Société des amis de Marcel Proust* 36 (1986): 569. In a personal communication, Viard—a distinguished Proust scholar—told me that it was only in 1915, after the death of Péguy, that Proust understood fully the role of Lazare in the Dreyfus Affair. See also Henri Bonnet, *La Matinée chez la Princesse de Guermantes: Cahiers du Temps Retrouvé*, critical ed., ed. Henri Bonnet with Bernard Brun (Paris: Gallimard, 1982). My thanks to Jacques Viard for bringing this work and reference to my attention.

194. Proust, *Matinée chez la Princesse de Guermantes*, 331.

195. See Jacques Kornberg, "The Dreyfus Legend," chap. 8 of *Theodor Herzl: From Assimilation to Zionism* (Bloomington: Indiana University Press,: 1993). In her famous 1942 essay, "Herzl and Lazare," Hannah Arendt made the case for Lazare against Herzl, in *The Jew as Pariah: Jewish Identity and Politics in the Modern Age*, ed. Ron H. Feldman (New York: Grove, 1978). This connection is taken up by Gabriel Piterberg in *The Returns of Zionism: Myths, Politics and Scholarship in Israel* (London: Verso, 2008).

196. Lazare, *Job's Dungheap*, 73.

CHAPTER 2

1. Amartya Sen, "We Can Best Stop Terror by Civil, Not Military, Means," *The Guardian*, 9 November 2007.

2. Sigmund Freud, "A Difficulty in the Path of Psycho-Analysis" (1917), *Standard Edition* (1955), 17:142.

3. Marcel Proust, "Notes for *Time Regained*," *Matinée chez la Princesse de Guermantes*, 429.

4. Yehuda Amichai, "Jerusalem," trans. Stephen Mitchell, *Poems 1948–62*, in *Poems of Jerusalem and Love Poems* (New York: Harper and Rowe, 1981), 5.

5. Josef Breuer and Sigmund Freud, *Studies on Hysteria* (1893–95), *Standard Edition*, vol. 2 (1955).

6. Breuer and Freud, "Preliminary Communication," in *Studies on Hysteria*, 2:7; original emphasis.

7. Ibid., 2:6; original emphasis.

8. Josef Breuer, "Case I: Fräulein Anna O," in *Studies on Hysteria*, 2:35.

9. Sigmund Freud, "The Psychotherapy of Hysteria," in *Studies on Hysteria*, 2:290.

10. Proust to Georges de Lauris, 29 July 1903, in *Letters of Marcel Proust*, 92.

11. Sarkozy has been explicit that his goal has been to foster a concept of "national identity," creating a Ministry for Immigration and National Identity, which he subsequently dissolved, and even apologized for, in a reshuffle of November 2010. He did not, however, change his policy, which included expelling seventy-nine Roma from France to Romania in August 2010.

12. Freud, "Psychotherapy of Hysteria," in *Studies on Hysteria*, 2:290.

13. Ibid., 2:290–91.

14. Sigmund Freud, "A Difficulty in the Path of Psycho-Analysis" (1917), *Standard Edition* (1955), 17:142.

15. Although I do not think the analogy works at all levels, Joe Cleary provides an interesting analysis of partition in relation to Ireland and Palestine in *Literature, Partition and the Nation-State: Culture and Conflict in Ireland, Israel and Palestine* (Cambridge: Cambridge University Press, 2002).

16. Sen, "We Can Stop Terror."

17. Proust, "Notes for *Time Regained*," *Matinée chez la Princesse de Guermantes*, 429.

18. Freud, "Splitting of the Ego in the Process of Defence" (1940 [1938]), *Standard Edition*, vol. 23 (1964).

19. Sigmund Freud, *Moses and Monotheism* (1939 [1934–38]), *Standard Edition*, vol. 23.

20. I discuss this in more detail in the introduction to the new translation of this work, *The Man Moses and the Monotheistic Religion*, trans. J. A. Underwood, in Freud, *Mass Psychology and Other Writings* (London: Penguin Modern Classics, 2004). The introduction is also available in Jacqueline Rose, *The Last Resistance* (London: Verso, 2007).

21. Sigmund Freud, "Charcot" (1893), in *Early Psycho-Analytic Publications, Standard Edition* (1962), 3:20.

22. Freud, "Splitting of the Ego," 23:276.

23. Ibid.

24. Ibid.

25. Ibid.; "Die Ichspaltung im Abwehrvorgang," *Gesammelte Werke* (Frankfurt: Fischer Verlag, 1941), 17:60.

26. Freud, "Splitting of the Ego," 23:277.

27. Ibid.

28. Herr, "A Monsieur Barrès," 243.

29. For a fuller discussion of this history, see Elisabeth Roudinesco, *Jacques Lacan: Esquisse d'une vie, histoire d'un système de pensée* (Paris: Fayard, 1993), 101–8; Roudinesco, *Jacques Lacan: Outline of a Life, History of a System of Thought*, trans. Barbara Bray (New York: Columbia University Press, 1997), 71–82.

30. Henri Dutrait-Couzon, *Joseph Reinach Historien: Révision de "L'Histoire de l'Affaire Dreyfus"* (Paris: Savaète, 1905), xx.

31. Proust to Mme Straus, c. January 1908, *Letters of Marcel Proust*, 216.

32. Thérèse Oulton, *Territory* (London: Marlborough Fine Arts Publications, 2010).

33. Blum, *Souvenirs sur l'Affaire*, 14.

34. Aamir R. Mufti, *Enlightenment in the Colony: The Jewish Question and the Crisis of Postcolonial Culture* (Princeton, NJ: Princeton University Press, 2007).

35. Ibid., 110.

36. Lazare, *Job's Dungheap*, 73.

37. Theodor Herzl, *Der Judenstaat* (1896); Herzl, *The Jewish State: An Attempt at a Modern Solution of the Jewish Question*, trans. Sylvie D'Avigdor (London: Zionist Organisation, 1934), 29; Herzl, "A Solution of the Jewish Question" (1896), in *The Jew in the Modern World*, ed. Paul Mendes-Flohr and Jehuda Reinharz, 2nd ed. (Oxford: Oxford University Press, 1995), 534.

38. Herzl, "Solution of the Jewish Question," 534.

39. Arendt, *Origins of Totalitarianism*, 302.

40. See, for example, Juliette Hassine, "L'Affaire Dreyfus et l'espace Romanesque," *Revue d'Histoire Littéraire de la France*, 1971; and Bouillaguet, who discusses Hassine at the end of her article "Marcel Proust devant l'Affaire Dreyfus," 40–41.

41. Proust to Reinach, dated shortly after 20 May 1906, in "Sixteen Letters of Marcel Proust to Joseph Reinach," by Watson, 594; Bouillaguet, "Marcel Proust devant l'Affaire Dreyfus," 40.

42. Bowie, *Proust among the Stars*, 141.

43. Proust, *Matinée chez la Princess de Guermantes*, 430.

44. Proust to Robert de Montesquiou, dated probably 1898, *Letters of Marcel Proust*, 54.

45. Marcel Proust, *Sodome et Gomorrhe, À la recherche du temps perdu*, 3 vols. (Paris: Gallimard, 1954), 4:680; *Sodom and Gomorrah, In Search of Lost Time*, trans. Scott Moncrieff and Terence Kilmartin, revised D. J. Enright, 6 vols. (London: Chatto & Windus, 1992), 4:92.

46. Proust, *Sodome et Gomorrhe*, 678–80; *Sodom and Gomorrah*, 90–92.

47. Proust, *Sodome et Gomorrhe*, 680; *Sodom and Gomorrah*, 92.

48. Proust, *Sodome et Gomorrhe*, 678–80; *Sodom and Gomorrah*, 90–92.

49. L'Archiviste, "Drumont et Dreyfus," 39.

50. Arendt, *Origins of Totalitarianism*, part 1, *Antisemitism*, 81.

51. Ibid., 87.

52. Ibid., 86.

53. Marcel Proust, *Le temps retrouvé*, vol. 3 of *À la recherche du temps perdu*, 3:840; *Time Regained*, trans. Andreas Mayor and Terence Kilmartin, rev. D. J. Enright, vol. 6 of *In Search of Lost Time* (London: Chatto, 1992), 184.

54. According to Elisabeth Roudinesco (*Retour sur la question juive*, 219), a 1966 survey by the French Institute found that 19 percent of those asked thought that Jews "were not French like the rest." Fifty percent said they would not vote for a Jew as president of the Republic.

55. Proust, *Le côté de Guermantes*, *À la recherche du temps perdu*, 2:288; *The Guermantes Way*, *In Search of Lost Time*, 3:330.

56. Proust, *Le côté Guermantes*, 2:288; *The Guermantes Way*, 3:330–31.

57. Proust, *Le côté Guermantes*, 2:235; *The Guermantes Way*, 3:267.

58. Reinach, *Histoire de l'Affaire Dreyfus*, 1:470.

59. Ibid., 469.

60. Wilson, *Ideology and Experience*, 155.

61. Proust, *Le côté Guermantes*, 2:288; *The Guermantes Way*, 3:331; *The Guermantes Way*, trans. Mark Treharne, *In Search of Lost Time*, 6 vols. (London: Allen Lane, 2002), 3:285.

62. Proust, *Le temps retrouvé*, 832; *Time Regained*, 175.

63. Proust, *Finding Time Again*, trans. Ian Patterson, *In Search of Lost Time*, 6:140.

64. Proust, *Le temps retrouvé*, 815; *Time Regained*, 154.

65. Proust, *Du côté de chez Swann*, 1:6; *Swann's Way*, 1:4.

66. Proust, *The Way by Swann's*, 1:9–10.

67. I discuss this question in "Zionism as Psychoanalysis," chap. 2 of *The Question of Zion* (Princeton, NJ: Princeton, 2005).

68. On this matter, literary critic F. R. Leavis's judgment was, I think, correct, but not his reading of the difficulty as a sign of aesthetic failure and certainly not his solution, which was to restore coherence to the work by cutting out the Jewish component altogether.

69. Rivière, cited in Woo, "Lecture de Proust," 71.

70. Edward Said, *Culture and Imperialism* (London: Chatto & Windus, 1993), 33.

71. Ibid., 28.

72. Benda, "L'Affaire Dreyfus et le Principe d'autorité," 175.

73. Dutrait-Couzon, *Joseph Reinach Historien*, xx.

74. Bowie, *Proust among the Stars*, 148.

75. Blum, *Souvenirs sur l'Affaire*, 14.

76. Proust, *Le côté Guermantes*, 290; *The Guermantes Way*, 332; my emphasis.

77. Proust, *Le côté Guermantes*, 238; *The Guermantes Way*, 271.

78. Proust, *Sodome et Gomorrhe*, 656; *Sodom and Gomorrah*, 65.

79. Proust, *Le côté Guermantes*, 235; *The Guermantes Way*, 268.

80. Arendt, *Human Condition*, 41.

81. Proust, *Le côté Guermantes*, 236; *The Guermantes Way*, 269.

82. Anne Michaels, *The Winter Vault* (London: Bloomsbury, 2009), 62.

83. Freud, "Some Points for a Comparative Study of Organic and Hysterical Motor Paralyses" (1893 [1888–93]), *Standard Edition* (1966), 1:164; original emphasis.

84. Ibid., 1:169.

85. Ibid., 1:171.

86. George Eliot, "The Modern Hep! Hep! Hep!" in *Impressions of Theophrastus Such*, ed. Nancy Henry (1874; London: William Pickering, 1994), 162, 160.

87. For a fuller discussion of Ahad Ha'am, see Rose, "Zionism as Psychoanalysis."

88. Eliot, "The Modern Hep! Hep! Hep!" 147.

89. Bouillaguet, "Marcel Proust devant l'Affaire Dreyfus," 40–41; for a discussion of Proust and Lazare, see Viard, "Proust, Bernard Lazare, Péguy et Romain Rolland."

90. Cited in Bouillaguet, "Marcel Proust devant l'Affaire Dreyfus," 41.

91. Proust, *Sodome et Gomorrhe*, 632, 620; *Sodom and Gomorrah*, 37, 24.

92. Herzl, *Jewish State*, 26.

93. Proust, *Jean Santeuil*, 2:87; trans., 297.

94. Proust, *Le temps retrouvé*, 879; *Time Regained*, 233.

95. See, for example, Julie Chamard-Bergeron, "L'Affaire Dreyfus dans le kaléidoscope d'*À la recherche du temps perdu*," *Bulletin de la Société des amis de Marcel Proust* 57 (2007): "The artist is not a political animal—he is called upon to determine himself through interiority" (61).

96. Proust, *Le temps retrouvé*, 879; *Time Regained*, 233.

97. See Wassenaar, *Proustian Passions*, for a discussion of how, between *Jean Santeuil* and *À la recherche*, politics disperses itself into, as well as revealing its inseparability from, the life of the mind.

98. See Rose, *The Question of Zion*, chap. 2.

99. Marrus and Paxton, *Vichy France and the Jews*, xii–xiii.

100. Lizzy Davies, "Draft of Memo Reveals Pétain's Personal War against the Jews," *Guardian*, 4 October 2010.

101. Ilan Pappé, *The Making of the Arab-Israeli Conflict, 1947–1951* (London: I. B. Tauris, 1992), 39–40.

102. Edward Said, "Zionism from the Standpoint of Its Victims," in *The Question of Palestine* (London: Vintage, 1980), 89.

103. Yehuda Amichai, "Jerusalem," trans. Stephen Mitchell, in *Poems of Jerusalem and Love Poems*, 5.

104. Edward Said, *After the Last Sky*, with photographs by Jean Mohr (London: Faber, 1986), 159.

105. It was only after writing the first draft of this chapter in 2007 that I read Gil Z. Hochberg's *In Spite of Partition: Jews, Arabs, and the Limits of the Separatist Imagination* (Princeton, NJ: Princeton University Press, 2007), which came out at around the same time. Hochberg's analysis of the power of literary writing to traverse political boundaries in the Middle East has many links with, as well as adding substance to, the argument I am making here, drawing on an impressive array of Hebrew and Arab sources, which I have much appreciated in my rewriting of this chapter.

106. Nur Masalha, *The Politics of Denial: Israel and the Palestinian Refugee Problem* (London: Pluto, 2003), chap. 6.

107. Amos Elon, *The Blood-Dimmed Tide: Dispatches from the Middle East* (New York: Columbia University Press, 1997), 38.

108. Ibid., 43.

109. Ibid., 44.

110. Ibid., 46.

111. Cited in Avi Shlaim, *The Iron Wall: Israel and the Arab World* (London: Allen Lane, 2000), 244–45.

112. Cited in Aluf Benn, "Territory Policy, Give or Take 40 Years," *Ha'aretz*, 8 October 2010, which reviews a collection of Dayan's speeches after the 1967 war.

113. Ibid., 46.

114. Mahmoud Darwish, "Palestine: The Imaginary and the Real," in *Innovation in Palestinian Literature: Testimonies of Palestinian Poets and Writers*, trans. Abdl-Fattah Jabr (Ramallah: Ogarit Cultural Centre, 2000), 20.

115. Glenda Abramson, cited in Joseph Cohen, "Yehuda Amichai," in *Voices of Israel*, ed. Joseph Cohen (Albany, NY: SUNY Press, 1990), 10.

116. Yehuda Amichai, "I Lived for Two Months in Quiet Abu Tor," *Poems of Jerusalem and Love Poems*, 24–27.

117. Yehuda Amichai, "National Thoughts," *Selected Poems*, trans. Chana Bloch and Stephen Mitchell (New York: Viking, 1987), 57.

118. Franz Rosenzweig, *Ninety-Two Poems and Hymns of Yehuda Halevi*, ed. Richard A. Cohen (Albany, NY: SUNY Press, 2000), 235.

119. Segev, *1967*, 19.

120. Proust also quotes these lines in the exordium to *Sodome et Gomorrhe*, to signal the inevitable exposure that awaits the closeted homosexual. It is another instance of his merging Jewish history with the plight of the homosexual. The words are also a partial anagram of Proust's own name. See Wassenaar, *Proustian Passions*, 120.

121. The day after the war was over, Amos Oz criticized Shemer in the daily *Davar*, pointing out that the marketplace was not empty but full of Arabs, as were the Temple Mount and Jericho road. Twenty years after the incident, in a newspaper supplement commemorating twenty years since the "reunification of the city," Shemer reiterated that Jerusalem devoid of Jews was mournful and in ruins and that the land of Israel without Jews was desolate. Naomi Shemer, "Eikh Nolad Shir" (How a Song Was Born), *Yediot Aharonot*, 22 May 1987.

122. Seamus Heaney, "The Redress of Poetry," in *The Redress of Poetry* (London: Faber 1995), 6.

123. Darwish, "Palestine: The Imaginary and the Real," 15.

124. Mahmoud Darwish, *Unfortunately, It Was Paradise: Selected Poems*, trans. and ed. Munir Akash and Carolyn Forché, with Sinan Antoon and Amira El-Zein (Berkeley: University of California Press, 2003), 63.

125. Raja Shehadeh, "Mahmoud Darwish," *Bomb* 81 (Fall 2002), http://bombsite.com/issues/81/articles/2520.

126. Mahmoud Darwish, Samih al-Qasim, and Adonis, *Victims of a Map*, trans. Abdullah al-Udhari (London: Al Saqi books, 1984), 11.

127. Shehadeh, "Mahmoud Darwish."

128. Reuvin Snir, "'Other Barbarians Will Come': Intertextuality, Meta-Poetry, and Meta-Myth in Mahmoud Darwish's Poetry," in *Mahmoud Darwish: Exile's Poet, Critical Essays*, ed. Hala Khamis Nassar and Najat Rahman (Northampton, MA: Olive Branch Press, 2008), 145.

129. Personal communication, Mohammed Shaheen.

130. Maya Jaggi, interview, "Mahmoud Darwish: Poet of the Arab World," *Guardian*, 8 June 2002; Mahmoud Darwish, "A Cloud from Sodom"; cited in Angelika Neuwirth, "Hebrew and Arabic Poetry: Mahmoud Darwish's Palestine: From Paradise Lost to a Homeland Made of Words," in *Mahmoud Darwish: Exile's Poet*, 186–87.

131. Cited in Hochberg, *In Spite of Partition*, 134–35.

132. Cited by Neuwirth, "Hebrew and Arabic Poetry," 185. In the discussion that follows, I am indebted to this article.

133. Mahmoud Darwish, *Selected Poems*, trans. Ian Wedde and Fawwaz Tuqan (Cheadle: Carcanet, 1973), 51. On the basis of discussion with

Mohammed Shaheen, I have slightly modified the translation. Mahmoud Darwish, *Collected Poems* (Beirut: Dar al-Awdah, 1977), 1:307–10.

134. Translation by Mohammed Shaheen, personal communication.

135. All quotations from this poem are taken from Darwish, *Unfortunately, It Was Paradise*, 165–68. Translation slightly modified on the basis of discussion with Mohammed Shaheen. Darwish, *Collected Poems*, 1:311–22.

136. The soldier was Shlomo Sands, author of the acclaimed and controversial *The Invention of the Jewish People* (London: Verso, 2009), which begins with an account of his own genesis, in terms of family, education, and experience, the ethnically and politically proscribed boundaries of the new nation. The friendship of Darwish and Sands predated 1967 (personal communication). Shlomo Sands, *Frontline*, London, 21 April 2009.

137. Darwish, "A Cloud from Sodom"; cited in Neuwirth, "Hebrew and Arabic Poetry," 186.

138. Shehadeh, "Mahmoud Darwish."

139. Breuer and Freud, *Studies on Hysteria*, 2:165.

CHAPTER 3

1. Pierre Nora, "Entre mémoire et histoire," *Les lieux de mémoire*, vol. 1, *La République* (Paris: Gallimard, 1984), xvii; "Between Memory and History," trans. Marc Roudebush, *Representations* 26 (1989): 7.

2. Ezekiel 37, inscribed on Nathan Rapaport's *Scroll of Fire*, Martyrs' Forest, outside Jerusalem (1971), cited in James Young, *Texture of Memory: Holocaust Memorials and Meaning* (New Haven, CT: Yale University Press, 1993), 223.

3. Esther Shalev-Gerz, "The Perpetual Movement of Memory," 24.

4. Frances A. Yates, *The Art of Memory* (London: Routledge & Kegan Paul, 1966).

5. Cited in ibid., 22.

6. Cited in ibid., 22.

7. Ed Pilkington, "'A bunch of dead muscles thinking,'" *Guardian*, 9 January 2010. The mnemonic system was brought from medieval Europe to China by Jesuits. See Jonathan Spence, *The Memory Palace of Matteo Ricci* (London: Faber, 1985).

8. Rachel Whiteread, "My Fairytale Landscape," *Guardian*, 8 May 2008.

9. Simon Hattenstone, "Ghosts of Childhood Past," *Guardian Weekend*, 10 May 2008.

10. Frances A. Yates, "Architecture and the Art of Memory," *Architectural Association Quarterly* 12 (1980): 573.

11. Yates, *Art of Memory*, 10.

12. John Hooper, "Berlusconi's Return in the Hands of Rome as Italians Go to the Polls," *Guardian*, 14 April 2008.

13. Cited in Tom Kington, "Unicef among Critics of Italian Plan to Fingerprint Roma Children," *Guardian*, 27 June 2008.

14. Judt, "What Have We Learned."

15. Tony Judt, *Postwar: A History of Europe since 1945* (London: Pimlico, 2007).

16. Walter Benjamin, "The Storyteller," in *Illuminations*, ed. Hannah Arendt (London: Jonathan Cape, 1970), 93–94.

17. Judt, "What Have We Learned," 20.

18. Pierre Nora, "Entre mémoire et histoire," in *Les lieux de mémoire*, ed. Nora, part 1, vol. 1, p. xxvi; "Between Memory and History," 13.

19. Nora, "La nation mémoire," *Les lieux de mémoire*, part 2, vol. 3, *La Nation*, 651.

20. Benda, "L'Affaire Dreyfus et le Principe d'autorité," 192.

21. Judt, "From the House of the Dead," *Postwar*, 826.

22. Judt, "What Have We Learned," 16.

23. Kate Connolly, "Remembrance Train Banned from Station," *Guardian*, 11 April 2008.

24. Brian Flynn, Tom Wells, and Neil Syson, "Beast of the Dungeon," *Sun*, 9 May 2009.

25. Ian Traynor, "Candidate to Lead Austria Vows to Uphold Holocaust Law," *Guardian*, 9 March 2010.

26. Stefanie Marsh and Bojan Pancevski, *The Crimes of Josef Fritzl: Uncovering the Truth* (London: HarperCollins, 2009), 12–13. I am indebted to this study for the details of the case.

27. Kate Connolly, "Plea to World: 'Keep Nation's Image Separate from Crime,'" *Guardian*, 1 May 2008.

28. Marsh and Pancevski, *Crimes of Josef Fritzl*, x.

29. Jess Smee, "Kampusch Buys House Where She Was Held," *Guardian*, 16 May 2008.

30. Judt, *Postwar*, 2.

31. Kate Connolly, "Police Call Former Residents of Fritzl House," *Guardian*, 2 May 2008.

32. Proust, *Du côté de chez Swann*, 1:6; *The Way by Swann's*, 1:10.

33. Proust, *Du côté de chez Swann*, 6; *The Way by Swann's*, 10.

34. Proust, *Du côté de chez Swann*, 6; *The Way by Swann's*, 10.

35. Walter Benjamin, "The Image of Proust," in *Illuminations*, 205.

36. Ibid., 207.

37. Proust, *Sodome et Gomorrhe*, 985; *Sodom and Gomorrah*, trans. John Sturrock, vol. 4 of *In Search of Lost Time*, 380–81.

38. Michael Wood, "Proust: The Music of Memory," in *Memory: Histories, Theories, Debates*, ed. Susannah Radstone and Bill Schwarz (Ashland, OH: Fordham University Press, 2010), 109–22.

39. Proust, *Le temps retrouvé*, 903; *Time Regained*, 263.

40. Proust, *Du côté de chez Swann*, 44; *The Way by Swann's*, 50–51.

41. Proust, *Le côté de Guermantes*, vol. 2 of *À la recherche du temps perdu*, 88; *The Guermantes Way*, trans. Scott Moncrieff and Terence Kilmartin, rev. D. J. Enright (New York: Modern Library, 1993), 94.

42. Samuel Beckett, "Proust" (1931), in *Proust and Three Dialogues with Georges Duthuit* (London: John Calder, 1965), 39. Beckett is citing Proust: *Sodome et Gomorrhe*, 195; *Sodom and Gomorrah*, 769.

43. Proust, *Du côté de chez Swann*, 44; *The Way by Swann's*, 51.

44. Shalev-Gerz, "Perpetual Movement of Memory," 24.

45. Nora, "Entre mémoire et histoire," xix; "Between Memory and History," 8.

46. Nora, "Entre mémoire et histoire," xvii; "Between Memory and History," 7.

47. Sigmund Freud, "Project for a Scientific Psychology" (1895), *Standard Edition* (1950), 1:382.

48. Ibid., 1:380–81.

49. Sigmund Freud, "On the Psychical Mechanism of Hysterical Phenomena: A Lecture" (1893), *Standard Edition* (1962), 3:31.

50. Judt, "From the House of the Dead," *Postwar*, 829. Judt is specifically addressing attempts to diminish German and Austrian historical accountability by the equation of Nazism and Stalin's communism. Saul Friedlander discusses this issue in relation to victims and perpetrators in his analysis of what came to be known as the "Historian's Quarrel" of the 1980s (*Historikerstreit*), in *A Conflict of Memories? The New German Debates about the "Final Solution"* (New York: Leo Baeck Institute, 1987).

51. Sigmund Freud, "Remembering, Repeating and Working-Through (Further Recommendations on the Technique of Psycho-Analysis)" (1914), in *Papers on Technique, Standard Edition*, vol. 12 (1958).

52. For the fullest discussion of this difficult issue in relation to the Holocaust, see Dominick LaCapra, *History and Memory after Auschwitz*

(Ithaca, NY: Cornell University Press, 1998), esp. chap. 1, "History and Memory: In the Shadow of the Holocaust."

53. Freud, "Remembering, Repeating and Working-Through," 12:154. For a discussion of the use of the word *tamed* in Freud's work, see editor's note to *Project for a Scientific Psychology*, 1:382.

54. Freud, "Remembering, Repeating and Working-Through," 12:155.

55. I discuss this issue more fully in "The Last Resistance," in *The Last Resistance* (London: Verso, 2007).

56. Proust, *Le temps retrouvé*, 875; *Time Regained*, 227.

57. James Strachey, editor's note, in "Remembering, Repeating and Working-Through," by Freud, 12:155.

58. Joan Rivière, "A Character Trait of Freud's," in *Psycho-Analysis and Contemporary Thought*, ed. John D Sutherland (London: Hogarth, 1958), 149. My thanks to Ian Patterson for bringing this to my attention.

59. Walter Abish, *How German Is It (Wie Deutsch Ist Es)* (New York: New Directions, 1979), 190, 163, 81, 170.

60. Ibid., 121.

61. Ibid.

62. Proust, *Le temps retrouvé*, 902–3; *Time Regained*, 263.

63. Reinach, *Histoire de l'Affaire Dreyfus*, 3:192.

64. James Young, *Texture of Memory*, 21. See also Stan Cohen, *States of Denial: Knowing about Atrocities and Suffering* (Cambridge: Polity, 2001); and also Jay Winter, *Sites of Mourning, Sites of Memory* (Cambridge: Cambridge University Press, 1995).

65. Ezekial 37, inscribed on Nathan Rapaport's *Scroll of Fire*, Martyrs' Forest, outside Jerusalem, 1971; cited by Young, *Texture of Memory*, 223.

66. Young, *Texture of Memory*, 210. See also, Hochberg, "Memory, Forgetting, Love: The Limits of National Memory," chap. 5 of *In Spite of Partition*.

67. Ehud Olmert, "A Tribute at 60: A Very Happy Birthday," *Jewish Chronicle*, 18 April 2008.

68. Naomi Tereza Salmon, "Transcription of Video," Esther Shalev-Gerz, *MenschenDinge / The Human Aspect of Objects* (Weimar: Gedenkstätte Buchenwald, 2006), 87.

69. Rory McCarthy, "West Bank Clashes over Israel's Heritage List Sites," *Guardian*, 27 February 2010.

70. Aluf Benn, "In Search of a Higher Purpose," *Ha'aretz, Week's End*, 12 February 2010.

71. Cited on the flyleaf to *Preliminaries*, by S. Yizhar, trans. Nicholas

de Lange (London: Toby Press, 2007); see also Lawrence Joffe, obituary of S. Yizhar, *Guardian*, 24 August 2006.

72. Tom Segev, *One Palestine, Complete: Jews and Arabs under the British Mandate*, trans. Haim Watzman (London: Little, Brown, 2000), 124.

73. Meron Benvenisti, *Sacred Landscape: The Buried History of the Holy Land since 1948*, p. 340; cited in Piterberg, *Returns of Zionism*, 213. See Piterberg for an extended and strong linking of Yizhar and Benvenisti.

74. Anita Shapira, "Hirbet Hizah," 24.

75. Ibid., 25, 31–32.

76. Ibid., 51, 39.

77. See Benny Morris, *The Birth of the Palestinian Refugee Problem* (Cambridge: Cambridge University Press, 1998); revised as Morris, *The Birth of the Palestinian Refugee Problem Revisited* (Cambridge: Cambridge University Press, 2004), 204; Shlaim, *Iron Wall*; Pappé, *Making of the Arab-Israeli Conflict*.

78. Shapira, "Hirbet Hizah," 10.

79. Ephraim Kleiman, "Hirbot Hizah ve-zikhronot lo neimim aherim" (Hirbet Hizehs and other unpleasant memories), *Prozah* 25 (1978): 24; cited in Shapira, "Hirbet Hizah," 47.

80. S. Yizhar, "Be-terem aharish," *Yediot Aharanot*, 24 February 1978; cited in Shapira, "Hirbet Hizah," 52.

81. Judt, "From the House of the Dead," *Postwar*, 815.

82. S. Yizhar, *Khirbet Khizeh*, trans. Nicholas de Lange and Yaacob Dweck (Jerusalem: Ibis, 2008), 92; partially translated by H. Levy in *Jewish Quarterly*, 1957, and reprinted in *Caravan: Hebrew Prose and Verse* (New York: Yoseloff, 1962). All subsequent quotes are from the 2008 translation.

83. Ibid., 104–5; Yizhar Smilansky, *Hirbat Hizha* (Tel Aviv: Zmora-Bitan, 2006), 75. (The inconsistencies in the spelling of the title stem from the fact that there is no one system for the transliteration of Hebrew.)

84. Smilansky, *Hirbat Hizha*, 75. As Adina Hoffman points out, these lines are strange, as the Palestinians are not yet an exiled people, but they become so as a result of what is being narrated in this story (personal communication).

85. Robert Alter, trans., *The Five Books of Moses: A Translation with Commentary* (New York: Norton, 2004), 912–13. Alter is citing scholar Jeffrey H. Tigay.

86. Frank Crüseman, *The Torah: Theology and Social History of Old Testament Law*, trans. Allan W. Mahnke (Edinburgh: T & T Clark, 1996), 204.

87. *The Torah: A Modern Commentary*, W. Gunther Plaut (New York: Union of American Hebrew Congregation, 1981), 1364.

88. S. Yizhar, "Midnight Convoy," trans. Reuven Ben-Yosef, in *Midnight Convoy and Other Stories* (Jerusalem: Israel Universities Press, 1969).

89. S. Yizhar, "Al meshorerei hasipuah" (On the Poets of Annexation), *Ha'aretz*, 8 December 1967; cited in Shapira, "Hirbet Hizah," 31.

90. Blum, *Nouvelles Conversations*, 136.

91. Yizhar, *Khirbet Khizeh*, 7.

92. Yizhar, *Khirbet Khizeh*, 7; Smilansky, *Hirbat Hizha*, 33.

93. Piterberg, *Returns of Zionism*, chap. 6, "The Bible, the Nakba and Hebrew Literature."

94. S. Yizhar, *Preliminaries* (1992), trans. Nicholas de Lange (London: Toby Press, 2007).

95. Ibid., 225–26. I wrote this chapter before reading Dan Miron's introduction to the novel, which also focuses on this passage.

96. Yizhar Smilansky, *Mikdamot* (Tel Aviv: Zmora-Bitan, 1992), 165.

97. Ibid.

98. Shalev-Gerz, "Perpetual Movement of Memory," 1.

99. Shalev-Gerz, "Reflecting Spaces/Deflecting Spaces," talk given at Dossin, Mechelen (a former barracks in Holland, where thousands of Jews, Roma, and Sinti were rounded up before being sent to concentration camps), 14 March 2007.

100. Young, "Countermonument: Memory against Itself in Germany," chap. 1 of *The Texture of Memory*, 30.

101. Jacques Rancière, "Die Arbeit des Bildes/The Work of the Image," in *MenschenDinge / The Human Aspect of Objects*, 9.

102. Ibid.; 22, 10, 16, 9, 9.

103. Shalev-Gerz, "Perpetual Movement of Memory," 2.

104. Shalev-Gerz, "The Judgement, A Philosophical Walk," proposition for a monument for the victims of the Nazi military tribunal in Murellenberg, Charlottenberg, Berlin, 2001, communication from the artist.

105. Shalev-Gerz, "Perpetual Movement of Memory," 5.

106. Stephen Fry, Harold Pinter, Stephen Rose, et al., "We're Not Celebrating," *Guardian*, 30 April 2008; Independent Jewish Voices

Steering Group, "60 Years: We Wish Everyone Could Celebrate," *Jewish Chronicle*, 9 May 2008.

107. Shalev-Gerz, "Proposition for Art Focus, Jerusalem 1997, 50 years of Israel," communication from the artist.

108. Rancière, "Die Arbeit des Bildes," 13.

109. Shalev-Gerz, *Daedel(us)*, North Inner City Dublin, Fire Station Artists' Studios, 2004.

110. Anthony Gormley, Ralph Rugoff, and Jacky Klein, "Field Activities: A Conversation between Anthony Gormley, Ralph Rugoff and Jacky Klein," in *Antony Gormley: Blind Light*, ed. Anthony Vidler, Susan Stewart, and W. J. T. Mitchell (London: Hayward Publishing, 2007), 55–56. For a discussion of Gormley which makes specific mention of Quintilian and the art of memory, see Stephen C. Levinson, "Space and Place," *Some of the Facts* (Cornwall: Tate St. Ives, 2001). I am grateful to Anthony Gormley for bringing this to my attention after I had completed this chapter.

CHAPTER 4

1. Samuel Beckett, "The Expelled" (1954), *The Expelled and Other Novellas* (New York: Penguin, 1973), 33.

2. Samuel Beckett, "Proust," 31.

3. Genet, *Un captif amoureux,* 347; *Prisoner of Love,* 211.

4. Beckett, "Proust," 33. Elsewhere, Beckett writes that Proust's material is "pulverised by time, obliterated by habit, mutilated in the clockwork of memory." "Proust in Pieces," in *Disjecta: Miscellaneous Writings and a Dramatic Fragment,* ed. Ruby Cohn (Dunbar, Scotland: Calder, 1983), 65.

5. Beckett, "Proust," 33, 33, 21, 19, 33, 22, 21.

6. Ibid., 20.

7. Ibid., 19; Sigmund Freud, "Our Attitude Towards Death," essay 2, "Thoughts for the Times on War and Death" (1915), *Standard Edition* (1957), 14:290.

8. Beckett, "Proust," 25.

9. Sigmund Freud, "A Disturbance of Memory on the Acropolis" (1936), *Standard Edition* (1964), 22:246.

10. T. W. Adorno, "Trying to Understand *Endgame*" (1958), *Notes to Literature,* 2, ed. Roy Tiedemann, trans. Shierry Weber Nicholson (New York: Columbia University Press, 1992), 250; Adorno, "Versuch das

Endspiel zu verstehen," *Noten Zur Literatur,* 2 (Frankfurt: Suhrkamp Verlag, 1961).

11. Susan Sontag, *Regarding the Pain of Others* (New York: Farrar, Strauss & Giroux, 2003).

12. Samuel Beckett, "The Unnameable," in *Molloy/Malone Dies/The Unnameable* (London: Calder, 1976), 288.

13. Samuel Beckett, *Endgame (Fin de partie)* (1957), Grove Centenary Edition, ed. Paul Auster, vol. 3 (New York: Grove Press, 2006), 150.

14. Chaim Levinson and Natasha Mozgovaya, "Likud MK: 'Hussein Obama' Can't Kick Us out of Hebron," *Ha'artez,* 2 April 2010.

15. Beckett, "Proust," 73.

16. Jean Genet, "Quatres Heures à Chatila," *Revue d'études Palestiniennes,* 1983; reprinted in *Revue d'études Palestiniennes,* special issue, *Jean Genet et la Palestine,* Spring 1997; Genet, "Four Hours in Shatila," *For Palestine,* ed. Jay Murphy (Danbury, CT: Writers and Readers, 1993); translation occasionally modified.

17. Genet, *Un captif amoureux; Prisoner of Love;* translation occasionally modified.

18. Edward Said, "Bases of Coexistence" (1997), in *The End of the Peace Process: Oslo and After* (London: Granta, 2000), 207.

19. Adorno, "Trying to Understand *Endgame,*" 251; "Versuch das Endspiel zu verstehen," 202.

20. See Hochberg, *In Spite of Partition,* chap. 5.

21. *Divine Intervention,* directed by Elia Suleiman, 2002. Michal Kapra, "I Saw an Amusing Palestinian," interview with Elia Suleiman, *Maariv,* November 1998; cited in Nurith Gertz and George Khleifi, *Palestinian Cinema: Landscape, Trauma and Memory* (Edinburgh: Edinburgh University Press, 1998), 179.

22. E. Khoury, *Gate of the Sun.*

23. Edward Said, "Jean Genet," in *On Late Style: Music and Literature against the Grain* (New York: Pantheon, 2006), 82; originally published in *Grand Street* 36, no. 9 (1990).

24. Dierdre Bair, *Samuel Beckett* (New York: Harcourt, Brace, Jovanovich, 1978), 29–30. Richard Begam, *Samuel Beckett and the End of Modernity* (Stanford, CA: Stanford University Press, 1996), 6.

25. Perloff, "'In Love with Hiding,'" 93, 85; Phyllis Gavney, "Normandy Landing," *Irish Times* 12 April 2010.

26. Beckett, *Disjecta,* 107.

27. See Edmund White, *Genet: A Biography* (New York: Knopf, 1993), 481–95.

28. Said, "Jean Genet," 82.

29. Genet, *Les Paravents* (1961) (Paris: Gallimard, 2000), 187; *The Screens*, trans. Bernard Frechtman (London: Faber, 1963), 124.

30. Genet, *Les Paravents*, 180; *The Screens*, 118.

31. Genet, *The Screens*, 201.

32. Gohier, "Le Péril," 168, 169.

33. Genet, *The Screens*, 127.

34. Herr, "A Monsieur Barrès," 243.

35. Beckett, *Endgame*, 112.

36. Ibid., 112–13.

37. Ibid., 122.

38. Ibid., 150–51.

39. Adorno, "Trying to Understand *Endgame*," 254.

40. Beckett, *Endgame*, 113.

41. In his introduction to *Samuel Beckett: "Waiting for Godot" and "Endgame"* (London: Macmillan, 1992), Stephen Connor picks out Adorno's essay, with its historical focus, as the notable exception to the majority of Beckett critics (p. 12). Adorno's reading is taken up by Josh Cohen in *Interrupting Auschwitz* (New York: Continuum, 2003).

42. Adorno, "Trying to Understand *Endgame*," 244; "Versuch das Endspiel zu verstehen," 192. In "Ending the Waiting Game: A Reading of Beckett's *Endgame*," Stanley Cavell, responding to the suggestion that the play might be situated in a bomb shelter, suggests such a reading leaves the most important question unasked: "Do these people want to survive?" Cavell, *Must We Mean What We Say?* (Cambridge: Cambridge University Press, 1969), 137.

43. Adorno, "Trying to Understand *Endgame*," 252; Shalev-Gerz, *MenschenDinge*.

44. Adorno, "Trying to Understand *Endgame*," 254.

45. Ibid., 254.

46. Beckett, *Disjecta*, 107.

47. Adorno, "Trying to Understand *Endgame*," 245.

48. Perloff, "'In Love with Hiding,'" 99.

49. For strong versions of this argument, see Pascale Casanova, *Samuel Beckett: Anatomy of a Literary Revolution* (London: Verso, 2006); Leo Bersani and Ulysse Dutoit, *Arts of Impoverishment: Beckett, Rothko, Renais* (Cambridge, MA: Harvard University Press, 1993); Leslie Hill,

Beckett's Fiction in Different Words (Cambridge: Cambridge University Press, 1990). See also Badiou, *L'increvable désir*. A useful summary of Beckett criticism is given by Andrew Gibson in "Samuel Beckett and Contemporary Criticism," in *Badiou on Beckett*, ed. Toscano and Power.

50. Samuel Beckett, "Three Dialogues," in *Disjecta*, 165.

51. Casanova, *Samuel Beckett*, 16.

52. Beckett, "German Letter of 1937," in *Disjecta*, 172.

53. Beckett, *Endgame*, 127.

54. Ibid., 150.

55. Ibid., 154.

56. Adorno, "Trying to Understand *Endgame*," 261; "Versuch das Endspiel zu verstehen," 217.

57. Adorno, "Trying to Understand *Endgame*," 247, "Versuch das Endspiel zu verstehen," 197.

58. For a critique of Blanchot, see also Gillian Rose, *The Broken Middle: Out of Our Ancient Society* (Oxford: Blackwell, 1992), chap. 1, part 1, "Unscientific Beginning," and chap. 2, part 1, "Confession and Authority."

59. Adorno, "Trying to Understand *Endgame*," 245–46.

60. Ibid., 248.

61. Ibid., 257.

62. Beckett, "Proust," 13.

63. T. J. Clark, "Madame Matisse's Hat," *London Review of Books* 30, no. 16 (14 August 2008), 30.

64. Jean Genet, "Interview with Laurent Boyer," 1991, cited in White, *Genet*, 169.

65. Marcel Proust, *Within a Budding Grove, In Search of Lost Time*, trans. C. K. Scott Moncrieff and Terence Kilmartin, rev. D. J. Enright (London: Chatto & Windus, 1992), 1.

66. White, introduction to *Jean Genet: Selected Writings* (Hopewell, NJ: Ecco Press, 1993), xi.

67. Jean Genet, "Une rencontre avec Jean Genet," *Revue d'études Palestiniennes*, 1983; reprinted in *Revue d'études Palestiniennes*, special Issue, *Jean Genet et la Palestine*, Spring 1997, 32.

68. Said, "Jean Genet," 78.

69. Genet, "Rencontre," 31.

70. Genet, "Rencontre," 27. See also Rashid Khalidi, *Under Siege: PLO Decision-Making during the 1982 War* (New York: Columbia University

Press, 1986): "Israel's role goes far beyond the indirect responsibility and sins of omission attributed to seven Israeli officials by the Kahan Commission" (178). The Commission itself cites these remarks by Chief of Staff Rafael Eitan before the Phalange were let into the camps: "It will be an eruption the likes of which has never been seen; I can already see in their eyes what they are waiting for." Yitzhak Kahan, Aharon Barak, and Yona Efrat, *The Commission of Inquiry into the Events at the Refugee Camps in Beirut, 1983, Final Report (Authorised Translation): The Beirut Massacre: The Complete Kahan Commission Report* (Princeton, NJ: Karz-Cohl, 1983), introduction by Abba-Eban, p. 27. See also Khalidi, *Under Siege*, chap. 6, "Wartime Decisions and Their Consequences," for an account of the accords between Israel, the United States, and the PLO resulting in the departure of the latter from Beirut, the assurances regarding the safety of the civilians, and the premature departure of the U.S. forces, followed by that of the French, Italian, and British forces, which left the Palestinians without the guaranteed protection.

71. Genet, "Rencontre," 26.

72. Amnon Kapeliouk, *Sabra et Chatila: Enquête sur un massacre* (Paris: Seuil, 1982), iii; Kapeliouk, *Sabra and Chatila: Inquiry into a Massacre*, trans. and ed. Khalil Jehshan, foreword by Abdeen Jabara (Belmont MA: Association of Arab-American University Graduates, 1984), 52. (As there are differences between the French and English versions, including an additional chapter 7 and a conclusion in the translation, wherever available, I give references to both.)

73. Amnon Kapeliouk, *Enquête sur un massacre*, iii; *Inquiry into a Massacre*, 52.

74. Genet, "Quatre Heures à Chatila," 7; "Four Hours in Shatila," 19.

75. The 1983 independent, international commission into the invasion, the MacBride Commission, concluded that Israel had committed acts of aggression contrary to international law. See Seán MacBride, Richard Falk, Kader Asmal, et al., *Israel in Lebanon: Report of the International Commission to Enquire into Reported Violations of International Law by Israel during Its Invasion of Lebanon* (London: Ithaca, 1983).

76. Kapeliouk, *Enquête sur un massacre*, ii; *Inquiry into a Massacre*, 10.

77. Kapeliouk, *Enquête sur un massacre*, ii; *Inquiry into a Massacre*, 12.

78. Kapeliouk, *Enquête sur un massacre*, 19; *Inquiry into a Massacre*, 15.

79. Kapeliouk, *Enquête sur un massacre*, 29; *Inquiry into a Massacre*, 14.

80. Kapeliouk, *Inquiry into a Massacre*, 100.

81. Kahan Commission, 24.

82. Kapeliouk, *Enquête sur un massacre*, 109; *Inquiry into a Massacre*, 51. See also Ze'ev Schiff and Ehud Ya'ari, *Israel's Lebanon War*, ed. and introduced by Ina Friedman (New York: Simon & Schuster, 1984), chap. 13, "Anatomy of a Slaughter." Thanks to Philip Hollander for bringing this text and others on the massacre to my attention, including Shimon Shiffer, *Opération boule de neige: Les secrets de l'intervention israélienne au Liban* (Paris: Jean-Claude Lattès, 1984); and Robert M Hatem, *Dans l'ombre d'Hobeika en passant par Sabra et Chatila* (Paris, Jean Picollec, 2003), which recounts the events from a Lebanese Christian dissident viewpoint. Now exiled in Paris, Hatem attributes sole responsibility for the massacre to the Lebanese Maronite Elie Hobeika and absolves Ariel Sharon of all responsibility.

83. Schiff and Ya'ari, 266. According to Shiffer, it was following a phone call from Schiff in the morning of 17 September that Mordechai Zapori, minister of post and telecommunications, attempted to alert Itzhak Shamir, the minister of foreign affairs, to the fact that a massacre had taken place. Shamir's failure to respond was criticized by the Kahan Commission, Shiffer, *Opération boule de neige*, 219, 268.

84. Kapeliouk, *Enquête sur un massacre*, 111; *Inquiry into a Massacre*, 51.

85. *Report of the Commission of Inquiry into the Events at the Refugee Camps in Beirut (The Kahan Commission)*, 57.

86. Kahan Commission, 60.

87. Kapeliouk, *Enquête sur un massacre*, 112; *Inquiry into a Massacre*, 52.

88. Kapeliouk, *Inquiry into a Massacre*, 58.

89. One section of the conclusion to the English translation is called "The Scene from the Seventh Floor." Kapeliouk, *Inquiry into a Massacre*, 57–60.

90. Kapeliouk, *Enquête sur un massacre*, 47; *Inquiry into a Massacre*, 22.

91. Kahan Commission, 22.

92. Schiff and Ya'ari, *Israel's Lebanon War*, 285.

93. Mahmoud Darwish, *Memory for Forgetfulness: August, Beirut, 1982*, trans. Ibrahim Muhawi (Berkeley: University of California Press, 1995).

94. For a discussion of the film in terms of its challenge to Israeli masculinist notions of military identity and authority, see Philip Hollander, "Shifting Manhood: Masculinity and the Lebanon War in *Waltz with Bashir* and *Beaufort*," unpublished paper.

95. Kobi Ben-Simhon, "Speak, Memory," *Ha'aretz*, 6 February 2009.

96. Ibid.

97. Ibid. Ze'ev Schiff reports hearing Operation Officer, Colonel Bezalel Treiber refuse a request to renew the illumination of the camps on the night of 16 to 17 September on the grounds that civilians were being killed. Schiff and Ya'ari, 265.

98. "Entretien avec Leila Shahid," *Genet à Chatila, texts réunis par Jérôme Hankins* (Arles, France: Solin, 1992), 36.

99. Genet is not alone in making this connection. The *Black Panthers* was the name taken by a second-generation Mizrahim protest movement in Israel in the 1970s. There have been a number of Palestinian films, such as Eli Hamo and Sami Chetrit's *The Black Panthers (in Israel) Speak* (2003) and Nissam Mossek's *Have You Heard about the Black Panthers* (2009) on this subject. For a full discussion, see Ella Shohat, preface to new edition, *Israeli Cinema: East/West and the Politics of Representation* (London, I. B. Tauris, 2010). I am grateful to Ella Shohat for letting me read this preface before publication.

100. Genet, "Rencontre," 32, 28, 32; original emphasis.

101. Ibid., 32.

102. Ibid., 34. For a discussion of some of the philosophical issues raised by Genet's discussion of language in relation to Sabra and Chatila, see Steven Miller, "Open Letter to the Enemy: Jean Genet's Holy War," *Diacritics* 34, no. 2 (Summer 2004).

103. Genet, "Quatre heures à Chatila," 22; "Four Hours in Shatila," 36–37.

104. Genet, "Quatre heures à Chatila," 19; "Four Hours in Shatila," 33.

105. "Entretien avec Leila Shahid," *Genet à Chatila*, 36.

106. Genet, "Rencontre," 36.

107. Said, "Jean Genet," 79.

108. Genet, *Un captif amoureux*, 445; *Prisoner of Love*, 272.

109. Genet, "Rencontre," 33.

110. Genet, "Quatre heures à Chatila," 8; "Four Hours in Shatila," 19.

111. Genet, *Un captif amoureux*, 11; *Prisoner of Love*, 3.

112. "Entretien avec Leila Shahid," *Genet à Chatila*, 49.

113. Genet, "The Palestinians," *Journal of Palestinian Studies*, 3, no. 1 (Autumn 1973), 27. The essay was put together from Genet's notes of a meeting in Paris in September 1972 with seven young Palestinians. Genet is referring to the expulsion of the Palestinians from Jordan in September 1970.

114. Genet, "Quatre heures à Chatila," 22; "Four Hours in Shatila," 37.

115. Genet, "Rencontre," 33.

116. Genet, "The Palestinians," 24.

117. Genet, *Un captif amoureux*, 432; *Prisoner of Love*, 264.

118. Genet, *Un captif amoureux*, 410; *Prisoner of Love*, 251.

119. "For the first time he felt happy in the milieu where he was living," "Entretien avec Leila Shahid," *Genet à Chatila*, 18.

120. Genet, "Quatre heures à Chatila," 23; "Four Hours in Shatila," 37.

121. Genet, "Quatre heures à Chatila," 23; "Four Hours in Shatila," 37.

122. Genet, *Un captif amoureux*, 248–49; *Prisoner of Love*, 149.

123. Genet, "Rencontre," 32.

124. Genet, *Un captif amoureux*, 504; *Prisoner of Love*, 309.

125. Genet, *Un captif amoureux*, 461; *Prisoner of Love*, 282.

126. Genet, "Quatre heures à Chatila," 15; "Four Hours in Shatila," 28–29.

127. Genet, *Un captif amoureux*, 504–5; *Prisoner of Love*, 309.

128. Genet, *Un captif amoureux*, 505; *Prisoner of Love*, 309.

129. Genet, "Rencontre," 36.

130. Elia Suleiman in informal conversation with Nadia Yaqub, Barbican, London, 1 May 2010.

131. Genet, "The Palestinians," 8.

132. Genet, *Un captif amoureux*, 308; *Prisoner of Love*, 186.

133. Genet, *Un captif amoureux*, 542; *Prisoner of Love*, 331.

134. Genet, *Un captif amoureux*, 347; *Prisoner of Love*, 211.

135. Félix Guattari, "Genet retrouvé," *Revue d'études Palestiniennes*, special issue, *Jean Genet et la Palestine*, Spring 1997.

136. Genet, *Un captif amoureux*, 347; *Prisoner of Love*, 211.

137. Genet, *Un captif amoureux*, 348; *Prisoner of Love*, 211.

138. "Entretien avec Leila Shahid," 39. Leila Shahid, cited in Edmund White, *Genet*, 610. In "Entretien avec Leila Shahid," 26.

139. Genet, *Un captif amoureux*, 314; *Prisoner of Love*, 190.

140. Guattari, "Genet retrouvé," 59.

141. Said, "Jean Genet," 85.

142. Guattari, "Genet retrouvé," 59.

143. Cited in Gertz and Khleifi, *Palestinian Cinema*, 187.

144. Hamid Dabashi, "In Praise of Frivolity: On the Cinema of Elia Suleiman," in *Dreams of a Nation: On Palestinian Cinema*, ed. Hamid Dabashi (London: Verso, 2006), 151 (from interview conducted by Dabashi, October 2002).

145. Genet, *Les paravents* (1961) (Paris: Gallimard, 2000), 173; *The Screens*, trans. Bernard Frechtman (London: Faber, 1963), 112.

146. Adorno, "Trying to Understand *Endgame*," 257.

147. Dabashi, "In Praise of Frivolity," 135; Olivier Joyard, "Dans l'oeil d'Elia Suleiman le nomade," *Cahiers du cinéma*, October 2002, 14.

148. Suleiman, "Illusions Nécessaires," 54. See also Frank Garbarz and Yann Tobin, interview with Elia Suleiman, "Elia Suleiman: Le plaisir de se demander pourquoi," *Positif* 500 (October 2001), 205. My thanks to Tim Kennedy for bringing these articles to my attention.

149. Dabashi, "In Praise of Frivolity," 142.

150. Bourland, "Cinema of Nowhere," 96.

151. Genet, *Un captif amoureux*, 347; *Prisoner of Love*, 211.

152. Dabashi, "In Praise of Frivolity," 154.

153. Genet, *Les paravents*, 71.

154. Genet, *Les paravents*, 257, 265; *The Screens*, 185, 191.

155. E. Khoury, *Gate of the Sun*; *Bâb al Chams*. Where relevant, references to the Arabic are given after the page number of the English translation. For an important discussion of Khoury's 1977 novel *Little Mountain*, see Edward Said's afterword to *Little Mountain*. For a discussion of *Gate of the Sun* in relation to Khoury's life and work, see Jeremy Harding, "Jeremy Harding Goes to Beirut to Meet the Novelist Elias Khoury," *London Review of Books* 28, no. 22 (16 November 2006).

156. Hanrahan, "Key to Memory."

157. Khoury in discussion with Jeremy Harding, World Literature Weekend, London Review Bookshop, 18 June 2010.

158. Hanrahan, "Key to Memory."

159. Raja Shehadeh, "Gate of the Sun by Elias Khoury," *Nation*, 19 April 2006.

160. Khoury, *Gate of the Sun*, 235.

161. Ibid., 239; 240–41.

162. Ibid., 241; 252.

163. Ibid., 239.

164. Ibid., 254; 268.

165. Ibid., 403.

166. Khoury in informal discussion, World Literature Weekend, 18 June 2010.

167. Khoury, *Gate of the Sun*, 404.

168. Ibid., 417.

169. Ibid., 415.

170. Ibid., 275.

171. Ibid., 274; 291.

172. Ibid., 275; 292.

173. Ibid., 274. In discussion, Khoury described this moment as the first in Arabic literature to present the Holocaust in terms of responsibility (World Literature Weekend, 18 June 2010). See also Gilbert Achcar, *The Arabs and the Holocaust: The Arab-Israeli War of Narratives* (New York: Metropolitan, 2009).

174. Genet, "The Palestinians," 32.

175. Bourlond, "Cinema of Nowhere," cited in Gertz and Khleifi, *Palestinian Cinema*, 172.

176. Suleiman, in conversation with Nadia Yaqub, Barbican, London, 1 May 2010.

Index